Treating the Chemically Dependent and Their Families

SAGE SOURCEBOOKS FOR THE HUMAN SERVICES SERIES

Series Editors: ARMAND LAUFFER and CHARLES GARVIN

Recent Volumes in This Series

Dennis C. Daley
Miriam S. Raskin
editors

Treating the Chemically Dependent and Their Families

SAGE SOURCEBOOKS FOR THE HUMAN SERVICES SERIES 16

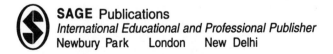

SAGE Publications
International Educational and Professional Publisher
Newbury Park   London   New Delhi

For information address:

SAGE Publications, Inc.
2455 Teller Road
Newbury Park, California 91320

SAGE Publications Ltd.
6 Bonhill Street
London EC2A 4PU
United Kingdom

SAGE Publications India Pvt. Ltd.
M-32 Market
Greater Kailash I
New Delhi 110 048 India

Printed in the United States of America

Library of Congress Cataloging-in-Publication Data

Main entry under title:

Treating the chemically dependent and their families / edited by
    Dennis C. Daley and Miriam S. Raskin.
        p.   cm.
    ISBN 0-8039-3297-9. — ISBN 0-8039-3298-7 (pbk.)
    1. Substance abuse—Treatment.   2. Substance abuse—Patients—
Family relationships.   I. Daley, Dennis C.   II. Series: Sage sourcebooks
for the human services series ; v. 16.
RC564.T735   1991
616.86′06—dc20   90-15562
                                                                            CIP

93 94 15 14 13 12 11 10 9 8 7 6 5 4 3 2

Sage Production Editor: Diane S. Foster

CONTENTS

To
Charles (Bud) Chettle
and
To DCD—for helping me become a
better teacher and a more asture social worker

We appreciate the major contributions of "Attila, the Hun" (IER). His numerous readings of the text and subsequent recommendations enhanced the final product. We value his professionalism, support and great sense of humor.

DENNIS C. DALEY
MIRIAM S. RASKIN

PREFACE

The media reminds us daily of the physical and emotional problems of addiction of many kinds. Clinical studies and polls document the large number of alcoholics and drug addicts in the United States. But in addition to the addicts themselves, many other people are affected by addiction: On the average, each addict adversely affects four to six other people.

Alcohol and drug addiction are associated with multiple medical, psychological, family, social, legal, financial, and spiritual problems. Addicted individuals are more likely to need medical care, enter the criminal justice system, or seek help for personal or family related problems caused or exacerbated by their addiction.

All of the helping professions encounter alcoholics and drug addicts, regardless of the initial presenting problems of the client. Professionals may function in a variety of roles to help addicts or their families, including identifying and assessing alcohol- and drug-related problems; informing patients and families about addiction and recovery issues; referring patients and families to appropriate professional or self-help programs; providing direct treatment; developing clinical and educational programs specific to the needs of addicts and their families; providing support and collaborating with other caregivers; and serving as advocates for clients.

This book is a practical guide for doctors, nurses, psychologists, social workers, family therapists, counselors, probation and parole officers, ministers, and other health care or social service professionals who work with addicted individuals and/or their families. The major issues relevant to addiction and recovery are reviewed from the perspectives of the addict, the addict's family, and the professional. The reader is guided in making a personal assessment of his or her own beliefs and behaviors in order to challenge possibly inappropriate enabling behavior.

The contributors to the book represent diverse disciplines, including medicine, nursing, social work, family therapy, psychology, counseling, and education. Each chapter represents a specialized area of clinical experience and integrates relevant literature.

Chapter 1 is an overview of alcoholism and drug addiction. Topics reviewed include prevalence of addiction, definitions and conceptual frameworks, effects of addiction, myths and misconceptions about addiction, professional enabling, types of addictive substances, and theories of addiction.

Chapter 2 focuses on assessment of addiction problems, with a discussion of the assessment process and its criterion. The use of laboratory tests, self-assessment questionnaires, and structured assessments administered by professionals are reviewed. Two case examples are presented to illustrate typical issues and problems in the assessment of addiction.

In chapter 3, Lou Gene Kingery-McCabe and Frances A. Campbell review the consequences to the addict of his or her addiction. They discuss the factors that determine how an individual is affected by addiction, including the physical, medical, psychological, social, and spiritual elements of addiction.

John D. Massella discusses "Intervention" in Chapter 4. He reviews the role of denial in addiction and the issue of "hitting bottom." The intervention process is described in discrete steps. Several different types of intervention are reviewed, including those by health care and social service professionals, by families with and without the assistance of professional intervention, and by employers. Examples are used to illustrate the practical aspects of the intervention process.

Chapter 5, by Tod R. Marion and Kathryn Coleman, addresses recovery issues and treatment resources. The authors discuss the principles of recovery from several perspectives. Treatment resources are reviewed, including professional and self-help programs, and resources used throughout the continuum of care, such as detoxification, outpatient treatment, and pharmacological adjuncts.

Relapse prevention and treatment effectiveness are the topics of chapter 6. Treatment outcome studies and methodological problems in research on relapse are discussed. The precipitants of relapse and several relapse treatment models are reviewed, including the psycho-

educational approach to relapse prevention developed by one of the authors. Relapse is also addressed from the family's perspective. Issues
in lapse and relapse intervention are discussed. Several case examples
are used to illustrate the major concepts described in this chapter.

In chapter 7, Ruth Ann Seilhamer reviews the literature on the effects
of addiction on the family. She discusses the impact of addiction on
spouses, children, and the family unit. Family assessment procedures
are presented. Dr. Seilhamer integrates case examples and information
from her research on families of alcoholics.

In chapter 8, Carol Koffinke discusses clinical issues in family
recovery. including overcoming family denial and enabling, and adjusting to the addict's sobriety. This chapter also reviews the process of
assessing the personal and familial impact of addiction. Professional
and self-help resources available for families are highlighted.

It is our hope that this book will serve as a practical guide to many
helping professionals. With realistic attitudes, knowledge, and skills, a
significant contribution can be made to helping alcoholics, drug addicts, and their families.

DENNIS C. DALEY
MIRIAM S. RASKIN

Chapter 1

INTRODUCTION AND OVERVIEW
OF ADDICTION

MIRIAM S. RASKIN
DENNIS C. DALEY

PREVALENCY

The number of individuals and families affected by drug and alcohol
abuse and addiction is staggering. A 1987 Gallup poll found that one in
four families reported a problem with alcohol abuse in the home. This
is twice the rate of 1974 ("Out in the Open," 1987, p. 83). Data from
the National Institute of Mental Health's Epidemiologic Catchment
Area Survey of 20,000 adults indicated that 13.7% of adults met current
or lifetime criteria for alcohol abuse or dependence, and 5.9% met
criteria for drug abuse or dependence.

Although there has been a gradual decline in illicit drug use since
the 1970s, drug addiction has been devastating to many individuals and
families. In 1982, the National Household Survey on Drug Use showed
that there were 21.6 million people who had at sometime used cocaine.
One fifth of the respondents identified themselves as current cocaine
users—these individuals had used the drug one or more times in the
month preceding the survey. The use of illicit drugs by high school
students is comparable with the use of alcohol: Almost one-half have
used one or more illicit drugs before they graduate from high school.

In the past decade, educators, employers, helping professionals,
and average citizens have become aware of and concerned about the

extensive damage that can occur to those who suffer from addictions. State governments have passed legislation that acknowledges the severity of the drug and alcohol problem and have taken steps to address the situation. For example, someone caught driving drunk in Maryland (even a first offender) has his or her driver's license taken away immediately. Nationwide the proportion of fatally injured drivers who were legally drunk dropped from 50% to 43% in 1984, but the rate is still too high. Keeping drunk drivers off the roads will save lives and motivate some to seek early intervention and treatment for themselves and their families.

Alcoholism is the third most prevalent public health problem in the United States. Chronic alcoholism was decriminalized in 1968 (Alcoholic Rehabilitation Act, P.L. 90-574) and recognized as a major health and social problem. It is not surprising that more than 50% of ninth graders have tried alcohol; by the senior year of high school, 93% have tried it. *Weekly Reader* reports that 36% of fourth graders were pressured by peers to drink. Many adolescents have drug or alcohol-related problems. On the other end of the continuum, however, Kola and Kosberg (1980) found that 85% of *elderly* alcoholics were unidentified and untreated.

EFFECTS OF ADDICTION

Addictive diseases affect the very fabric of our society. The addicted individual, the family, and society each experience adverse effects of addiction in a variety of ways. These effects range from mild to very severe. The individual with alcoholism or drug addiction is at greater risk for a multiplicity of problems, including medical, psychological, psychiatric, interpersonal, social, occupational or academic, family, spiritual, and financial complications (Daley, 1988). Addiction causes tremendous personal suffering; many deaths are related to alcoholism or drug addiction (medical diseases, accidents, overdoses, etc.). Alcoholism has been found to contribute to more family problems than any other factor. Between 25% and 50% of violence between spouses is due to alcohol.Alcohol is also found to be a contributing factor in one-third of child molestation cases. Children are particularly affected when there is alcoholism in the family. They are vulnerable to a multiplicity of psychosocial problems (Daley, 1988).

Alcoholism is responsible for many accidents and deaths, although only 3% of recorded deaths are officially attributed to causes directly linked to alcohol. It is estimated that one third to two thirds of all boating fatalities were alcohol related, as were 30% of the 30,000 suicides in 1985. A study by the National Institute on Alcohol Abuse and Alcoholism (NIAAA, 1981) reported that mortality rates for alcoholics are 2.5 times higher than for the general population.

Society is affected by the great economic costs of alcohol and drug addiction. The annual cost to American society of cocaine abuse is estimated at $25 billion to $35 billion. Alcoholism costs the United States approximately $117 billion annually in medical bills and lost productivity. The courts and prisons report that they deal with high proportions of alcoholics. Almost 50% of the arrests in the United States are alcohol related. Many people take cocaine at work, and this has become a major concern in business, industry, and the professions. Costly mistakes to the individual and society include stealing, embezzlement, or padding expense accounts.

AIDS-related deaths and drug overdoses have exacted a toll on society. Approximately 1,000 people die each year in the United States from heroin overdoses. Intravenous drug users accounted for one-third of all new AIDS cases in the first half of 1985, and the proportion of the AIDS population who are intravenous drug users is increasing.

MYTHS AND MISCONCEPTIONS
ABOUT ADDICTION

Informational and attitudinal myths have evolved about alcohol and drug addiction, partly as a result of media messages such as: Drinking is sophisticated and a necessary part of success; drinking and masculinity are synonymous; the alcoholic is a"skid row bum"; or drinking beer does not lead to alcoholism. As society has become more health conscious, and as medical discoveries related to addictions have contributed to further understanding of the disease, some of these myths have begun to change.

Mass media campaigns alone have not been found to change health behaviors, but measures such as raising the legal drinking age in many states have been found to reduce alcohol-related traffic accidents. Evidence that such legislation reduces the alcohol consumption of young people is less conclusive. Changes in information and attitudes can be discerned by a recent Gallup poll that found the great majority of American adults are convinced that alcoholism is an illness rather than a sign of moral weakness.

A myth that has often delayed needed treatment is that the alcoholic or drug addict must "hit bottom" before treatment can begin. Another part of this myth is that the alcoholic or drug addict needs voluntarily to initiate and seek help on his or her own. There is growing evidence that referrals to treatment in an employment situation, rather than disciplinary action, can be as effective as self-initiated or self-referral treatment.

Other misconceptions hold that addiction is caused by mental illness, that addicts can be cured, and that addiction is a secondary disease caused by some other disorder. Addiction is treatable, but not curable at this time. It is a progressive disease that usually does not get better without treatment. A person seeking treatment will not be cured but may be in recovery even after many years.

PROFESSIONAL ENABLING

Enabling refers to any behavior on the part of the professional that directly or indirectly contributes to the continuation of the alcohol or drug problem. Enabling behaviors may be *passive* (e.g., ignoring the problem and not doing anything to help the person; or failure to ask appropriate questions to ascertain if an alcohol or drug problem exists), or *active* (e.g., giving inappropriate advice to an alcoholic or drug addict concerning continued substance use).

Professionals often inadvertently enable, even when their intention is to help the client. Enabling may be caused by a lack of understanding of the addiction, inadequate training, or overfunctioning on the part of the professional. Following are some common examples of professional enabling that impede the helping process:

1. *Failure to get the history of related or drug use and/or family history of alcohol- and drug-related problems.* On one extreme are cases in which no information is obtained regarding substance use. In other cases minimal or inadequate information may be obtained. For example, an intake worker at a community mental health clinic took extensive histories of psychiatric symptoms on all new clients, yet asked very few questions about substance abuse or any symptoms indicating a possible problem. A staff member in a hospital specializing

in treating high-risk infants reported that alcoholism and other types of drug addiction were present in a substantial number of cases. Yet, it was not uncommon for the medical records not to have any information concerning substance abuse, even in cases where it was common knowledge among the staff that a particular parent was addicted.

This form of enabling can also occur when a family member rather than the individual with the substance abuse problem is the one seeking help. Many families of alcoholics and drug addicts seek help for a multiplicity of problems that result directly from the addiction. For example, the wife of a heroin addict and alcoholic became quite depressed and despondent because her husband's addiction caused considerable problems in her family. She finally decided to seek help for herself and arranged to see a psychiatrist. Her treatment consisted of antidepressant medications and occasional supportive sessions aimed at reducing her depressive symptoms. A detailed evaluation of her husband's addiction was not conducted. As a result, her feelings of rage, guilt and shame were not addressed in treatment. She received no education about addiction, and no referral to support groups or to a professional interventionist to help pressure her addicted husband to seek help.

Appropriate information about substance use should be integrated in the intake or evaluation/assessment procedures. This will help in identifying addiction-related problems.

2. *Waiting for the person with the alcohol or drug problem to "hit bottom."* Professionals often believe the myth that a person with a chemical dependency problem cannot be helped unless he or she "hits bottom" or asks for help. The problem is that the vast majority of individuals with substance abuse problems do not acknowledge the problem or voluntarily seek help. One could easily interpret this stance as meaning these people have not yet hit bottom. However, because untreated substance abuse may lead to severe problems (medical and/or psychosocial) for many, a heavy price is paid waiting for these people to hit bottom. Many people with alcohol or drug problems have successfully been pressured to seek help through the process of intervention. (This process is discussed in greater detail in Chapter 4.) Professionals who adopt the attitude that clients with substance abuse problems can be helped before they hit bottom even if they do not initially want help, will be more likely to take steps to help these clients.

3. *Failure to include the alcohol or drug problem in the treatment plan.* In some instances, alcohol or drug problems are identified

and acknowledged, but specific strategies to deal with them are not incorporated in the treatment plan. When a substance abuse problem is identified, it is the professional's responsibility to ensure that the treatment plan addresses it, even if this is not the person primarily involved in the treatment of this client. In many instances, a person's drug alcohol problem is intimately connected with "other" problems that lead him or her to a professional for service.

4. *Giving simple advice.* Telling an alcoholic or a drug addict to stop using drugs will most likely have little, if any, lasting impact. The nature of addiction is such that continued substance use occurs despite the evidence that it is pathological and causes problems for the individual or others. Additionally, many chemically dependent people experience irrational and compulsive desires to use, which defy logic and do not respond to simple advice. Rather than give advice to stop using, the professional can make a greater impact by advising the individual to seek help and by facilitating the person's use of this help if possible (e.g., referring to a chemical dependence treatment program or a self-help program, or working with the individual on achieving abstinence).

5. *Bailing the person out of trouble or assuming his or her responsibilities.* Professionals can fall into the same trap as families with respect to shielding the person from consequences of behaviors by bailing them out of trouble. Many caregivers help clients through advocacy actions and sometimes fall prey to enabling in this area. For example, a social worker went to great lengths to help a young cocaine-addicted client in trouble with the law by convincing the family to pay fines and court costs. The social worker went through with this plan despite the client's repetitive history of not learning from his or her mistakes. It helped to reinforce the client's view that he could get others to bail him out of trouble.

In another instance, an alcoholic woman was in deep financial trouble because she had spent the family's finances on a drinking binge. In desperation, she went to her minister for financial help and for help in getting her creditors off her back. Even though the minister knew of her history of alcoholism and subsequent problems, he felt compelled to "help" her by getting her a loan and calling several creditors to arrange for reduced payment of her bills. Her responsibilities were assumed by her minister, and she was shielded from the negative effects of her drinking and subsequent irresponsible behaviors.

Professionals can be more helpful in the long run by not bailing clients out of difficulty and by helping them to see the relationship between their substance abuse and their life problems. They can further help clients by putting the responsibility back on them to solve the problems caused by substance abuse. While they can facilitate the process by providing support, professionals should let clients take responsibility for themselves.

6. *Assuming that severe or multiple problems have to exist for the person to be considered addicted.* The severity of addiction varies widely among people. Where as some will show all or most of the symptoms of dependency and severe medical or psychosocial sequelae, others will show fewer symptoms of addiction with less severe impairment. Cases in the latter stages of addiction typically are easier to detect because of the presence of many problems. Earlier stages of addiction, especially cases in which the pattern of substance abuse is episodic rather than continual, are more difficult to identify. Medical and/or psychosocial problems may be fewer or less severe for these people. Even then, however, an individual can still meet the criteria for addiction. Professionals must guard against taking the stance that the pattern of substance abuse must be a daily one or characterized by loss of control of substance intake during all episodes of use. Not all areas of functioning have to be adversely affected for addiction to be present.

7. *Accepting the chemical dependency as symptomatic of other problems.* While most addicted individuals manifest problems in emotional or interpersonal functioning, this is not to say that resolving these will eliminate the addiction. Even if a given individual has a concurrent psychiatric disorder, the substance use disorder is a problem in its own right that requires treatment. If the addiction problem is not addressed as a primary problem, and the person continues to use the substances, addressing other problems will likely be futile, both for the clinician and the client.

8. *Assuming that if the addicted individual becomes abstinent from substances, recovery is in motion.* Many alcoholics and addicts temporarily stop substance use for a variety of reasons. However, this does not ensure recovery nor indicate that the person is even in the recovery process. It is recommended that professionals adopt the stance that although abstinence from substances is an appropriate goal, behavioral and/or life-style change is also needed.

9. *Telling families that they cannot do anything to help an addicted member until he or she is "ready" for help.* The success of interventions in pressuring chemically dependent people to seek help illustrates that families do not have to accept addiction passively and wait for the

impaired member to seek help. In reality, there are many actions families can take to influence the addict. For example, getting help themselves from professionals and/or self-help programs often has an impact on the dynamics within the family and makes the addicted member uncomfortable, sometimes leading him or her voluntarily to seek help. Or families can obtain the help of a professional and plan an intervention with the aim of pressuring the addicted member to seek treatment. Because addicted individuals' judgments are impaired, many factors prevent them from being "ready" for help. In fact, professionals would probably be better off assuming that most addicted people will never be ready for treatment until others (professionals, employers, the courts, families, etc.) "make them ready."

10. *Assuming that if the chemically dependent member seeks help, the family will no longer experience pain, and improvements will occur.* Although there are sometimes immediate positive benefits within a family when an addicted member gets help, adverse effects unfold as time progresses, particularly when families do not get treatment when it is needed. Individual family systems and members within families vary in how they are affected by addiction. Often, they have recovery needs of their own that do not get resolved simply because the addicted person is in treatment.

The reality is that many professionals have at one time or another "enabled" an addicted person. The aforementioned list certainly is not all-inclusive, and readers are encouraged to think of other ways of enabling. A positive step easily taken by professionals is acknowledging enabling behaviors and making a commitment to stop.

TYPES OF ADDICTIVE SUBSTANCES

Many different substances are used and abused. These include legal and nonlegal substances as well as those prescribed by physicians for medical purposes. It is not unusual, for example, for an individual to become addicted to a tranquilizer prescribed to reduce anxiety or an analgesic medicine prescribed to reduce pain. Many addicted people have problems with more than one substance (National Institute on Drug Abuse [NIDA], 1987).

Substances are ingested in a variety of ways. They may be taken orally, snorted, smoked, or injected with a needle. The route of ingestion determines how quickly the effect of the substance is experienced.

Following is a brief review of the different types of substances abused. For a more detailed review of pharmacology and specific effects of each type of compound, the reader is advised to consult more detailed texts (e.g., Schuckit, 1989; NIAAA, 1987; NIDA, 1987)

Alcohol

All alcoholic beverages contain ethanol, which is a depressant of the central nervous system. Wine, beer, and liquor all contain ethanol. One half ounce of ethanol is found in 4 oz. of wine, in 12 oz. of beer, and in 1 oz. of 100 proof liquor. Alcohol is also found in mouthwash, vanilla extract, cough syrup, and rubbing alcohol. Some alcoholics resort to using these.

Although a depressant of the central nervous system, alcohol has a stimulating effect when used in small quantities. Depending on the amount used and the individual's unique reaction, alcohol may impair coordination, judgment, or mood. Alcohol may also affect sleep, appetite, energy level, and sexual interest or ability. Of all the substances used or abused, alcohol remains the number one problem among the chemical dependencies.

Depressants

These are sedative-hypnotic, antianxiety, and tranquilizing drugs used for a variety of medical and psychiatric disorders. About 90% of medical or surgical patients hospitalized receive antianxiety or sedative hypnotics during their hospital stay (Schuckit, 1989). They include short, intermediate, and long-acting barbiturates (Pentothal, Nembutal, Seconal, Leminol, etc.), antianxiety drugs (benzodiazepines, such as Librium, Valium, or Ativan, and carbamates such as Miltown and Equanil), and other depressants (Paraldehyde, Placidyl, Doriden, etc.). Depressant drugs may show effects similar to those of alcohol. Some are safer than others, and some are less likely to lead to tolerance or to produce physical addiction (Schuckit, 1989). However, the potential for abuse or addiction for many depressants is high.

Opiates

Opiates or narcotic analgesics, are very addictive drugs used by physicians to treat pain, coughs, and diarrhea. These include natural substances, such as morphine, codeine, and opium; semisynthetic compounds, such as heroin, dilaudid, and Percodan; and synthetic compounds, such as methadone and Darvon.

Opiates produce drowsiness, mood changes, and analgesia. In high doses depression of the central nervous system may occur. The person may experience nausea and vomiting and can become restless. If large doses of an opiate are taken, breathing slows down, pupils become smaller, and it is difficult to awaken the individual. Some of the medical and physical difficulties a user can develop include congested lungs, skin abscesses, and infection of the heart lining and valves. Infections can also develop from the use of unsterile syringes, needles, and solutions.

Heroin accounts for much of the opiate abuse in the United States, and there are an estimated 500,000 heroin addicts. Heroin is a powder, which the user usually dissolves in water and injects. Dependence is likely if there is heavy use or if there is occasional use over long periods of time.

Cocaine

Cocaine is a stimulant of the central nervous system and is used medically as a local anesthetic. Cocaine is usually found in powder form and is sniffed or snorted. When inhaled, it reaches the brain and neurons of the sympathetic nervous system in three minutes. Some users prefer to inject or smoke cocaine. Smoking cocaine is known as freebasing. By injecting, the user can be affected in 15 seconds; by smoking, in seven seconds.

Terms used for cocaine include: coke, C, snow, blow, toot, nose candy, and The Lady. Sometimes substances such as flour, baking soda, talc, and sugar are used to cut or dilute cocaine. In the mid-1980s, a highly potent form of cocaine ("crack") began to appear in the United States. This is an inexpensive form of cocaine, which has become a drug of choice for many adolescents. Some children are being born "crack addicted," to be left in hospitals by mothers who are unable to care for them. Some of these children are now reaching school age, and the long-term effects of crack cocaine on development, attention span, and learning are yet to be determined.

It is estimated that between four and six million people are current users of cocaine, while approximately one million are addicts. In low doses cocaine can enhance sexual desire, increase energy, and decrease appetite. The negative effects of cocaine use include increase in blood pressure, heart rate, body temperature, and breathing rate. Daily users experience anxiety, depression, confusion, and impaired thinking. Heavy use can cause angina and may bring on a heart attack. Although cocaine can be a sex-enhancing drug, high doses can lead to sexual dysfunction.

From 1981 to 1984, the number of reported cocaine related deaths in the United States increased from 195 to 578 a year (NIDA, 1986). As cocaine use has increased, there has been a concomitant rise in the number of people suffering from dual addictions. The most common drug used with cocaine is alcohol.

Stimulants

In addition to cocaine, there are many other stimulant drugs. These include the amphetamines (e.g., Benzedrine), dextroamphetamines (e.g., Dexedrine), methamphetamines (e.g., Desoxyn), caffeine, and stimulants such as Preludin or Ritalin. These compounds affect the central nervous system, peripheral nervous system, and cardiovascular system. They cause euphoria, increase energy, decrease fatigue, increase sexual desire, decrease appetite, and decrease the need for sleep. Like other drugs, they may also impair judgment and cause physiological or behavioral changes.

Cannabis

Cannabis is one of the most widely used and abused drugs. It is estimated that as many as 1,692,000 Americans may be dependent on marijuana (Roffman, Stephens, & Simpson, 1989). Types of cannabis include marijuana ("pot") and hashish. This drug is usually smoked in a cigarette or pipe, although it can be eaten. It produces euphoria, feelings of relaxation, heightened sexual arousal, perceptual changes, and increase in hunger. Chronic, heavy use can cause loss of appetite, sleep disturbance, anxiety, paranoia, nausea, depression, cravings for more of the drug, and respiratory problems. Chronic marijuana abusers sometimes experience loss of motivation.

Hallucinogens

These include LSD (acid), mescaline (peyote), psilocybin, and synthetic compounds (such as DOM, STP, or DMT) produced in laboratories. These drugs do not cause physical dependency. They produce changes in perceptions of the outside world or a person's internal world (i.e., how one sees, hears, smell, feels, or tastes). An altered body image and decreased ability to differentiate between oneself and the world (i.e., loss of boundaries) may also occur. Panic reactions, flashbacks, and temporary psychoses may be experienced, necessitating emergency interventions (Schuckit, 1989).

Phencyclidine (PCP)

This drug is an animal tranquilizer that can be ingested orally, smoked, or injected intravenously. It is sometimes sprayed on other drugs such as cannabis. This is probably the most unpredictable of all the drugs in terms of its effects on various individuals. Disorganization, panic, paranoia, psychosis, and manic behavior may occur. Chronic PCP abusers show increased rates of aggressiveness and violent behaviors (Schuckit, 1989).

Other Substances

A variety of other compounds may be used or abused by individuals with alcoholism or drug addiction. These include volatile or organic solvents such as gasoline, kerosene, glues, cleaning solution, and aerosols; amyl or butyl nitrites; deliriants such as nutmeg or morning glory seeds; and over-the-counter medicines such as nonprescription hypnotics, diet pills, and analgesics.

DEFINITIONS AND CONCEPTUAL FRAMEWORKS

The predominant historical view of the addicted individual is that he or she is morally weak, could stop drinking or using drugs if he or she were really motivated, and could "reform" if he or she had a strong will. Although many professionals now accept addiction as a disease, the historical view of addiction as a moral, ethical, or psychological problem still has many adherents. Empirical research about addictions has been of such short duration that terms are not yet sufficiently differentiated and are often used interchangeably. For example, the following terms are used in the professional literature to describe alcohol and other drug problems: alcoholism, alcohol abuse, alcohol dependence, problem drinking, excessive drinking, drinking problem, drug abuse, drug addiction, drug dependence, chemical abuse, chemical addiction, chemical dependence, substance abuse, and substance dependence. The problem with the use of multiple terms and definitions has been compounded by differing conceptual frameworks used in the treatment of alcohol and drug addiction (Davies, 1976).

It can be difficult for the clinician to begin with problem definition when the field has not been clear in its definition of substance abuse. For example, 104 different definitions have been recorded for alcoholism (Rogers & McMillin, 1984). There are many definitions for drug abuse or drug addiction as well. Definitions have developed from the medical, psychological, nursing, and psychiatric perspectives.

Jellinek (1960) has been credited with the development of the disease concept of alcoholism and a classification scheme for the addiction. The early type of alcoholic is labeled the *Alpha Alcoholic* in which psychological dependence exists, but there is no loss of control or of the ability to abstain. In *Beta Alcoholism* there is evidence of medical complications such as cirrhosis of the liver, gastritis, or polyneuropathy. This type of alcoholism typically develops when the socially accepted custom of drinking accompanies poor nutritional habits. *Gamma Alcoholism* was seen by Jellinek as the most characteristic pattern of American alcoholics. This type shows physical dependence, cravings, loss of control, and increased tissue tolerance. A slight distinction is made between Gamma Alcoholism and *Delta Alcoholism*: Instead of loss of control, there is only "inability to abstain." The last classification is *Epsilon Alcoholism*, a pattern characterized by periodic drinking and bouts that may last days or weeks.

The National Council on Alcoholism (NCA, 1972) classified alcoholism according to various stages. NCA developed three diagnostic levels. A person is classified as an alcoholic if he or she meets one or more of the major Diagnostic Level 1 criteria (physiological and clinical). Some of these include: physiological dependence, evidence of tolerance to the effects of alcohol, and major alcohol related illnesses. Under Diagnostic Level 2 (behavioral, psychological, and attitudinal), a person who satisfies this criteria is suspected of alcoholism, but other modes of assessment need to be made. Under Diagnostic Level 3, the person is possibly an alcoholic, but substantial additional evidence is needed before a diagnosis can be made. This evidence can include self-reports, biochemical markers, and interviews with the family members and significant others.

Definitions of addiction have ranged from the more theoretical, with clinical classifications, to the more practical, used by self-help groups such as Alcoholics Anonymous (AA) and Narcotics Anonymous (NA). AA views alcoholism and NA views addiction as diseases of the body, mind, and spirit. Addiction is characterized by an individual's "powerlessness" over alcohol or drugs—the substance controls the person's life and takes away "choice." Powerlessness over substance use results in "unmanageability" in the individual's life, and problems in living occur because of the use of substance (Alcoholics Anonymous, 1976; Narcotics Anonymous, 1983).

Experts have offered other definitions. Twerski (1984) defines addiction as the dependence of normal functions (such as work, eating, sex, or sleeping) on alcohol or drugs regardless of the quantity or effects of the drugs on behavior. Talbot (1984) sees addiction as a disease rather than a weakness or symptom of something else. The major symptom is compulsion, wherein the addict continues "to use alcohol or drugs despite the experience, logic, insight and advice" (p. 150). Talbot provides seven criteria for diagnosing addiction (p. 152):

1. Compulsive drinking or drug use
2. Changing tolerance
3. Withdrawal
4. Blackouts
5. Physical destruction
6. Psychological destruction
7. Sociocultural destruction

Wallace (1985) defines alcoholics as those who "cannot consistently control their drinking and cannot predict their personal and social behavior once they start to drink" (p.10).

The American Psychiatric Association classifies substance use disorders into two categories: (1) substance *abuse;* and (2) substance *dependence.* A person is substance dependent if he or she exhibits three or more of nine specific symptoms for a minimum period of 30 days (see Chapter 2 for a listing of these nine symptoms). The diagnosis of "abuse" is used if less than three symptoms are present. This new classification system allows a person to be diagnosed as dependent without necessarily having physiological symptoms, such as marked tolerance change or withdrawal symptoms, when substance use is stopped or reduced significantly.

THEORIES OF ADDICTION

During the past decade there have been major advances in our knowledge of the biological, psychological, and behavioral underpinnings of addiction. What has not occurred is a similar acceleration in society's perception of the disease as illness, nor in the strategies used to prevent and treat both the disease and related social and environmental factors.

The reasons that people become addicted have perplexed scientists, physicians, psychiatrists, and other human-service personnel for decades. Their debates have led to many theoretical models that claim to explain why some people become addicted and others do not. It has been especially difficult to separate and isolate the hereditary and the environmental components of addiction. In April 1990, the *New York Times* reported that "scientists generally accept the notion that alcoholism is based on complex genetic, cultural and social factors" (Altman, 1990, p.A18). The existence of multiple theories necessitates that the clinician keep abreast of changes in ongoing research and new medical evidence related to a genetic predisposition to alcoholism.

There are numerous theories of addiction. These include social learning, psychodynamic, genetic, rational-emotive, and multivariate. In this section, a brief summary of the major theories of addiction is provided. For in-depth exploration of these theories, the reader is encouraged to consult the bibliography.

Social Learning Theory

Social learning theory is one branch of conditioning theory. This school of thought does not view alcoholism as a disease or as a personal deficiency. It proposes that individuals who experience a great deal of stress learn that alcohol decreases anxiety and tension. This learned response to decreasing stress becomes a positive reinforcer, and the individual continues to use it until physical dependence develops. Unless a person continues to drink, withdrawal will occur. In order not to experience the adverse effects of withdrawal, the withdrawal symptoms become the stimuli for continued drinking (Anderson, 1987).

In a social learning model, addicts are seen as having learned from past experience and through social conditioning to anticipate that alcohol (or drugs) will solve their problems. Addictive behavior is seen as a response to highly emotional states of an individual or highly charged settings (Peele, 1987). Alcoholism is a learned behavior that results from reinforcement of pleasurable experiences or from avoidance of negative ones.

Learning theorists believe that drinking patterns and alcoholism can be explained through social sanctions and norms of society related to drinking behavior. In addition, these components of learned behavior also contribute to unlearning behaviors.

Because behavior is learned through stimuli, aversion techniques are utilized in addiction treatment. For example, electric shock treatments or nausea-inducing drugs such as Antabuse may be prescribed for drug- and alcohol-dependent individuals (Nardi, 1982).

Psychodynamic Theory

Psychodynamic theory views the alcoholic as a person whose early childhood deprivation or overindulgence causes an unconscious need for nurturance. Very often these dependency needs cannot be met, and the individual becomes anxious and develops the need for power and control. Although alcohol is used to reduce anxiety, it also creates a false sense of power. When the person is sober, he or she becomes overwhelmed with feelings of anxiety and failure, which lead to continued drinking.

One major criticism of this theory is that "although early childhood deprivation or overindulgence may increase vulnerability to the development of alcoholism, these experiences are not specific to alcoholism. In fact, they are reported by adults with a variety of psychosocial problems" (Anderson, 1987, p. 136).

In addition to being oral dependent, alcoholics also have been considered latent homosexuals and deficient in ego functions. Although the psychodynamic model focuses on individual dysfunction, it does not exclude the impact of social factors and significant individuals in the development of the addiction.

Physiological/Genetic Theory

The idea that alcoholism has a genetic basis has been postulated for a long time. Genetic theorists believe that alcoholism is an inherited disease. In 1956, the American Medical Association classified alcoholism as a disease because it fit the classical definitions of a disease. That is, it affects a large number of people, and it has a cluster of symptoms, a predetermined outcome, and a prescribed treatment. This view is supported through observations and studies that show that alcoholism runs in families; racial differences seem to exist in alcohol sensitivity (Wolff, 1972); and adopted children who have an alcoholic biological parent have higher rates of alcoholism than adopted children who do not have an alcoholic biological parent (Goodwin, Schulsinger, Hermansen, Guze, & Winokur, 1973).

The mechanism of inheritance of alcoholism is not yet definitely known. Some perspectives include: an inherited weak constitution leading to a proneness for the disease (Jellinek, 1960); a glandular disorder that leads to an endocrine imbalance as the individual continues to drink (Tintera & Lovell, 1949); a neurochemical deficiency that has early childhood manifestations such as minimal brain damage and hyperactivity (Cantwell, 1972); and a biochemical explanation of alcoholism that views alcoholism as a food addiction.

The etiology of a genetic link to alcoholism has been speculative because, until recently, researchers have not been able to isolate a specific gene. *The New York Times* reported that "a gene that puts people at risk of becoming alcoholics has been identified for the first time (Altman, 1990). The gene found to be linked to alcoholism was the receptor gene for dopamine. The study, carried out by Dr. Ernest P. Noble (UCLA) and Dr. Kenneth Flume (University of Texas Health Science Center), studied the brains of 35 people who died of alcoholism and 35 others who were not alcoholics. The gene was present in 77% of the alcoholics and 28% of the nonalcoholics. The researchers do not believe that one gene causes all forms of alcoholism. However, this research may lead the way for new methodologies of prevention and treatment. Further research along the lines of this study may eventually lead to a determination of what role genetics play in abuse, addiction, and damage to vital organs, and of what role culture and environment play in alcoholism.

The genetic model does not attribute alcoholism to psychological or family problems. Alcohol contributes to the alcoholic's inability to cope with daily problems of living and causes pathological behaviors. Tarter and Edwards (1986) advocate a behavior-genetic basis of alcoholism etiology. "Alcohol consumption in predisposed individuals may be the only one of a variety of available coping strategies and . . . its selection over other drugs may reflect the involvement of nonbiological factors (i.e., sociocultural influences and alcoholic beverage availability)" (p. 355).

Rational-Emotive

The rational-emotive approach theorizes that irrational beliefs impact on low frustration tolerance, causing anxiety and discomfort in the individual. Overindulgence in alcohol or other drug use occurs as a way of handling these feelings of frustration or anxiety. The addict believes, for example, that he or she cannot function without a drink or a drug, or that abstaining is too painful. A feeling of deprivation results from decisions to abstain from using. This in turn leads to experiencing low frustration tolerance. Examples of irrational beliefs leading to feelings of frustration include "I cannot stand avoiding a drink," "I must have a drink or I can't go on," and"I must not abstain when it's so enjoyable to imbibe" (Ellis, McInerney, DiGiuseppe, & Yeager, 1988).

The rational-emotive approach views alcohol or drug intoxification as a way of coping with problems or stresses. Alcohol or drugs enable the individual to avoid or escape from problems. The person believes that alcohol or drug use is a way of relaxing and reducing tension. Irrational beliefs that may contribute to use include "I can't stand being upset," or " I'm too weak to stand this upsetting emotion."

Addicts may believe that they are in a hopeless situation and judge themselves as worthless. Such thinking leads to feelings of guilt or depression; substance abuse is perceived as a way to relieve the emotional discomfort temporarily. The rational-emotive approach views addiction as a result of using alcohol or drugs to seek excitement. These individuals cannot stand boredom or monotony and use drugs as a way of providing excitement (Ellis, McInerney, DiGiuseppe, & Eager, 1988).

Multivariate Approach

This approach theorizes that addiction is a multivariate syndrome. Rather than view the addiction as a unitary phenomenon, it acknowledged that there are multiple patterns of substance use occurring in multiple types of personalities, with a variety of adverse consequences. Individuals will have multiple prognoses and may require different treatment interventions. Pattison and Kaufman (1982) base this model on current scientific evidence. They espouse the following propositions (pp. 24-26):

1. Alcohol dependence (addiction) subsumes a variety of syndromes defined by drinking patterns and adverse consequences.
2. Use occurs on a continuum from nonuse to various degrees of deleterious drinking.
3. The development of alcohol problems follows variable patterns over time.
4. Abstinence bears no relation to rehabilitation.
5. Psychological and physical dependency are not separate and not necessarily related phenomena.
6. Continued drinking of large doses over time is likely to lead to physical dependence.
7. The population of individuals with alcohol problems is multivariate.
8. Alcohol problems are interrelated with other life problems.
9. Treatment should also emphasize the drinking environment of the individual.
10. Treatment and rehabilitation services should provide for continuity of care over an extended period of time.
11. Evaluation of treatment outcome should recognize degrees of improvement.

The available evidence suggests that there is a multiplicity of factors that contribute to the development and maintenance of alcoholism or other drug addictions. It is probably an interaction among multiple factors that ultimately determines whether or not a given individual develops an addiction. These factors include genetic vulnerability, individual differences in drug response, metabolism, brain chemistry, learning factors, personality, coping mechanisms, drug availability, and the influence of family, culture, and environment (Daley, 1988; Goodwin, 1988; Marlatt & Gordon, 1985; Mule, 1981; NIDA 1988a, 1988b; Pattison & Kaufman, 1982).

REFERENCES

AA World Services. (1976). *Alcoholics Anonymous.* New York: Author.
Altman, L. K. (1990, April 18). Scientists see a link between alcoholism and a specific gene. *The New York Times,* pp. A1, A18.
Anderson, S. C. (1987). Alcohol use and addiction. *Encyclopedia of social work* (18th ed., pp. 132-142). Silver Spring, MD: National Association of Social Workers.

Cantwell, D. (1972). Psychiactric illness in the families of hyperactive children. *Archives of General Psychiatry, 27,*414-417.

Daley, D. (1988). *Surviving addiction.* New York: Gardner.

Davies, D. L. (1976). Definitional issues in alcoholism. In R. E. Tarter & A. Sugarman (Eds.), *Alcoholism: Interdisciplinary approaches to an enduring problem* (pp. 53-73). Reading, MA: Addison-Wesley.

Ellis, A., McInerney, J. F., DiGiuseppe, R., & Yeager, R. (1988). *Rationale-emotive therapy with alcoholics and substance abusers.* Elmsford, NY: Pergamon.

Goodwin, D. (1988). *Is alcoholism hereditary?* (2nd ed.). New York: Ballantine.

Goodwin, D. W., Schulsinger, F., Hermansen, L., Guze, S. B., & Winokur, G. (1973). Alcohol problems in adoptees raised apart from biological parents. *Archives of General Psychiatry, 28,* 238-243.

Jellinek, E. M. (1960). *The disease concept of alcoholism.* New Haven, CT: Hillhouse.

Kola, K., & Kosberg, J. (1980, May). *A model for the assessment of community service delivery systems for the elderly alcoholic.* Paper presented at the Annual Forum of the National Conference of Social Welfare, Cleveland, OH.

Marlatt, G. A., & Gordon, J. (Eds.). (1985). *Relapse prevention.* New York: Guilford.

Mule, S. J. (Ed.). (1981). *Behavior in excess.* New York: Free Press.

NA World Services. (1983). *Narcotics Anonymous.* Van Nuys. CA: Author.

Nardi, P. (1982). Alcoholism and homosexuality: A theoretical perspective. *Journal of Alcohol and Homosexuality, 7*(4), 9-25.

National Council on Alcoholism, Criteria Committee. (1972). Criteria with the diagnosis of alcoholism. *American Journal of Psychiatry, 129,* 127-135.

National Institute on Alcohol Abuse and Alcoholism. (1981). *Fourth special report to the U.S. Congress on alcohol and health* Washington, DC: U.S. Department of Health and Human Services.

National Institute of Alcohol Abuse and Alcoholism. (1987). *Alcohol and health.* Rockville, MD: Author.

National Institute on Drug Abuse. (1986). *Cocaine use in America. Prevention network* (p. 10). DHHS, Publ. No. (ADM) 86-1433. Rockville, MD: Author.

National Institute on Drug Abuse (1987). *Drug abuse and drug abuse research.* Rockville, MD: Author.

National Institute on Drug Abuse. (1988a). *Biological vulnerability to drug abuse.* Rockville, MD: Author.

National Institute on Drug Abuse. (1988b). *Learning factors in substance abuse.* Rockville, MD: Author.

Out in the Open. (1987, November 30). *Time,* pp. 80-90.

Pattison, E. M., & Kaufman, E. (1982). The alcoholism syndrome: Definitions and models. In E. M. Pattison & E. Kaufman (Eds.), *Encyclopedia handbook of alcoholism* (pp. 3-30). New York: Gardner.

Peele, S. (1987). *The meaning of addiction: Compulsive experience and its interpretation.* Lexington, MA: D. C. Heath.

Roffman, R. A., Stephens, R. S., & Simpson, E. E. (1989). Relapse prevention with chronic marijuana smokers. In D. Daley (Ed.), *Relapse: Conceptual, research and clinical perspectives.* New York: Haworth.

Rogers, R., & McMillin, C. (1984). *Don't help—A guide to working with the alcoholic.* West Friendship, MD: Education and Training Intitute of Maryland.

Schuckit, M. (1989). *Drug and alcohol abuse: A clinical guide to diagnosis and treatment.* New York: Plenum.

Talbot, G. D. (1984). Substance abuse and the professional provider: The need for new attitudes about addiction. *Alabama Journal of Medical Sciences, 21*(2), 150-155.

Tarter, R., & Edwards, K. (1986). Antecedents to alcoholism: Implications for prevention and treatment. *Behavior Therapy, 17,* 346-361.

Tintera, J., & Lovell, H. (1949). Endocrine treatment of alcoholism. *Geriatrics, 4,* 274-280.

Twerski, A. (1984). *Self-discovery in recovery.* Center City, MN: Hazeldon.

Wallace, J. (1985). *Alcoholism: New light on the disease.* Newport. RI: Edgehill.

Wolff, P. H. (1972). Ethnic differences in alcohol sensitivity. *Science, 175,* 449-450.

Chapter 2

ASSESSMENT OF
ADDICTION PROBLEMS

MIRIAM S. RASKIN
DENNIS C. DALEY

INTRODUCTION:
PROFESSIONAL PERSPECTIVE

The assessment of client problems has subjective and objective elements. With clients who have drug and alcohol problems, the subjective elements—the personal reactions and feelings of the helping professional toward a client—may be anger, hostility, or frustration. Not all clinicians are comfortable with clients who deny their alcohol or drug problems. Clients may come to the interview intoxicated, or they may be hostile or resistant to treatment. Some clinicians choose to work with a population or a problem area that would not ordinarily involve contact with certain groups such as alcoholics, homosexuals, adolescents, or handicapped individuals. However, because drug and alcohol addiction is pervasive and causes problems in virtually any area of functioning, it is impossible to avoid working with addicted clients or their families.

The professional literature amply documents negative attitudes toward clients with alcohol and other drug problems (Chappell, Veach, & Krug, 1985; Googins, 1984; *Human Behavior,* 1972; Knox, 1971; Mendelson et al., 1964; Milam & Ketcham, 1985; Talbott, 1984). Negative attitudes often result from personal experiences with an addicted family member, friend, patient, or client that were painful or difficult for the worker. Such attitudes may also result from the influence of other professionals (e.g., supervisors or colleagues) who display negative attitudes toward addicted people. Clinicians who believe that alcohol or other drug use is "bad" or "wrong," or that those with addictions are "weak," are very susceptible to judging these clients in negative ways.

Attitudes and perceptions should be examined to clarify how the professional views alcohol, other drug use, and people who have addiction problems. Self-exploration can help reduce the likelihood of a negative attitude interfering with the clinician's ability to help addicted clients or their families. For example, if unresolved anger is felt toward a parent, these feelings can be unconsciously displaced from the clinician to the person seeking help. Even though the clinician may not be aware of this process, it can result in decreased interest in helping the client or in inappropriate anger with the client. If prior attempts to help an alcoholic or drug addict have failed, the professional may begin to feel that addicts cannot be helped. If an attempt to help fails, the blame may be placed on the client rather than on the worker's lack of knowledge or skills. If a clinician has been manipulated by addicted people, he or she may also adopt a negative or hostile attitude toward these clients. The professional essentially projects negative feelings about himself or herself onto clients.

In examining the potential bias of negative attitudes, the clinician can consider the following questions:

1. What substances have you used? What were the results?
2. What role do substances currently play in your life?
3. Does your religion influence your use or nonuse of alcohol or other drugs? If yes, how?
4. Have you personally known any drug addicts or alcoholics?
5. If you have known such people, how has their addiction affected your life?
6. Do you believe in addiction as a disease?
7. Do you think addiction is treatable?
8. Do you think an addicted person must "hit bottom" or admit to having a problem before he or she can be helped?
9. How do you feel about working with a client who is an alcoholic or a drug addict?
10. How do you feel about working with an alcoholic or drug addict who doesn't want help?

In order to make an accurate assessment and effective intervention with addicted clients, it is important to combine knowledge and skills with empathy, objectivity, and realistic expectations. The professional must believe that addiction and related problems are treatable. If the helping professional is moralistic about addiction problems, intimidated by addicted clients, angry or hostile with them, feels they are hopeless, or is overly protective or enabling, then clients may not be properly assessed and/or treated.

Negative attitudes toward addicted clients or their families may be overcome by self-assessment and by increasing knowledge and understanding of addiction, relapse, and recovery. The clinician can attend "open" group meetings of Alcoholics Anonymous, Narcotics Anonymous, Al-Anon, or Nar-Anon; attend professional workshops; read professional literature; or visit addiction treatment centers. Talking with people who are successfully recovering from addiction is of tremendous value. If the professional continues to experience negative feelings or reactions toward addicted clients, or if he or she struggles with personal problems associated with a significant other's addiction, personal therapy should be undertaken. Some practitioners and treatment centers offer a range of educational and therapeutic programs that help individuals deal with personal issues or problems in their relationships with addicted people.

The following account of a clinician's personal experiences illustrates some of these attitudinal issues and their impact on professional work:

I grew up in a home with an alcoholic mother. My four siblings and I had a lot of difficulties because of her alcoholism and my father's absence from the home. He dealt with her problem by avoiding it. The sad thing was that he avoided us all as well. This experience growing up in an alcoholic family definitely was a major factor in my decision to become a social worker. I wanted to help others who had problems.

My first paid job was in a family service agency where I worked with a wide range of problems with children, parents, and families. Although in retrospect I can say that a good number of these families were having problems because of a parent's addiction, in my work at the time I seldom even discussed anything related to the addiction. There were some cases, for example, where the alcoholism was blatant. Yet I still didn't face it. I always felt uncomfortable with the idea of talking about someone's alcohol problem. I remember having a lot of negative, judgmental thoughts towards my addicted client. These were the same feelings I had towards my alcoholic mother. I also had a tendency to become very impatient with the spouses of these clients because I figured they put themselves into the situation, and could get out of it if they really wanted to. Again, I likened their situations to that of my father. Somehow, deep down, I harbored the belief that he could have done something about my mother's alcoholism.

Until I understood and accepted alcoholism as a disease, and healed from my personal emotional wounds, I was ineffective with clients or families with alcoholism or other drug addiction problems. I finally was able to achieve this acceptance, and to forgive my parents, through personal growth experienced in a group of adult children of alcoholics and in personal therapy. Much of my anger, guilt, and shame was resolved, although it took a long time. The result has been that I am much more astute at assessing addiction-related problems, and much more effective with my clients. Had I not achieved this personal growth, I am convinced that I would still be having difficulties helping clients with problems related to an addiction.

—Al, son of an alcoholic, age 32

INTRODUCTION TO ASSESSMENT

Assessment can be one of the most difficult steps in the helping process, especially when addiction is the "hidden" problem. Googins (1984) states that, "because problem drinking is 'problem causing,' it is not surprising that human service staff most often encounter alcoholism shrouded by many other social problems" (p. 161).

The addicted person may seek help in a medical setting, a crisis clinic, a mental health agency, a family service agency, or from a private practitioner or a public assistance agency. In the medical setting, the presenting problem may be pancreatitis, liver disease, traumatic injury, or broken bones. In the mental health setting, the person may present depression, suicidal feelings, self-destructive behavior, anxiety, psychotic symptoms, or problems associated with an organic brain syndrome. Each of these problems may be a result of alcoholism or drug addiction. The professional must recognize that the problem may not be resolved if the addiction is not confronted and proper treatment is not initiated. Or, if the problem is resolved, other serious difficulties related to the addiction are likely to continue if the addiction is not treated. For example, an alcoholic's gastritis may be treated in the medical setting, but his or her family may continue to suffer adverse emotional and financial consequences as a result of the alcoholism.

In agencies where the primary focus is the treatment of addiction, clinical interviews and assessment instruments are geared toward direct questions about addiction. However, in settings where problems other than addiction are usually presented (e.g., schools, family services, mental health agencies, juvenile courts) clinicians routinely need to incorporate specific questions about substance use in the assessment process in order to recognize the presence of an addiction and to formulate an effective treatment plan.

The next two sections of this chapter will review assessment criteria and the assessment process. The reader will be introduced to paper-and-pencil assessment tools that can be used in the beginning stages of problem definition. Sample questions about addiction that can be adapted to most health, mental health, social service, and other settings will be provided. The chapter will also include case examples of assessment interviews with the addicted individual as well as with significant others (e.g., family or friends). The components of the clinical interview will be discussed, including problems the clinician will face and possible strategies the interviewer can use in conducting diagnostic interviews.

ASSESSMENT CRITERIA

According to the updated criteria (DSM-III-R) of the American Psychiatric Association, substance-use disorders fall into one of two categories: substance dependence or substance abuse. Dependence is generally regarded as a more serious form of the disorder than is abuse. A diagnosis of dependence is given if three or more of the following nine symptoms are present for a minimum of 30 days (APA, 1987):

1. Repeated effort or persistent desire to cut down or control substance use.
2. Often intoxicated or impaired by substance use when expected to fulfill social or occupational obligations, or when substance use is a hazard (e.g., doesn't go to work because of being hung over or high; goes to work high; drives when drunk).
3. Tolerance: need for increased amounts of substance in order to achieve intoxication or desired effect with continued use of same amount.

4. Withdrawal: substance-specific syndrome following cessation or reduction of intake of substance.
5. Frequent preoccupation with seeking or taking the substance.
6. Has given up some important social, occupational, or recreational activity in order to seek or take the substance.
7. Often uses a psychoactive substance to relieve or avoid withdrawal symptoms (e.g., takes a drink or diazepam to relieve morning shakes).
8. Often takes the substance in larger doses or over a longer period than originally intended.
9. Continuation of substance use despite a physical or mental disorder or a significant social or legal problem that the individual knows is exacerbated by the use of the substance.

One of the major changes from DSM-III to DSM-III-R criteria is that an individual can now be diagnosed as having a dependency problem without the presence of physiological criteria such as withdrawal symptoms or significant tolerance changes.

THE ASSESSMENT PROCESS

In order to determine if an addiction exists and what type of treatment is indicated, the health care professional will need to obtain a thorough history from the client, family, and/or other sources (e.g., records and referents). This history is an ongoing process, and it may take more than one interview to evaluate the client. Although the clinician can get accurate information from the client, collateral sources of information often help in developing a comprehensive assessment and initial treatment plan. Specific information is needed about the pattern of substance use in terms of:

- specific substances used
- age at first use
- date of last use
- usual pattern of use (e.g., daily, weekly, variable)
- methods of use (for certain drugs—oral, smoke, injection)
- if needles are used to inject drugs, are they clean? are they shared with others?
- any significant tolerance change (increase or decrease)

- any withdrawal symptoms experienced when use is stopped or cut markedly
- any complications related to use such as overdoses, blackouts, or convulsions

The history of substance use should include the use of prescribed drugs as well as illicit drugs. The clinician can further ask the client which substance(s) is(are) preferred and whether multiple substances are used in order to "boost" the effects. The client should also be asked about the duration and circumstances of any significant period of complete abstinence from substance use (e.g., did this period occur while recovering from a physical problem, while incarcerated, or was it self-initiated?)

It is best to be specific when asking the client about substance use (e.g., "Mr. Smith, I am going to ask you about your use of tobacco, alcohol, and other drugs, including prescribed medications and over-the-counter substances") rather than ask general questions, such as "Do you use drugs?" Questions asked in general terms to a person who is addicted are likely to evoke erroneous information because of the way the client may interpret the question. For example, the client can take the question "Do you use drugs?" to mean "Am I currently (today or this week) using drugs? Am I using 'hard' drugs? Am I using illegal drugs?" Because of denial associated with addiction, these kinds of client responses are very common. Older alcoholics very often do not perceive excessive use of prescription drugs as "drug abuse," even when they are dependent on these drugs.

Patterns of Substance Use

There is a wide variation in the pattern of substance use among people. Figure 2.1 illustrates a continuum of substance use and the accompanying consequences. For example. nonproblematic use includes medicinal drugs or social drinking. Misuse may take many forms, including seldom drinking but getting intoxicated at a New Year's Eve party, or taking more of a drug than prescribed. Any form of substance misuse, abuse, or dependence may have consequences that vary from mild to fatal. The following brief examples illustrate different degrees of problems and medical/social effects of substance use:

A Continuum of Substance Use

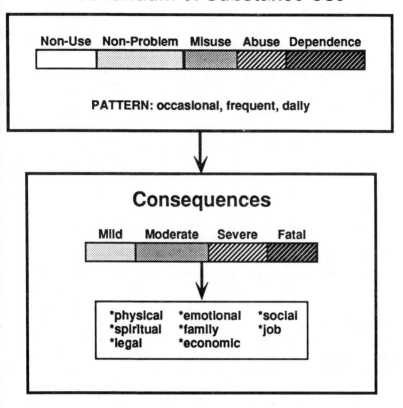

Figure 2.1 A Continuum of Substance Use

Substance Misuse/Abuse

Case 1: Ethel is a 67-year-old retired librarian who has been receiving tranquilizers and sleeping pills from her doctor for several months. When she gets extremely nervous, she will sometimes take two or three times the dosage prescribed, or have a couple of glasses of wine to help her relax.

Case 2: Gene is a 45-year-old minister who is respected in his community. He drinks alcohol in social situations about four times a year. Last New Year's Eve he and his wife attended a party during which time he had several mixed drinks. On the way home, he wrecked his car and was charged with driving under the influence. This was one of the few times in his life that Gene was drunk.

Case 3: Ralph is a 34-year-old married father of two children and has his own wallpapering business. He seldom drinks during the week but drinks heavily on weekends, especially when his friends drop by. When drinking, he will occasionally instigate a fight with his wife or children. His weekend drinking has been a source of friction between him and his family for several years. His wife feels that Ralph ignores the family and complains that it's difficult to get him to go places on the weekend. Recently, he experienced blackouts and doesn't seem to be able to control his alcohol use as he has in years past.

Substance Dependence

Case 1: Bob is a 38-year-old heroin addict with a 20-year-plus history of addictive use of multiple substances. He injects $200 to $300 worth of heroin daily and often uses other opioid and depressant drugs as well as alcohol. To support his addiction, Bob sells drugs and sometimes resorts to robbery. He estimates he's committed hundreds of robberies over the years to support his addiction. Bob's life is controlled totally by his addiction. As a result, he's lost contact with his family, has not held a steady job in over nine years, has been arrested and sent to prison twice, and was once stabbed in a fight over drugs. He hangs out solely with addicts and often goes to "shooting galleries" where others inject drugs into his veins. His drug use has resulted in several overdoses, poor physical health, and periods of depression. He's suffered through severe withdrawal discomfort dozens of times. Bob has also been detoxified 14 times from heroin, alcohol, and other drugs, and has completed a rehabilitation program. His longest "clean time" has been four months.

Case 2: Larry is an alcoholic and pill addict who managed to avoid problems resulting from his addiction until several months ago. He has had a number of blackouts following binges, where he cannot remember what he said or did. Although he's gotten sick after heavy drinking binges, Larry has only experienced mild physical withdrawal symptoms. Because of failure to seek treatment, he was recently suspended from the company where he had worked for 24 years as an engineer. This action enraged him so much he went out and got drunk. He then wrecked his car and got arrested for driving under the influence. Larry must now seek treatment, or he will lose his job and face jail time.

Case 3: Bart is a 47-year-old chronic alcoholic who drinks several quarts of wine a day. He sleeps in local church shelters, abandoned buildings, or under bridges. He hasn't held a job in 10 years or seen any relative for more than 6 years. When Bart eats, it's usually in a soup kitchen. He sometimes panhandles for money. He looks much older than his age, has few teeth left, is grossly underweight, and has an enlarged liver. Bart has been in the hospital and detoxification facilities over 50 times. He cannot be without wine for more than eight hours or he gets nervous, sick, and shakes badly. He's had DTs (delirium tremens) many times.

Effects of Substance Use

In addition to information about the patterns of substance use, the clinician will need to get informⱥtion on the effects of substance use on several areas of functioning: physical and medical condition; eating patterns and diet; emotional and psychological health (e.g., moods, self-esteem); interpersonal and family relationships; work and/or school; social activities; financial condition; legal status; and spirituality. The professional can then inquire as to whether or not the client has participated in any type of professional treatment such as medical or social detoxification, inpatient or outpatient rehabilitation, a halfway house or therapeutic community, outpatient counseling, methadone maintenance, or pharmacotherapy such as bromocriptine (cocaine addicts), naltrexone (opioid addicts), or disulfiram (Antabuse; alcoholics).

It is also valuable to ask about participation in self-help recovery programs such as Alcoholics Anonymous, Narcotics Anonymous, Cocaine Anonymous, Women for Sobriety, and others. The clinician needs to determine when and where the client attended meetings, for how long, and what type (e.g., lead, discussion, 12-step meetings). It is important to know if the client had a "sponsor" or worked the "12-step program" of recovery, and how participation in professional treatment or self-help programs has affected the client. For relapsed alcoholics and drug addicts, a review of prior treatment facilitates the development of goals and plans for the prevention of relapse.

A significant percentage of addicted clients have psychiatric disorders (Daley, Moss, & Campbell, 1987; Hesselbrock, Meyer, & Keener, 1985; Rounsaville, Spitzer, & Williams, 1986). Therefore, the clinician should determine if mental health problems currently exist, or if there has been treatment of such problems. The clinician can explore factors precipitating previous treatment and related outcome.

Because addictions run in families, it is important to find out if the client has any relatives with a history of substance abuse or psychiatric disorders. Family history of treatment in professional or self-help programs should also be assessed.

The clinical interviews provide the opportunity to assess the client's perception of the problems and motivation for treatment. Clients with addiction problems frequently do not perceive themselves as having a problem requiring treatment, regardless of the type of agency or setting. These clients often come to substance abuse treatment settings as the result of external pressure from their family, employer, or court (e.g., as a result of a charge of driving while intoxicated). Initial motivation for treatment is not necessary (Carroll, & Schnoll, 1982; Daley, Moss, & Campbell, 1987; Laundergan, Spicer, & Kammeier, 1979). How the client perceives both his or her problems and his or her needs are critical variables in the helping relationship.

An assessment of the strength and weaknesses of the client is part of the initial screening process. This helps the professional in the development of the treatment plan. Assessment is an ongoing process for those clinicians who will see a client over a period of time, and it is not unusual to uncover important pieces of information over time.

The professional should pay particular attention to the client's social network as a critical variable in defining problems and determining treatment goals. Many addicted clients are part of dysfunctional social systems in which all or most relationships are with others who abuse, or are addicted to, substances. This is especially common for those clients whose life-styles revolve around the planning and use of substances.

Because there will be some clients who will not be honest about their history of substance use, biochemical screens of blood and urine may help to establish most recent drugs used. One client presented a history of alcoholism while denying use of any other substances. Results of urine tests indicated he had a very high level of THC (the active ingredient of marijuana) in his system. Upon presentation of this finding, he reluctantly admitted to an extensive history of dependence on marijuana. His intent was to discuss his alcoholism in treatment and ignore his marijuana use. With the additional information from the urinalysis, the clinician was able to explore issues pertinent to the client's marijuana addiction. The worker should be aware, however, that laboratory tests vary in their accuracy, and that some substances can only be detected within hours of their use.

BIOCHEMICAL MARKERS

Two laboratory tests used in conjunction may be useful in early detection of alcoholism. These are the GGTP (gammaglutamyl transpeptidase) and the MCV (mean corpuscular volume) tests. The GGTP is used to detect heavy alcohol use. The accuracy of this indicator is affected by "coexisting liver pathology, drug use, and individual metabolic differences among alcohol abusers" (NIAAA, 1987, p. 110).

A worker needs to become familiar with laboratory tests that have been shown to have some accuracy in discriminating between alcoholics and nonalcoholics. Blood samples or urinalysis can help establish current drug levels within the system, but no single biochemical marker has been found that can sufficiently screen alcoholics in the general population. It would be important to request that clients have biochemical tests done when other assessment tools (1) seem vague and inconclusive, (2) are contradictory in their results, and (3) seem to be pointing to alcoholism, and the worker wishes to have a more complete picture by using a combination of clinical, psychosocial, and medical/laboratory tests.

SELF-ASSESSMENT QUESTIONNAIRES

Paper-and-pencil self-assessment instruments also are used to gather data from clients. Questionnaires have been developed for purposes of assessment, treatment planning, and research. A brief review of several of these instruments follows.

Michigan Alcoholism Screening Test (MAST)

Researchers and practitioners have become increasingly interested in early diagnostic and screening instruments for alcoholic individuals. Some symptoms such as alcohol-related accidents and escape drinking may appear early in an alcoholic's drinking history. The MAST is a self-administered instrument consisting of 25 true/false statements, which takes approximately 5 to 10 minutes to complete. It was devised to detect alcoholism through a quantifiable, structured interview instrument. The statements describe medical, social, and behavioral problems associated with excessive drinking. The MAST distinguishes male alcoholics from nonalcoholics. The simplicity and gender specificity of this instrument place limits on its usefulness for general population screening. In addition, it allows the respondent to falsify answers deliberately or through unconscious denial (NIAAA, 1987). The questions of the MAST are clearly related to alcoholism. It could be used in an addiction-focused agency, or in an agency or hospital whose expressed purposes are something other than to treat alcohol-related problems. The MAST has been used in medical settings to identify patients with alcohol-related problems. Following are five sample questions from the MAST:

1. Do you feel you are a normal drinker?
2. Have you ever awakened the morning after some drinking the night before and found you could not remember a part of the evening before?
3. Have you ever lost a job because of drinking?
4. Do you ever have a drink before noon?
5. Have you ever been arrested, even for a few hours, because of drunk behavior?

Drug Abuse Screening Test (DAST)

The DAST is designed to provide a brief instrument to screen clinically individuals with problems related to drug abuse. This is a self-administered questionnaire consisting of 20 items. A 10-item DAST is also available.

The total DAST score gives a quantitative index of the severity of the problem. It takes five minutes to complete and is inexpensive to administer. The DAST has diagnostic value for screening and assessment in substance abuse treatment and other settings (Skinner, 1984).

The DAST can differentiate among clients who have either drug problems only, alcohol problems only, or mixed drug/alcohol problems. Those clients with alcohol-related problems typically score five or below, and those with drug problems or mixed alcohol/drug problems score six or above.

The DAST could be used to complement data gained through clinical interviews and/or lab tests. The DAST is minimally influenced by biases of denial and social desirability in treatment centers. These biases may have more of an impact on client responses in an employ-ment or criminal justice setting. The reader should review the DAST instrument to determine if it is appropriate for the client population in a particular agency. Following are five questions from the DAST that refer to the past 12 months in the client's life:

1. Have you used drugs other than those required for medical reasons?
2. Can you get through the week without using drugs?
3. Have you engaged in illegal activities in order to obtain drugs?
4. Have you ever experienced withdrawal symptoms (felt sick) when you stopped taking drugs?
5. Have you been involved in a treatment program specifically related to drug use?

Dr. G. Douglas Talbot's Questionnaire

The Talbot Questionnaire is an assessment tool used for *adults* to help them determine if they have a problem with alcohol or drugs. It is a three-step self-assessment that requires an individual to respond to a 29-item questionnaire. If three or more answers in the questionnaire are "yes," then a seven-day diary is kept that describes specific activities such as conversations about drinking, amount of money spent for alcohol/drugs, and what other people who are close to the client think about his or her drinking or drug use. The third step is a self-assessment that involves asking oneself whether drinking or drug usage signifi-cantly interferes with physical health, psychological and emotional health, family life, religion, employment, and money and finances. If the answer is "yes," the individual is warned that he or she may be addicted and need help.

The self-assessment, like many others, requires the person to be honest and to be able to read and write at a reasonably high level, and it requires a person to be disciplined enough to keep an accurate diary (Twerski, 1982). This is suitable for individuals expressing concern over substance use who are not certain if they need help. Following is a sample of questions from the questionnaire:

1. Is drinking or drug use associated with fights or arguments at home with your spouse or children?
2. When you miss your accustomed drink or drugs, do you become nervous and shaky until you have had some alcohol or a pill?

3. Are you having trouble sleeping now?
4. Is your business or are your bills going badly since you started drinking or taking drugs?
5. Are you having trouble with your sex life since you started drinking or taking drugs?

Substance Abuse Problem Checklist (SAPC)

The SAPC is a self-administered inventory. The checklist, according to its developer, Dr. Jerome F. X. Carroll, is cost-effective, pragmatic, and reflects AA's and NA's philosophy of taking a personal inventory. The SAPC is appropriate for treatment, research, and administrative uses. It can be completed in approximately 40 to 45 minutes and can reliably provide relevant clinical information.

The SAPC adds the dimension of ecological dysfunction ("problems in living") to the ordinarily collected data that relate to physical and psychological problems. The statements are specific—"I need someone to take care of my children," rather than "I have family problems" (Carroll, 1984).

The checklist is grouped into eight major categories with 377 total problem statements. The categories are:

1. motivation for treatment
2. health
3. personality
4. social relationships
5. job
6. leisure time
7. religious or spiritual
8. legal

There are three additional questions at the end of the instrument. They ask the respondent to identify which of the problems marked in the booklet (1) have the *most* to do with his or her drinking and/or use of drugs, (2) he or she is willing to work on while in treatment in this program, and (3) he or she and the treatment staff should work on *first*. The SAPC can be used in inpatient or outpatient substance abuse treatment contexts and is most useful in identifying problems early in treatment. When clients participate in a self-inventory, they become participants in identifying and developing individualized treatment plans. Because the SAPC identifies environmental issues, it can be used by the practitioner in developing aftercare plans for clients leaving treatment.

The following is a sample of the Substance Abuse Problem Checklist (SAPC):

Directions: Inside this booklet are different kinds of problems that alcoholics and addicts typically have when they enter treatment. Please read each problem statement and decide whether you have that problem. If you do, *underline* the number next to the problem statement. If the problem is *especially* troublesome to you, circle the number next to the problem statement. If you do *not* have that problem, *do nothing* and go on to the next item.

Motivation

M11 I'm only here because someone has pressured me to enter treatment.

M16 I'm not sure I really want to change my way of doing things.

Health

H5 I don't eat a balanced diet.

H48 I have been generally neglectful of my physical health.

Personality

P72 Sometimes it's hard to separate what's real from what's not real.

P84 When I am under pressure and I have to compete, I give up.

Social Relations

S29 I find it hard to stand up for my rights and opinions at home.

S31 My family doesn't understand me.

Job

J4 I have tried to avoid personal problems by working too many hours or at too many jobs.

J47 I have often gotten into arguments with people at work.

Leisure Time

A15 I'm generally too tense to relax and enjoy physical activities and sports.

A30 I find it hard to relate to people unless I've had something to drink and/or taken some drugs.

R10   I feel very guilty about things I've done in the past which my present or former religion regards as sinful.

Religious or Spiritual

R19   I've never had any religious instruction.

Legal

L5   The courts are threatening to take away or have taken my child(ren) away.

L10   My driver's license has been suspended or revoked.

Alcoholics Anonymous (AA) and Narcotics Anonymous (NA) Approach

Narcotics Anonymous considers a person to be an addict if his or her life is "unmanageable" as the result of drug use. NA views the addiction as a disease with physical, psychological, and spiritual components. Because NA (like AA) is a self-help program, joining it means that the individual recognizes that a problem exists. A pamphlet titled *Am I an Addict* (Narcotics Anonymous, 1983), is a 45-question self-assessment. Narcotics Anonymous suggests that if five or more questions are answered positively, the person may want to find out what it is like to live without drugs and is encouraged to seek the fellowship of NA. Following are sample questions written by a cross section of addicts in the worldwide fellowship of NA.

- Do you spend money on drugs rather than food and other necessities?
- Do you get more drugs when your supply is running low or as soon as you run out?
- Do you use something to help you get going in the morning or to slow you down at night?
- Have you been arrested for drinking or drunk driving?
- Did you smoke your plant before it was two feet tall?
- Do you do things while under the influence that you would not do while straight?
- Do you think you must be high to have a good time?
- Do you use drugs to overcome your fear of people?
- Do all of your activities center around drugs?
- Do you want to stop using, but can't do it alone?

PROFESSIONAL ASSESSMENTS

McAndrew Alcoholism Scale (MAC)

The clinician may wish to utilize other assessment tools in addition to, or in lieu of, self-assessments. The McAndrew Alcoholism Scale (MAC) is an MMPI (Minnesota Multiphasic Personality Inventory) subscale that has been empirically derived and reliably differentiates alcoholics from nondrug abusing, psychiatric patients. This scale is stable over time and does not appreciably change with changes in drinking status. The MAC was found to have some ability to predict posttreatment drinking behavior at six months. In addition, this scale is able to differentiate alcoholics with a history of parental alcoholism (Sher & McCrady, 1984). Given that the outcome of alcohol problems is variable, an instrument such as the MAC, which can assist alcohol treatment counselors and other professionals in measuring prognosis, is of great utility.

Addiction Severity Index (ASI)

The Addiction Severity Index (ASI) is another instrument that the health care professional may use during the assessment process. The ASI has been used extensively as an assessment, diagnostic, and research instrument with alcohol- and drug-abusing clients. It has demonstrated reliability and validity. A trained technician can administer the index in less than an hour, and a detailed instruction manual is available from the National Institute on Drug Abuse (Cacciola, Griffith, & McLellan, 1985).

The ASI produces a problem severity profile for each client by analyzing six areas that result in treatment problems: (1) drug/alcohol use, (2) medical, (3) psychological, (4) legal, (5) family/social, and (6) employment/support. Objective questions are asked in each area. The index measures the number, extent, and duration of symptoms within the last 30 days and in the client's lifetime. Because the ASI can differentiate clients into subgroups with different patterns of treatment problems, it can be used to compare different forms of treatment and to match patients to treatments.

The Joint Commission on Accreditation of Health Care Organizations accepts the ASI as a "model instrument" for satisfying its requirements for comprehensive patient admission assessment and resulting individualized treatment plan. Three subgroups, however, are inappropriate for assessment by the ASI. These groups are older substance abuse patients (generally alcoholics who have evidence of cognitive impairment); clients who are younger with a history of criminal involvement; and adolescents less than 16 years old supported by their parents. The ASI is designed primarily for the older adolescent and adult populations.

The ASI is most suitable in substance abuse treatment settings. It is useful in clinical practice and in research. The developers of the ASI found that alcohol- and drug-abusing patients have particular and different constellations of treatment problems, and that *psychiatric* problems of patients rather than alcohol or drug problems are the most consistent predictors of treatment outcome (McLellan et al., 1985).

Other instruments that can be used in structured clinical interviews include the Alcadd Test (Manson, 1949), the Mortimer-Filkins Test (Kerlen, Mortimer, Mudge, & Filkins, 1971), the Alcohol Use Questionnaire (Wanberg, Horn, & Foster, 1973), the Drinking Profile (Marlatt, 1976), and the Substance Use Disorders Diagnostic Schedule (Harrison & Hoffman, 1989). The professional can take advantage of the many self-assessment or structured inventories when conducting an assessment in an addiction-focused agency. Several of these tools can also be adapted in agencies where addiction treatment is not the primary focus or service provided.

Self-assessment instruments have many potential benefits as well as some specific limitations. In general, they are cost-effective, can be completed in a relatively short period of time, and can save the clinician time by providing information on the existence of a drug/alcohol problem or an index of the extent or severity of drug abuse problems. Instruments can be used for screening in clinical assessment and treatment evaluation research. Utilization of inventories that include the client in the process of identifying his or her own problems can assist the worker in beginning a therapeutic dialogue as well as in establishing rapport. Another benefit of the self-assessment questionnaire is that the worker can feel fairly confident in the use and results of these instruments because many have been tested for reliability and validity.

A major limitation of all self-administered assessments is that they cannot be used by those who do not read or speak English. Even for English-speaking individuals, the instruments are limited when the reading level is below the fourth grade. The client can be given the tests orally, and a translation orally and/or in writing can be provided to non-English-speaking populations. Another limitation is the ability of the clients to fake results. This means that the worker should not use the inventory as a substitute for other diagnostic tools, including the clinical interview, physical and psychological evaluations, and information from collateral contacts.

Table 2.1 provides a summary of self-assessment and technician-administered inventories.

RECOGNITION OF ADDICTION: CASE EXAMPLES

The latter stages of addiction are easier for both professionals and lay persons to recognize. However, few health care and social service professionals receive specific training in recognizing the earlier stages of alcoholism or drug addiction. The two interviews described below involve a clinician who fails to recognize the problem and another who recognizes and deals with alcoholism.

Case 1

Mrs. Kathleen Young is a 35-year-old, white, Protestant, married, mother of two sons, ages 6 and 10, and one daughter, age 8. She sought help at her local mental health clinic as a result of frequent arguments with her husband and his increased episodes of violence. Following are excerpts from the initial interview:

Social Worker (SW): "Mrs. Young, my name is _____, a social worker at _____, and I'll be talking to you this morning to find out what problems bring you to our clinic. From the information you share with me we will determine how we might be of help to you. I'd like to begin by asking you to tell me what brought you to our clinic."

Mrs. Young (Y): " Things at home are getting worse. I'm frustrated with my kids, my 'old man' ain't never home. When he is at home we fight a lot. He's hitting me and the kids again. I got mad and reported him to child welfare and they told me to get help, but he wouldn't come today. He's hanging out at the club with his old cronies again, spending money we don't have, probably getting loaded. I just paid $65 for a ticket he got and we can barely pay our rent and bills. I just can't stand it any more, it's getting me down. If he don't straighten out, I'm kicking his ass out."

SW: "Mrs. Young, tell me about his hitting you and the kids."

Table 2.1

Summary of Self-Assessment and Technician-Administered Inventories

Inventory	Time	Problem Assessed	Target Population	Methods of Administering	Benefits	Limitations	Uses
Michigan Alcoholism Screening Test (MAST)	5-10 min.	Alcoholism	Adult males	Self-administered	Cost effective; easy to administer; can distinguish male alcoholics from non-alcoholics; free from response-style bias	Gender specific, alcohol related only	Clinical screening and assessment; treatment evaluation research
Drug Abuse Screening Test (DAST)	5 min.	Alcoholism, drug abuse	Adults	Self-administered	Cost effective; easy to administer; can differentiate individuals with drug only, alcohol only, mixed alcohol/drug problems	Read English above fourth grade; speak English; can falsify answers	Clinical screening and assessment treatment evaluation research
Georgia Doctor's Test	10 min.; 7-day diary	Alcoholism	Adults	Self-administered; Diary	Puts client in position of honestly evaluating substance use	Read and write English at a *high* level	Treatment
Substance Abuse Problem Checklist (SAPC)	40-45 min.		Adults	Self-administered	Cost effective; ecological dysfunction dimension included	Read English; speak English; can falsify answers	Treatment; research

(continued)

Table 2.1

Summary of Self-Assessment and Technician-Administered Inventories (Continued)

Inventory	Time	Problem Assessed	Target Population	Methods of Administering	Benefits	Limitations	Uses
Cocaine Addiction Questionnaire	15-20 min.	Cocaine use	Adults	Self-administered	Cost effective; gives explanation why a "yes" answer may be a problem for respondent	Limited to cocaine	Assessment
Am I an Addict (Narcotics Anonymous)	15-20 min.	Drug addiction	Adults	Self-administered	Practical	Drug related	Self-assessment; join self-help groups
McAndrew Alcoholism Scale (MAC)	1 hour	Alcoholism	Adults	Psychologist administered	Stable over time		Predict posttreatment drinking behavior
Addiction Severity Index (ASI)	1 hour	Alcohol and drug addiction	16 yrs. and older	Professionally administered	Can predict treatment outcome	Can't be used with older alcoholics with cognitive impairment; younger drug-addicted clients; adolescents younger than 16 supported by their parents	Assessment; match patients with treatment; research; treatment

Y: "When we was first married, Dan used to slap me around a lot. But after I had my first baby I told him I wouldn't put up with it no more. He stopped for a while. When the kids was young, he started hitting them sometimes."

SW: "Do you know what made him hit them?"

Y: "For anything. They'd be bad or make too much ruckus at home and get on his nerves."

SW: "You said he's hitting you and the kids again. When did this start?"

Y: " I remember it started late on a Sunday night. He came home from the club and was steaming mad because his football team lost and his dinner wasn't ready. Do you believe he started talking like it was my fault or something that the damn football team lost? He's got some nerve. Anyways, I walked away from him, which is what I usually do when he's this way, and he started cussing me out. And I didn't even do nothing wrong. He came after me, pushed me and slapped me twice. When I started crying and yelling at him my oldest came downstairs and told him to stop. That's when he smacked him in the face and told him he better get back to his room or he'd get a good licking."

SW: "What happened the next day when you first saw your husband in the morning?"

Y: "I didn't say nothing and he acted normal, like it never happened or something."

SW: "Since that episode, how many times has he hit you or the kids?"

Y: "He hits me more than the kids. I saw him hit our youngest twice. He's pushed me a couple of times and smacked me six or eight times. Gave me a black eye. The next day he acted innocent and had the nerve to ask me how I got the black eye. Can you believe that?"

As the interview progressed, there were several indicators that a drinking problem was present, although the worker did not focus on it. The problems that were present in this family were (1) the husband's drinking, (2) physical violence towards the wife and kids, (3) the wife feeling tired and overwhelmed with all that's happened in the home, (4) the wife's belief that her husband doesn't spend enough time with her or their children, (5) poor communication between the husband and the wife, and (6) the wife's lack of awareness of the role of his drinking in these problems.

She agreed to return later in the week and bring her husband with her. The worker was surprised that the husband was so pleasant and cooperative during the interview. Although he downplayed the violence, he agreed that it should stop. He readily admitted that he and his wife weren't getting along. Both agreed to come for regular sessions to try to work some of their problems out.

The worker saw them together weekly for three months, and occasionally he saw them individually. The violence stopped, but they continued to argue over many things. The wife often flew off the handle at her husband in the sessions and freely vented her rage. Just when they seemed to be making progress, arguments would erupt. Although these arguments most often followed excessive drinking on his part, neither the worker nor the couple spent time discussing it. They focused more on the many "problems" the couple presented. However, the worker did finally get her to agree not to bring up his many past transgressions for which she was still upset.

Discussion of Case History

As the initial interview progressed, it became increasingly clear that the husband's drinking was a significant factor in many of the presenting problems. However, the worker did not pick up on the clues and instead chose to pursue other issues.

Following is a review of several clues the wife presented during the initial interview that the worker could have used at the time they were presented, or later in the interview, to ask more questions about the husband's drinking and the effects on him and his family.

1. Where did the client spend his time that he was seldom at home? How much time was spent drinking or at the club?
2. What kind of "help" did child welfare recommend? Did it include AA or counseling for a drinking problem?
3. How often does he go to the club? For how long? What is meant by "old cronies" (drinking buddies)?
4. What does she mean when she says he is "probably getting loaded?" How often does this occur? What is he like when loaded? When drinking but not loaded? How does this differ from his behavior when he doesn't drink?
5. What did he get the ticket for? Was it a "driving under the influence" ticket?
6. Was he more likely to hit the kids if he had been drinking, or after he was intoxicated?
7. How late did he come home and how long had he been at the club? Had he been drinking? Was he intoxicated?

8. When he "acted innocent," did he give the impression that he did not remember what happened? Does she recall similar incidents in the past where he did things but then seemed to forget that he had done them (possible blackouts)?

As a result of the worker's failure to assess the drinking problem (severe alcoholism) properly during the course of treatment, an inappropriate treatment plan was developed. Although treatment did lead to some improvements, they tended to be transitory. As treatment progressed, more evidence of the husband's alcoholism became apparent, but the worker and the couple continued to ignore this problem.

Four months after the initial session, the worker got a call from the wife, who frantically reported that her husband stabbed her the previous day with a knife. In a drunken state, the husband had chased their 10-year-old around the dining room table with the knife. After she notified the police, the department of child welfare was called, and the children were placed in foster care homes until a hearing was set.

This example represents a case in which it was fairly obvious that alcoholism was a problem, although the clinician did not focus on it. There will be many situations in which a person or family member who has a substance abuse problem may present very obvious signs, such as patterns of excessive use and intoxication, blackouts, aggressive behaviors, tickets for driving under the influence, spending inordinate amounts of time at drug-use parties, and job problems. However, there will also be many situations in which the signs are not so obvious, and the problem is uncovered only because the worker explores certain avenues of questioning. The next case will illustrate how the substance abuse problem was gradually uncovered by the worker over several sessions.

Case 2

Mr. Jack Cohen is a 43-year-old high school teacher referred to the local mental health clinic by his supervisor, who felt Jack "hadn't been himself" lately and seemed to feel under a lot of stress.

Clinician (W): "Mr. Cohen, my name is _____ and I'm a therapist at the clinic. I'll be talking with you today about the concerns or problems that have brought you to our clinic. After our meeting, we will be able to determine how we might best be of help to you. Can you tell me how you came about coming to our clinic?"

Mr. Cohen (C): "Well, the vice principal at school, who is my supervisor, felt that I've been under a lot of pressure lately and that it might help to talk to someone. He suggested your clinic because one of the other teachers got a lot of help here last year. I don't really know if I need to be here, though."

W: "Can you tell me about the 'pressure' you've been experiencing lately?"

C: "I just don't seem to have been myself the past couple of months. Me and my wife aren't getting along, we are strapped financially, and I don't seem to be enjoying my job anymore. To be honest, I think maybe I'm burned out with teaching, tired of the same old routine. The administrators are always hassling us, making our job more difficult. I don't look forward to going to school anymore."

W: "Mr. Cohen, have you been missing more work these past few months or going in late?"

C: "I don't go in late because I'm in a car pool. But I've missed a few days lately when I didn't feel well."

W: "What was the nature of your 'not feeling well' when you took off?"

C: "I had the flu and generally felt lousy and run-down."

W: "How many days did you miss so far this year, would you say?"

C: " I don't know exactly. Maybe seven or eight."

W: " Mr. Cohen, would these occur on any certain day of the week?"

C: "It could be any day. I think a few were after weekends, on Monday. I'll tell you what really bothers me is that my wife is always bugging me about something."

W: "Like what, can you tell me the most recent examples of her bugging you?"

C: "Well, we just seem to argue about everything. Money, the kids, cutting the grass, the car, you know, things most people argue about."

W: "How about the last couple times she bugged you. What was it about?"

C: "She got mad at me for coming home late and not calling her. She's so controlling at times."

W: "How late were you that she got mad?"

C: "Oh, a couple of hours I guess. I went out with some of my friends after work for chicken wings."

W: "So where did you go for the chicken and what time did you actually get home that night?"

C: "We went to the Do Drop Inn. I guess I got home at about 9:30 or so."

W: "Did you have anything to drink that night?"

C: "Just a few beers. My wife nagged me about that, too."

W: "What exactly do you recall her saying about having a few beers?"

C: "That I ought to be at home with the family instead of out drinking beer. You know, I work hard at school and need to unwind now and then. Don't you think we all do?"

W: "Has she ever complained before about drinking?"

C: "Yeah, even when I have a few at home when I watch a baseball game on the tube. She tries to tell me sometimes I promise to do things and then forget about them. Just can't please a wife, can you?"

W: "Why do you think she is so concerned with you having a few beers? Can you help me understand that?"

C: "Like I said, it's hard to please wives, you know how they are."

Over the course of the next month, the worker saw John each week. As John became more comfortable sharing information with the worker, it became increasingly clear that alcoholism was his main problem. When his wife came in for a session, additional information was gathered and verified, facilitating the worker's conclusion that John was an alcoholic. The clinician gradually was able to identify the following symptoms:

1.   Numerous episodes of intoxication, averaging about two each week.
2.   An increased tolerance. John was now drinking much more than he had in the past and could handle large amounts of liquor.
3.   John was drinking much more than he intended and was having trouble sticking to his occasional self-imposed limits of no more than three drinks on any one occasion.
4.   Blackouts followed some drinking bouts.
5.   John was having increased marital discord over his drinking and related behaviors, yet continued to drink and upset his family.
6.   He would sometimes miss work following a heavy weekend drinking binge.

When the worker was certain that alcoholism was a significant problem, he discussed this with John and his wife. Both initially had difficulty accepting the worker's assessment and the recommendations that John stop drinking and attend AA, and that their counseling focus on issues pertaining to sobriety. It took several more sessions before John was willing to accept these recommendations. He eventually was able to quit drinking and stay sober with the help of AA and counseling. His wife was very supportive of his efforts and found comfort in attending Al-Anon, where she began to focus on her own behaviors and feelings.

ASSESSING A CLIENT WHO IS INTOXICATED

A thorough assessment in an addiction-focused agency involves clinical interviews coupled with possible self-assessments and laboratory and medical examinations. An accurate diagnosis and treatment plan can be hampered if the client comes to the interview intoxicated. Dean (1985) recommends that if a client is using alcohol during the interview, detoxification may be necessary because cognition, responses, and testing accuracy may be impeded. Caddy (1985) states that "it is typically quite useless, in my view, to attempt any interaction with an intoxicated patient beyond providing a general level of concern and support. . . . A second visit should be scheduled with the patient as soon as possible after the initial contact" (p. 166). Because a client who is intoxicated will often be accompanied by a friend or family member, Caddy feels it would be beneficial to use this time to get background information on the client and establish a relationship with a significant other who might later encourage the client to return to the agency. Both Caddy and Dean agree that it is important for the client to understand that effective service cannot be provided unless the client is sober.

In his book "Confrontation in Psychotherapy with the Alcoholic," Forrest (1987) stresses that the worker must require clients to be sober at therapy sessions: "While this may seem rather elementary, it must be stressed that confronting alcoholic patients can only be effectively accomplished when the patient is sober" (p. 19). Some professionals in the alcohol field recommend even stronger measures than confrontation. Caddy (1985) requires all his patients to undergo breath analysis at the assessment interview and at the beginning of each subsequent interview (p. 168). He recognizes that many professionals do not like this procedure because they feel it is offensive to the client. However, he has found little resistance from his clients and observes that a sober client provides more accurate data. Breath testing is standard procedure at each session, presumably maximizing the chances that a client will come to therapy in a sober state.

A comprehensive assessment cannot be accomplished when the client is intoxicated. One or several measures must be taken to assist the client in becoming sober and returning to the agency. This can be facilitated by eliciting the assistance of friends, family members, or significant others of the client. The clinician needs to express genuine concern about the client but be firm in establishing ground rules for receiving services.

If the health care professional determines that the addiction is severe enough to warrant detoxification, then immediate steps need to be taken to refer the client to a medical or social detoxification service. Detoxification should be considered if:

1. The client has a known history of withdrawing from substances (e.g., a history of DTs or convulsions).
2. The client has medical problems or symptoms requiring immediate attention, such as elevated blood pressure.
3. The client has psychiatric problems or symptoms requiring immediate attention, such as psychosis, severely depressed mood, or suicidal plans.
4. The client has a history of being unable to stop substance use without the help of supervised detoxification.
5. The worker believes that detoxification is needed if the client is to be motivated to accept other help for his or her addiction.

INTERVIEWS WITH FAMILY MEMBERS AND SIGNIFICANT OTHERS

Gathering detailed and accurate data about a client is important for a worker in any agency, but especially critical in an addiction-focused agency. Details and accuracy may have to be supplemented by a client's family, friends, or significant others. Clients often do not come for help voluntarily and may be brought to the agency by a family member. In general, the literature supports the use of reports from family members and significant others to enhance the diagnostic interview. For example, Caddy (1985) states, "I routinely begin the diagnostic process by interviewing the patient and other(s) together, initially and thereafter, separately" (p. 169). These interviews, according to Caddy, facilitate the evaluation process, determine the functioning of significant others and their personal agendas, and frequently get the support of family members while the client is in therapy. Gerard and Saenger (1966) report that the likelihood that the alcoholic will continue in treatment can be significantly affected if the spouse is interviewed.

Milby and Rice (1985) offer support for interviewing family members and others, but also offer a note of caution: "Reports from significant others can provide important diagnostic information. They can corroborate self-reports, provide new observations and historical detail, and provide important information about the role of relationship factors and the social support available during intervention" (p. 191). However, based on the research of Rounsaville, Kleeber, Wilber, Rosenberger, and Rosenberger (1981), Milby and Rice (1985) caution that significant others tend to underreport problems, and that clients themselves are more aware of dysfunction than relatives or friends.

Interviews with family members can include, but are not limited to, their knowledge and perception of the history of substance abuse, legal problems, physical and psychological problems, occupational and mental functioning, family and spiritual problems, previous attempts by the addicted person to seek treatment, and their outcome. Inconsistencies with information provided by the addicted person can be reviewed. Weinberg (1973) urges the worker or counselor to maintain occasional contact with the spouse of an addicted client (with the client's knowledge): "It is virtually imperative for the counselor to have an independent source of information about the client's behavior outside the interview situation. The client may be reporting sobriety when he has been drinking, or he may indicate that everything is rosy at home when he has actually been moody and irritable, perhaps getting close to a slip" (p. 85).

By interviewing the family members and significant others, the worker can begin to determine the degree of denial that exists in the family. In establishing a relationship with the spouse, children, and significant others, the social worker may be able to use referrals to therapy or self-help programs for nonaddicted members. The following is a case example from a family member about the client's addiction and its effect on family functioning.

Mrs. Baker sought help at a family service agency at the advice of a friend because she was "depressed and disgusted" and was "flying off the handle" too easily with her children. The following are excerpts from the first two interviews:

Worker (W): "Mrs. Baker, please tell me what things are bothering you that bring you to our agency for help."

Mrs. Baker (B): "I've been feeling very frustrated and depressed lately. I'm just not happy with my life. It's so depressing."

W: "Could you describe your feelings of depression to me, Mrs. Baker?"

B: "I'm tired and worn out. I don't feel like anything is going well in my life anymore. I've lost my patience with my children, and I'm worried that I'm snapping too much at them."

W: "Do you know why?"

B: "Not really. It's just that the past year or so, things have gone downhill and I've felt more depressed lately."

W: "How long have you felt this way?"

B: "At least three months, since the (Christmas) holidays."

W: "I'm going to ask you some questions about your feeling depressed."

Upon further questioning, the worker determined that Mrs. Baker's mood had worsened significantly during the past several months, and for the first time in her life she couldn't shake off her depression by herself. Other depressive symptoms reported by her included difficulty falling asleep, loss of energy, significant decline in her interest in social life and personal hobbies, total loss of sexual drive, and feelings of uselessness and worthlessness. Because these symptoms began sometime during the Christmas holidays, the worker tried to find out what the holidays were like for her.

W: "Mrs. Baker, did anything happen over the holidays that contributed to the feelings you've described to me? By this I mean anything unusual or different, or any problems in your family?"

B: "Well, to be honest, I was hoping this year the holidays would be different, that our family could enjoy them together. But there was too much arguing and fighting, just like the other ones."

W: "Who was arguing and fighting in your family and about what?"

B: "Mainly me and Rick [her husband]. But nothing seemed to please him."

W: "When would he argue with you? And do you know why?"

B: "Rick always gets a bit argumentative when he drinks. He promised to take it easy over the holidays. He was doing good for a couple of months, but then broke his promise."

W: "It sounds like you're saying Rick has a drinking problem. Is that correct?"

B: "I don't know if I would say that. He doesn't drink every day. Sometimes he gets carried away."

W: "Mrs. Baker, how much does your husband usually drink each week on the average?"

B: "Well, he only drinks beer. He stops after work a couple times a week, and he drinks sometimes at home on the weekends."

Upon further questioning, the worker discovered that Rick is an episodic drinker, who sometimes goes several weeks or months without drinking alcohol. However, his pattern of drinking is alcoholic. He often gets drunk during weekends, consuming about a case and a half of beer each weekend that he drinks. He has told his wife that he would have just a few beers but instead consumed half a case or more. Rick has experienced blackouts, broken many promises to his family, and has said negative, hurtful things to his wife when he has been drinking. After obtaining information about Rick's alcohol use and his behavior, the worker then began inquiring more about Mrs. Baker and the family system.

W: "Mrs. Baker, have you found yourself thinking a lot about your husband's drinking even when he hasn't had anything to drink for a few days or weeks?"

B: "I always worry about when he'll start up again. He always does."

W: "Have you ever 'covered up' for his drinking and done things like calling his boss to report him sick?"

B: "A lot of times. I had to. I was worried he might lose his job."

W: "Tell me, Mrs. Baker, how do you think Rick's drinking has affected you?"

B: "It gets me upset and I get down."

As the worker talked with Mrs. Baker, it was clear that the family system accommodated her husband's drinking and upset everyone. Because he went for periods without drinking, the family would get a false sense of hope that things would get better. Mrs. Baker cut herself off from her friends, complained too much about her husband's drinking to her teenage kids, and directed some of her anger toward her husband at them. It was clear that many of her feelings and problems were directly related to the alcoholism. The worker also inquired about how her teenage children viewed the drinking and gained additional information substantiating the alcoholism problem in her family.

The importance of forming a relationship with the nonalcoholic family members has already been stressed. The health care professional needs to keep in mind that some time should be used in diagnostic interviews to corroborate information provided by the addicted person. Attention needs to be directed at family members, their needs, feelings, and behaviors.

An assessment tool has been developed for children of alcoholics. The Children of Alcoholics Screening Test (CAST) is able to distinguish latency age, adolescent, and adult children of alcoholics (Jones, 1982). The instrument has 30 items that measure children's feelings, attitudes, perceptions, and experiences related to their parents' drinking behavior. Children nine years of age or older can complete the CAST. This inventory is cost-effective, can be administered with ease, and can be used in a variety of settings.

If the worker does not formally administer the CAST, key questions can be asked in order to identify children of alcoholics. Frequently, the worker only asks the adolescent or young adult what their experience is with drugs and alcohol. Parental or caretaker addictions are often not brought to the surface or even seen as significant to the treatment plan. Talking with children about the questions on the CAST "can be diagnostic and therapeutic" (Pilat & Jones, 1984-1985, p. 280).

When the worker establishes the existence of alcoholism or other drug addiction, an initial treatment plan will need to be developed. The specifics of this plan will be contingent upon several factors:

1. Which person presents for treatment—the addicted client, a family member, or both.
2. How long the addiction has been present, and how severe it is in terms of amount or frequency of substance use.
3. The effects of the addiction on the person's physical, psychological, social, family, occupational, legal, and spiritual functioning.
4. The effects of the addiction on the family system and the individual members.
5. The motivation of the addicted person to participate in treatment.

6. The accessibility and availability of treatment resources (professional services will sometimes be dependent on insurance coverage or access to funds to pay for the cost of service).

Appropriate referral for additional services requires the worker to be familiar with professional and self-help resources available for addicted clients and families. Given that addiction will take many forms, the worker and client need access to a broad range of services. One case may require an immediate, emergency hospitalization. Another may require referral to a residential treatment program or to a self-help program. Good judgment about the treatment needed for the addicted client requires a complete assessment. In subsequent chapters, specific treatment issues and resources will be discussed in depth to familiarize the reader with the treatment of addiction.

REFERENCES

American Psychiatric Association. (1987). *Diagnostic and statistical manual of mental health disorders (DSM-III-R)* (rev. 3rd). Washington, DC: Author.

Cacciola, J., Griffith, J., & McLellan, A. J. (Eds.). (1985). *Addiction severity index instruction manual* (4th ed.). Rockville, MD: National Institute of Drug Abuse.

Caddy, G. R. (1985). *Alcoholism*. In M. Hersen & S. Turner (Eds.), *Diagnostic interviewing* (pp. 161-182). New York: Plenum.

Carroll, J. F. (1984). *Subsstance abuse problem checklist*. Eagleville, PA: Eagleville Hospital.

Carroll, J. F. X., & Schnoll, F. H. (1982). *Mixed drug and alcohol population*. In E. M. Patterson & E. Kaufman (Eds.), *Encycolpedia handbook of alcoholism* (pp. 742-758). New York: Gardner.

Chappell, J. N., Veach, T. R., & Krug, R. F. (1985). The substance abuse attitude survey. An instrument for measuring attitudes. *Journal of Studies on Alcohol, 46*(1), 48-52.

Daley, D., Moss, H., & Campbell, F. (1987). *Dual disorders: Counselling clients with chemical dependency and mental illness*. Center City, MN: Hazelden.

Dean, J. A. (1985). Multivariant assessment and treatment technique for alcohol problems. *The International Journal of the Addictions, 20*(8), 1281-1290.

Forrest G. G. (1982). *Confrontation in psychotherapy with the alcoholic*. Holmes Beach, FL: Learning Publications.

Gerard, D. J., & Saenger, G. (1966). *Outpatient treatment of alcoholism: A study of outcome and its determination*. Toronto: University of Toronto Press.

Googins, B. (1984). Avoidance of the alcohol client. *Social Work, 29*(2), 161-166.

Harrison, P. A., & Hoffman, N. G. (1989). *Substance use disorders diagnostic schedule*. St. Paul, MN: Cator.

Hesselbrock, M., Meyer, R,. & Keener, J. (1985). Psychopathology in hospitalized alcoholics. *Archives of General Psychiatry, 42*, 1050-1055.

Human Behavior. (1972). *1*(1), 39.

Jones, J. W. (1982). *The children of alcoholics screening test (C.A.S.T.).* Chicago: Family Recovery Press.

Kerlen, M. W., Mortimer, R. G., Mudge, B., & Filkins, L. D. (1971). *Court procedures for identifying problem drinkers* (Publication No. DOT-HS-800-632). Ann Arbor: Highway Safety Research Institute, University of Michigan.

Knox, W. J. (1971). Attitudes of psychiatrists and psychologists toward alcoholism. *American Journal of Psychiatry, 127,* 1675-1679.

Laundergan, J., Spicer, J., & Kammeier, M. (1979). *Are court referrals effective?* Center City, MN: Hazelden.

Manson, M. P. (1949). *The Alcadd Test.* Beverly Hills, CA: Western Psychological Service.

Marlatt, G. A. (1976). The drinking profile: A questionnaire for the behavioral assessment of alcoholism. In E. J. Mash & L. G. Terdal (Eds.), *Behavior therapy assessment: Diagnosis, design and evaluation* (pp.121-137). New York: Springer.

McLellan, A. T., Lubrorsky, L., Cacciola, J., Griffith, J., Evans, F., Barr, H., & O'Brien, C. P. (1985). New data from the addiction severity index reliability and validity in three centers. *Journal of Nervous and Mental Disease, 173*(7), 412-423.

Mendelson, J. R., Wexler, D., Kubzansky, P. E., Harrison, R., Leiderman, H., & Solomon, P. (1964). Physicians' attitudes to alcoholic patients. *Archives of General Psychiatry, 11,* 392-399.

Milam, J. R., & Ketcham, K. (1985). *Under the influence: A guide to the myths and realities of alcoholism,* New York: Bantam Books.

Milby, J. B., & Rice, J. A. (1985). Drug abuse. In M. Hersen & S. Turner (Eds), *Diagnostic interviewing* (pp. 183-204). New York: Plenum.

Narcotics Anonymous. (1983). *Am I an addict?* Van Nuys, CA: Author.

National Institute of Alcohol Abuse and Alcoholism. (1987). *Alcohol and health.* Rockville, MD: Author.

Pilat, J. M., & Jones, J. W. (1984-1985, Winter). Identification of children of alcoholics: Two empirical studies. *Alcohol Health and Research World,* pp. 27-36.

Rounsaville, B., Kleeber, H. D., Wilber, C., Rosenberger, D., & Rosenberger, P. (1981). Comparison of opiate addicts' reports of psychiatric history with reports of significant other informants. *American Journal of Alcohol Abuse, 8,* 51-69.

Rounsaville, B., Spitzer, R., & Williams, J. (1986). Proposed changes in DSM-III substance use disorders: Description and rationale. *American Journal of Psychiatry, 143*(4), 463-468.

Sher, K. J., & McCrady, B. S. (1984). The McAndrew alcoholism scale: Severity of alcohol abuse and parental alcoholism. *Addictive Behaviors, 9,* 99-192.

Skinner, H. A. (1984). Instrument for assessing alcohol and drug problems. *Bulletin of the Society of Psychologists in Addictive Behavoiors, 3,* 21-33.

Talbot, G. D. (1984). Substance abuse and the professional provider. *Alabama Journal of Medical Science, 21,* 150-155.

Twerski, A. J. (1982). *It happens to doctors, too.* Center City, MN: Hazelden.

Twerski, A. J. (1984). *Self-discovery in recovery.* Center City, MN: Hazelden.

Wanberg, K. W., Horn, J. L., & Foster, F. M. (1973). A different model for the diagnosis of alcoholism: Scales of the Alcohol Use Questionnaire (selected papers). *Proceedings of the general session, twenty-fourth annual meeting of the Alcohol and Drug Problems Association of North America.* Bloomington, IN.

Weinberg, J. (1973). Counseling recovering alcoholics. *Social Work, 18*(4), 84-93.

Chapter 3

EFFECTS OF ADDICTION ON THE ADDICT

LOU GENE KINGERY-McCABE
FRANCES A. CAMPBELL

MEDIATING VARIABLES

The effects of addiction are variable. Some individuals experience minor complications when using substances, whereas others experience major medical or psychological problems. Some are adversely affected in a relatively short time, whereas others use substances for many years without suffering negative consequences. Factors that mediate the impact of addiction include genetic predisposition, cultural influences, amount and frequency of substance use, age, gender, diet, physical and mental health, and life-style (Daley, 1988).

Each individual has a unique genetic makeup that influences vulnerability to illnesses such as diabetes, schizophrenia, heart disease, and cancer. Evidence for genetic predisposition to alcoholism and drug abuse continues to grow. This evidence comes from data from studies of high-risk children, familial alcoholism or drug abuse, twins, adoptees separated at an early age from their biological parents, and animal breeding (NIAAA, 1987; NIDA, 1988).

Genetic predisposition affects how a given individual's body responds to the ingestion of substances. The result may be, for example, the development of a high tolerance for substances, or a reduction of the severity of hangover symptoms following excessive drinking (Pickens & Svikis, 1988).

Cultural factors mediate the impact of alcohol or drug use. For example, Hispanic-American men have high rates of alcoholism and high rates of mortality from cirrhosis. Native Americans and Alaskan natives also have very high rates of alcoholism; the former are three times more likely to experience alcohol-related illness and injury than the general population. Liver cirrhosis is the fourth leading cause of death among native Americans. On the other hand, Asian-Americans have very low rates of alcoholism, especially women. Although physiological factors may partially account for some of these differences, cultural norms regarding substance use and abuse are also important variables. Intoxication, for example, is less acceptable among certain groups. Although genetic predisposition determines how the body may react to certain substances, the type, amount, and frequency of substances used also affect reaction.

Addiction typically affects four major areas of functioning: (1) physical and medical, (2) psychological or emotional, (3) social or family, and (4) spiritual. Each of these areas is discussed briefly in the following sections.

PHYSICAL AND MEDICAL EFFECTS
OF ADDICTION

Tolerance

Many psychoactive drugs lose their effect with repeated use. This phenomenon is called *tolerance*. It refers to the need for increasing amounts of a substance to achieve the desired effect, or to a diminishing effect from using the same dosage. Many addicts develop a high tolerance, which allows them to consume large amounts of substances.

Withdrawal Syndrome

Withdrawal syndromes can be classified in several different ways. One is by the chemical used (i.e., alcohol, sedative, hypnotic, opioids, or cocaine). The opioid withdrawal syndromes are associated with discrete and measurable physiological changes in the body, such as blood pressure, whereas the cocaine withdrawal syndrome is primarily associated with changes in mood and behavior pattern, such as sleeping and eating. Withdrawal effects for a given drug also vary within the addicted population and for a given individual at various times in his or her life.

The essential features of *alcohol or other depressant drug withdrawal* following cessation of, or reduction in, heavy prolonged drinking or drug ingestion are a coarse tremor of the hands, tongue, and eyelids, and at least one of the following: nausea and vomiting, malaise or weakness, tachycardia, sweating, elevated blood pressure, anxiety, depressed mood or irritability, and orthostatic hypotension (APA, 1987).

Withdrawal from alcohol or other depressant drugs is potentially more severe than other types of drug withdrawal. Treatment of withdrawal consists of a good physical evaluation, general supportive care (rest, nutrition, vitamins), and pharmacological treatment of the withdrawal symptoms (Schuckit, 1989). Alcohol withdrawal is usually managed with benzodiazepines such as Librium or Valium. These drugs reduce the risk of seizures or delirium tremens and add to the general comfort of the patient during withdrawal. Barbiturate withdrawal is usually managed with a barbiturate drug. A short-, intermediate- or long-acting compound may be used, depending on the clinical presentation of the individual patient.

A history of previous delirium tremens or seizures is the single best predictor of severity of alcohol withdrawal. Concomitant medical illness such as pneumonia is another important risk factor in the prediction of complications during alcohol withdrawal.

Opioid withdrawal refers to the syndrome dramatically protrayed in *Man with the Golden Arm* and is the condition many people associate with all types of drug withdrawal. Although dramatic at times, opiate withdrawal is not life threatening and presents less of a medical emergency than alcohol withdrawal. Symptoms of opiate withdrawal include yawning, tearing, runny nose, and anxiety. As the withdrawal progresses, the person develops "goose flesh," hot and cold sweats, abdominal cramping, nausea, vomiting, diarrhea, and muscle cramps. Elevations in blood pressure, pulse, temperature, and respiratory rate are experienced. It is not uncommon for opiate addicts to appear at the hospital emergency room when the quality or availability of heroin on the street declines.

Clinical management of opioid withdrawal includes rest, nutrition, physical and laboratory exams, and reassurance (Schuckit, 1989). Two common medications used are methadone or clonidine. Methadone is a long-acting opiate that is employed in decreasing doses over a period of several days. The patient may experience very few symptoms until discontinuation of the last dose, after which insomnia is the most common complaint. A more rapid method of detoxification employs the nonopiate, antihypertensive agent clonidine, which inhibits sympathetic outflow from the midbrain. This agent greatly reduces the automatic nervous system effects associated with opiate withdrawal. However, it is less effective than opiate drugs in relieving discomfort and pain, and it produces sedation and hypotension (Schuckit, 1989).

Cocaine withdrawal syndrome is generally thought to be a three-part process involving a "crash," withdrawal, and extinction (Gawin & Kleber, 1985). Cocaine withdrawal ordinarily is not life threatening, and symptoms usually resolve within several days. Occasionally, following chronic high doses of stimulants such as cocaine, one sees agitation, paranoia, and hallucinations requiring a brief course of low-dose neuroleptics such as Haldol. More typically, symptoms of cocaine withdrawal mimic severe depression, particularly in the "crash" period. During this period, suicidal thoughts are frequently expressed, as the craving for cocaine turns into craving for sleep. Sleep remains elusive, however, because of associated anxiety and agitation. A period of hypersomnolence follows the agitation and lasts two to four days.

Following the crash period, severity of withdrawal symptoms depends largely on the amount of cocaine used. From four to seven days after the crash, symptoms include reduced energy and lowered interest in the environment.

Blackouts

Blackouts, or amnesia, are generally considered an ominous sign in the progression from social drinking to compulsive alcoholic drinking, an indicator of physical dependence rather than mere abuse.

In the alcoholic, amnesia may account for violence, accidents, or indiscretions the individual cannot recall. Considerable variability exists in the presence and extent of this phenomenon, and a component of denial or even hysterical forgetting of embarrassing events may further complicate the picture.

Consequences for Organ Systems

The effects of addiction on overall health are *indirect*, attributable to neglect, poor diet, or omission of routine care, and *direct*, attributable to toxic effects of the substance used. Approximately 20% to 45% of patients in medical-surgical hospitals suffer from alcohol-, drug-, and tobacco-related problems. It is critically important to diagnose the underlying primary condition and not merely provide treatment for a secondary medical complication.

Alcohol and drugs can adversely affect the metabolism and efficacy of medications, contributing to, or exacerbating, medical or psychiatric problems. For example, alcohol and other central nervous system depressants enhance the effects of analgesics and interfere with actions of antidepressant or psychotropic medications (Schuckit, 1989).

Many organ systems are damaged by addiction, increasing the risk of a multiplicity of diseases. Over 30 diseases are associated with alcoholism. A brief review of the major medical consequences of addiction on various organ systems follows.

Digestive System

Alcohol affects the function and structural integrity of the stomach and the intestinal tract. Chronic high doses can irritate the gastric lining and lead to changes in intestinal mobility, metabolism, cellular structure, and blood circulation. Associated conditions are gastritis, malabsorption of vitamins and nutrients, diarrhea, and damage to the pancreas and liver. The liver is the primary site of alcohol metabolism, and alcohol abuse can cause changes in the form of fatty liver, alcoholic hepatitis, and cirrhosis. Alcohol abuse is the principal cause of cirrhosis, the ninth leading cause of death in the United States (NIAAA, 1987).

There is much less conclusive evidence indicating specific damage to the digestive system from use of the various drugs. However, heavy cocaine use has been linked to impairment of blood circulation to the bowels. Effects of this ranged from colitis to gangrene of the bowel, which resulted in death despite repeated surgery (Fishel, Hamamoto, Barbul, Jiji, & Efron, 1985; Nalbandian, Sheth, Deitrich, & Geogiou, 1985). Chronic ingestion of opiates cause constipation and may lead to intestinal obstruction or impaction.

Cardiovascular System

Heavy alcohol consumption has been shown to increase mortality from coronary heart disease and the general risk of cardiovascular diseases. This is thought to result from direct toxic effects of ethanol on the heart as well as other systemic effects, such as increased lipids (fats) in the blood, carbohydrate intolerance, and altered calcium and mineral metabolism (NIAAA, 1987). Claims of possible protective effects of moderate alcohol consumption against coronary heart disease have recently been questioned, as has the mechanism proposed to account for the protective effects of alcohol. It is premature to assume that moderate alcohol consumption has a protective effect.

The effects of cocaine on the cardiovascular system are attributable to cocaine's vasoconstrictor properties and its indirect stimulation of the heart through action on the sympathetic nervous system. There is a dramatic elevation of blood pressure and heart rate at particularly high doses of cocaine. An increase in normal heart rate can occur, and changes in heart rhythm can result in a very irregular pattern of the heartbeat, chest pain, and permanent damage to the heart muscle (myo-cardial infarction).

Effects of opiates on the heart in the normal person are not signifi-cant. The heartbeat is either unaffected or only slightly increased, and the EKG is not altered. There is, however, an effect on the peripheral blood vessels, causing them to dilate and making the body less able to respond to changes in blood pressure. This results in orthostatic hypo-tension, which can cause a person to faint if he or she stands up suddenly (Goodman & Gilman, 1985). A more serious consequence of opiate use, which may accompany intravenous use, is damage to the heart and its valves from infection through use of contaminated needles.

Marijuana use causes tachycardia (increased heart rate) following deep inhalation of the smoked product. This appears to be self-limited and is of some diagnostic interest, but it is not known to result in permanent damage to the heart or blood vessels.

The cardiovascular effects of benzodiazepines (e.g., Valium, Lib-rium, etc.) are minor except in severe intoxication. Hallucinogens and inhalants represent a very large and diverse group of substances that vary in their effects depending on the chemical structure of the specific compound.

Nervous System

The effects of alcohol are first seen on the brain and secondly on the peripheral nerves. Brain changes are reflected in neurochemical changes, and the neuronal membrane is the place where the effects are seen (NIAAA, 1987). The acute intoxicating actions of alcohol may be mediated by its disruption of membrane lipids and subsequent alteration in the function of membrane proteins. Chronic heavy alcohol use also results in structural change, including loss of volume in brain substance (evidenced in brain scans and autopsies) and changes in the electrical activity of the brain (measured by evoked potentials on EEG). Cognitive defects commonly associated with heavy alcohol consumption are short-term memory loss, visual spatial problems, and abstract reasoning impairment. Recent studies suggest that the primary disruption of alcohol is in the initial "encoding" phase of memory formation (NIAAA, 1987). If alcohol is administered after an event has been encoded, it has been found to enhance memory consolidation, the translation of memories into a long-lasting form. Further delineation of alcohol effects on memory systems, including the controversial issues of reversibility and long-term effects of moderate "social drinking," are areas requiring additional research.

Other neurological consequences associated with chronic alcoholism are Wernicke-Korsakoff Syndrome (global confusion, staggering gait, and abnormal eye movements), cerebellar degeneration (staggering, and speech and limb movement abnormalities), and seizures related to alcohol withdrawal. Alcohol-related injuries and accidental falls can cause blood clots, brain hemorrhage, or skull fractures. Damage to the peripheral nerves by long-standing alcohol abuse may result in loss of sensation in hands and feet ("stocking and glove" pattern), burning sensations, and diminished tendon reflexes.

Cocaine affects the nervous system by blocking the uptake and delaying the breakdown of various neurotransmitters. This causes the euphoria commonly associated with cocaine use and results in the sympathetic nervous system effects seen throughout the body (i.e., dilated pupils and tremors). There is an increase in energy and a decrease in appetite and ability to sleep. Toxic doses may result in elevated temperature, marked agitation, seizures, panic states, and paranoid psychosis.

The powerful effects of cocaine (narrowing of blood vessels) disrupt normal blood supply. The combination of the stimulant effect, which causes more blood to be needed, and the simultaneous restriction of blood vessels accounts for the brain hemorrhage and stroke associated with extremely high cocaine dosages. The depression that often follows initial abstinence in heavy cocaine users is believed to result from depletion of brain neurotransmitters.

Opioids (e.g., morphine and heroin, Percodan, Demerol) produce pain relief, drowsiness, and changes in mood and mental state. Moderate doses do not necessarily change the pain threshold of the person but markedly increase his or her ability to tolerate the pain (Goodman & Gilman, 1985). These properties are mediated by action of opioids on specific receptors in the brain. Other effects of opioid drugs are the reduction in releasing hormones, which control other hormones in the body, and the suppression of REM sleep as measured by EEG. A persistent complaint of opioid addicts in early recovery is inability to sleep. This is due to a "REM rebound" effect associated with cessation of long-time use.

Abuse of heroin and related drugs remains a significant public health problem with associated antisocial behavior. Current data from the Drug Abuse Warning Network indicate that deaths related to drug use are higher for opioid analgesics than for any drug category (NIDA, 1987).

Marijuana affects the brain by increasing and slowing alpha waves, which is consistent with the drowsiness induced by the drug. Brain atrophy was indicated in studies of monkeys given doses of marijuana equivalent to one joint a day for five years. This raises the possibility of permanent change in humans, although there is no evidence of this (NIDA 1987).

Marijuana intoxication impairs intellectual performance, including ability to perform cognitive tasks and transfer of information from immediate to long-term memory. It is not clear whether any effects are irreversible. Clinical experience with long-term marijuana users, however, frequently indicates memory impairment. Other problems include altered time sense, paranoia, and lack of motivation (i.e., the "amotivational" syndrome).

The hallucinogens and inhalants represent a broad category of drugs composed of differing chemical structures. Substance abusers seeking a "unique" psychedelic experience are keenly interested in these chemicals. Desired effects include mind expansion and heightened awareness and perception. "Bad trips" can result in intense paranoia and delusions that persist far beyond the period of intoxication and may slowly or incompletely remit over time. Considerable progress has been made in identifying brain receptors and neurotransmitters involved in the mediation of these drug effects.

Endocrine and Reproductive Systems

Alcohol affects reproductive systems differently in males and females. The female hormone estrogen is not suppressed by alcohol, but both acute and chronic alcohol use suppress the male hormone testosterone. Disruption of the H-P-G function (hypothalamus, pituitary, gonadal) in female alcoholics leads to menstrual disturbances, infertility, and loss of secondary sex characteristics (NIAAA, 1987).

Alcoholic men show decreased testosterone because of the direct toxic effects of alcohol on the testicular cells that produce the hormone, and the indirect suppression mediated through disruption of the H-P-G axis. This may lead to testicular atrophy, infertility, and impotence. "Feminization" of chronically alcoholic men is characterized by breast enlargement and female hair patterns and results from liver disease and the overall reduction in testosterone. Alteration of adrenal and thyroid hormones in both sexes has been observed (NIAAA, 1987).

Despite cocaine's "aphrodisiac" qualities, sexual dysfunction is common among heavy cocaine users. Cocaine supplants sexual gratification by directly affecting brain pleasure centers and by indirectly affecting physical and mental functioning.

Opioids affect the secretion of pituitary hormones controlling sex hormones, resulting in diminished sexual drive and impotence in males and menstrual irregularities and sterility in females. Opioids have long been regarded as suppressors of ADH, a pituitary hormone involved in regulation of body fluids (Goodman & Gilman, 1985).

It is now generally believed that marijuana affects reproductive functioning in males and females through its action on sex hormones. In females, this includes a decrease in estrogen and disruption of ovulation and the menses. In males, there is a decrease in sperm production and an increase in abnormal sperm forms (NIDA, 1987).

Finally, alcohol and each of the other drugs discussed adversely affect the unborn fetus. Further information on this may be obtained by consulting references cited at the end of this chapter.

Respiratory System

Chronic alcohol abuse is associated with higher incidence of respiratory infections. This may result from the addict's life-style, as well as altered immune status and nutritional and metabolic causes. Cocaine's effects on the respiratory system depend on the amount and route of ingestion. Chronic "snorting" of cocaine damages nasal passages, causing ulceration and perforation of the nasal septum. Smoking of free base or crack damages the lungs. Toxic doses smoked or injected may result in pulmonary edema, a life-threatening complication.

Opioids depress respiration centrally (i.e., via the brain). Death due to overdose is most often a result of respiratory depression.

Marijuana smoking irritates the lungs in a manner similar to tobacco. However, recent studies have shown two to three and a half times more tar in marijuana cigarettes than in tobacco cigarettes of the same weight. Depending on the quality and purity of the marijuana smoked, it may contain considerable foreign materials, often resulting in wheezing and asthma-like symptoms. At least one evaluation of the lungs of heavy marijuana smokers showed scarring and inflammatory changes much greater than changes in the lungs of tobacco smokers who died at similar ages.

Immune System

Observed immune deficiencies in alcoholics may be attributable to life-style, liver disease, poor nutrition, and the effects of alcohol. Evidence of altered immune status includes a decrease in the number and activity of cells used by the body to combat infections (NIAAA, 1987). A manifestation of this is the greater susceptibility of alcoholics to respiratory diseases.

There is an increased incidence of certain cancers in the alcoholic. Alcohol- related tumors include those of the mouth, throat, voice box (larynx), esophagus, lung, colon, stomach, pancreas, liver, and rectum. Alcohol and tobacco have been found to make independent and different contributions to cancers of the mouth and throat (NIAAA, 1987). This refutes the misconception that smoking, which often accompanies the alcohol, and not the alcohol itself, is linked to cancer.

There is no current evidence of a relationship between the immunological effects of alcohol consumption and the progression of disease in persons infected with the AIDS virus. Intravenous drug users are at increased risk for AIDS (Schuckit, 1989).

Evidence that marijuana smoking increases human susceptibility to disease remains inconclusive. Animal studies to date, however, suggest this possibility.

Hematologic

Laboratory tests performed on alcoholics demonstrate a number of changes in chemical profile and blood count that accompany heavy alcohol use. Decreased platelet count leads to clotting problems and increases the risk of bleeding. A decreased blood count may lead to anemia and increase the risk of infection.

PSYCHOLOGICAL AND EMOTIONAL EFFECTS OF ADDICTION

Addiction affects virtually every area of psychological functioning, including cognitive, emotional, and behavioral areas. The alcoholic or drug addict typically utilizes defense mechanisms (e.g., denial) that allow the addiction to continue. Self-esteem is adversely affected, and developmental tasks may be impeded or delayed as a result of impairments associated with the addiction. And, in many cases, addiction can exacerbate or mask psychiatric disorders.

Psychological Defenses

In order to live with the consequences of their addictions, addicts utilize certain defense mechanisms such as: (1) *denial*—refusing to acknowledge what is obvious to other people because awareness would be painful (e.g., insisting "I'm not drunk," while staggering and slurring speech); (2) *rationalization*— justifying attitudes, beliefs, or behavior that might otherwise be unacceptable by incorrect appplication of reasons (e.g., justifying being fired from a job because of drinking by saying the boss was intolerable); and (3) *intellectualization*— using an excess of thinking to avoid anxiety caused by unacceptable impulses or behavior (e.g., to avoid feeling guilty about drug use, an addict may engage in philosophical debates about what's wrong with society's drug laws). Denial is considered to be the "fatal aspect" of the disease of addiction (Anderson, 1981).

Cognitive Effects

Cognition refers to the processes that involve symbolic operation— perceiving, remembering, imaging, and thinking (Kaplan, 1988). Deficits in short-term memory, visual-spatial orientation, and abstract thinking are often identified as areas of deficit in formal testing of chronic alcoholics. Also, alcoholics are often subject to malnutrition, head trauma, seizures, and a number of systemic disorders making it difficult to distinguish between direct and indirect effects of the disease. Brains of severe alcoholics may lose volume or substance. This is demonstrated on a CAT scan as enlargement of the ventricles and widening of sulci and folds. In other words, the spaces get bigger as the "gray matter" shrinks. This is similar to the effects of normal aging but is greatly accelerated in alcoholics.

A very dramatic and fortunately uncommon condition associated with alcohol is Wernicke-Korsakoff's encephalopathy. This develops because of deficiency of a vitamin B (thiamine) and, if untreated, can result in permanent dementia. This condition is marked by mental confusion, loss of recent memory, ataxia, ophthalmoplegia, and confabulation.

Stimulants and hallucinogens can produce short-lived toxic psychosis. The hallucinogens have been known to produce long-lasting psychoses with accompanying cognitive distortions. Chronic use of PCP and cannabis can lead to paranoia, memory loss, poor concentration, and altered sense of time.

Emotional Effects

Alcohol or other drug use may exaggerate or distort emotions. For example, mild anger may be expressed as intense hatred, or mild attraction may be expressed as deep love (Daley, 1988). Substances may give the addict "permission" to express feelings to others, even in cases when to do so is clearly inappropriate. Emotional states may be caused by the physiologic effects of substances, such as the depressant effects of alcohol or tranquilizers, or emotions may be affected by the consequences of addiction, as in the case of feeling depressed after losing a job or significant relationship (Daley, 1988).

Certain emotional states are consistently identified as problematic by people seeking therapy. This is because of inability directly to feel and express them, or habits of expression that create problems for themselves or others. Many addicts have trouble dealing with anger, and they may use substances to give them courage to display anger or to deny it. Fear or anxiety (one is specific, the other generalized) are also part of most people's life experience. Fear may become crippling for some people and, by increasing vulnerability to whatever seems to make one feel "better," may serve as the underlying reason for substance use and abuse.

AA and NA have used the acronym "HALT"—to remind the addict not to get too hungry, angry, lonely, or tired. These are the states identified as vulnerable ones for many recovering individuals. In the authors' experiences, it is the avoidance of negative feelings by self-medication that becomes a deeply ingrained pattern. Addicts learn that they can control their feelings (albeit temporarily) by use of chemicals and therefore never develop alternate, healthier coping strategies. Because such feelings are a part of life, the newly clean and sober adult feels like he or she has been asleep for years and can't master even the simplest situation without craving the emotional "crutch" or drug of choice.

Effects on Behavior

Addiction was defined earlier as "overlearned behavior." The human organism is capable of a wide range of behaviors, some of which are self-selected and/or environmentally reinforced, and, therefore, tend to increase in frequency. As certain behaviors increase in frequency, others are excluded.

An animal allowed free access to cocaine will self-administer the drug until he dies—the administering of the drug occurs to the exclusion of other behaviors. Severe cocaine addicts will self-administer the drug until their supply is gone, and they may become suicidal when more substance is unavailable. When the cocaine supply is exhausted, the addicts "escape" by using alcohol or tranquilizers to induce sleep.

Addicts often use drugs or alcohol to "loosen up" in the beginning of their years of usage, that is, to be more talkative at a party, more spontaneous, more sexual, or more uninhibited on the dance floor. What appears in the early stages of recreational use to be "increased flexibility" degenerates into "very predictable and inflexible behavior" as the addiction progresses.

The rigidity or inflexibility of pathological behavior is evidenced in the extreme by the person who drinks to oblivion or self-injects repeatedly until his or her supply of drugs is gone.

Because substances impair judgment, an addict is capable of exhibiting *any* behavior, even if it is quite uncharacteristic. As control lessens, the addict is more prone to inappropriate or impulsive behaviors. Behaviors that are taboo while sober, such as incest or violence, are more likely to occur when an addict is impaired by substances. Many addicts report a "Dr. Jekyll-Mr. Hyde" pattern of behavior in which their behavior while under the influence of substances is markedly different from their behavior while sober.

Effects on Self-Esteem

The process of addiction is devastating to self-esteem or self-worth. Given that most addicts identify low self-esteem as a problem leading to use of chemicals, a vicious cycle results.

Self-esteem often has very little or no basis in reality. An individual may be intelligent, successful in his job, and attractive and still feel unworthy of his accomplishments. Like a fraud or an actor, he may be convinced that he will ultimately be unmasked. This can become a self-fulfilling prophecy, because it is enormously difficult to behave in ways that are contrary to our strongly held beliefs.

As addiction progresses there may be losses and events in the life of the addict to cause shaky self-esteem to spiral downward. Facing a failed marriage, alienated children, and a job loss contribute to an already fragile self-esteem.

Many addicts grew up in alcoholic families where caregivers may have been preoccupied with their own internal chaos, not to mention external chaos in the family. Addicts participating in Adult Children of Alcoholics groups frequently report a lack of positive reinforcement from parents for their accomplishments and an excessive amount of criticism. This contributes to low self-esteem.

Dual Diagnoses

Numerous studies on both community and clinical populations have documented high rates of addiction and psychiatric comorbidities (Rubinstein, Campbell, & Daley, in press). The Epidemiologic Catchment Area (ECA) Survey of the National Institute of Mental Health studied approximately 20,000 adults in five communities in the United States. This survey reported that 47% of alcoholics had at least one additional diagnosis. Psychiatric disorders occurred more frequently in the alcoholic than the nonalcoholic population (Helzer & Pryzbeck, 1988). Numerous clinical studies also give support to high rates of dual diagnosis. A study of 431 hospitalized alcoholics reported that 77% had at least one additional psychiatric diagnosis (Hesselbrock, Meyer, & Keener, 1985). Another study of 501 drug abusers found that almost

80% of patients had an additional disorder (Ross, Glasen, & German-son, 1988).

Although there is some debate on the "chicken or egg" issue of which disorder came first, there are several possible relationships between addiction and psychiatric illness (Meyer, 1986).

First, psychiatric disorders may serve as a risk factor for addiction. For example, individuals with affective disorders or certain personality disorders have a greater incidence of addiction than those without these disorders.

Second, psychiatric disorders can modify the course of an addiction in terms of rapidity of course, responses to treatment, symptoms, and long-term treatment outcome. For example, "male-limited" alcoholics tend to develop substance abuse problems earlier than "milieu-limited" alcoholics (Cloniger, 1987). Patients with higher scores of "psychiatric severity," as measured by the Addiction Severity Index, are more prone to relapse than patients with lower scores (McLellan et al., 1985).

Third, psychiatric symptoms may result from chronic intoxication. For example, cocaine addicts may experience depression following cocaine binges; PCP abusers may become psychotic following use of this drug; and alcoholics may become depressed as a result of the effects of alcohol on the central nervous system.

Fourth, psychiatric symptoms may result from consequences of substance abuse. For example, many addicts experience depression following the loss of their family, job, financial security, health, or self-esteem. Many negative losses are associated with addiction.

Fifth, substance abuse and psychiatric symptoms, whether ante-cedent or consequent, often become meaningfully linked over the course of time. In some patients, it is extremely difficult to separate the two disorders because of their interrelationship.

Finally, there are two instances in which the psychiatric disorder and addiction are not related. An alcoholic may develop an episode of major depression after a prolonged period of recovery from addiction. A person with bipolar disease may become addicted to cocaine long after being stabilized from the affective disorder.

Impact on Developmental Tasks

Many addicts identify the mid-teen years (14-16) as the age at which substance use and abuse began. The adolescent years are marked by intense physiological maturation and psychosocial vulnerability. The process of deciding "who am I," which Erik Erikson labels *identity versus identity confusion,* is the developmental task of adolescence. Mind- and mood-altering substances frequently interfere with the adolescent's internal perception of who he or she is. A healthy sense of self does not develop in conjunction with heavy drug or alcohol use.

The status of adulthood is typically one in which the individual develops intimate and satisfying *interpersonal relationships.* From the social/peer focus of adolescence, there is movement to intense sharing in a relationship without loss of personal boundaries. A sense of personal isolation is the defect resulting from failure to work through this developmental task. Addicts in recovery describe their hollow, shallow previous relationships and recognize that substance use helped to prevent them from fully knowing another person or allowing themselves to experience intimacy.

Another stage described by Erikson in adulthood is *generative versus stagnation.* This phase involves recognition and expression of personal gifts for the benefit of others. The primary goal is enrichment of the life of others, and the defect is seen as selfish self-absorption and self-indulgence. Addictive behavior appears very self-absorbed to families and friends of the user.In the later stages of an addiction the addict is totally absorbed with obtaining and using his or her drug of choice.

Integrity versus despair marks the final developmental stage. It is difficult to see much integrity in a life ravaged by the effects of drugs or alcohol. Integrity requires a firm sense of self, and this is often absent by default because of arrest in the earlier developmental stages.

Despair and self-contempt indicate a profound failure in the search for meaningfulness in life. Recovery can be the beginning of the road back from self-contempt to integrity.

SOCIAL AND FAMILIAL EFFECTS OF ADDICTION

There is an abundance of self-help, clinical, and research literature delineating negative effects of addiction on the family and society (Ackerman, 1982, 1987; "Al-Anon Faces Alcoholism," 1984; Black, Bucky, & Wilder-Padilla, 1986; Daley, 1987, 1988, 1990; Kaufman & Kaufmann, 1979; NIAAA, 1982; Seixas & Youcha, 1985). Although the destructive effects may initially be denied by those involved with the person who is addicted, it would be unusual for those in the environment not to be affected in some adverse ways. Because the addicted person is not functioning in the same manner while not using, those around him or her feel the change. It may be confusing at first for family members, friends, and co-workers to see clearly that the person has changed. But, as the disease of addiction progresses, the change becomes more obvious and is hard to deny.

Family and Relationship Problems

As addicts becomes more involved with substance use, they are less available to others in their lives. Many recovering persons describe chemicals as their "lover," "best friend," and something they turn to when seeking comfort or solace. Consequently, those who previously offered comfort and concern are not relied upon. Spouses, children, and others are emotionally abandoned as the substance becomes the primary relationship for the addicted individual, causing feelings of confusion and anger.

The substance abuse may precipitate behaviors in the individual that are unfamiliar and unacceptable to family and friends. Angry outbursts, rages, and selfish, demanding behaviors may surface. Violence toward spouses and children may occur. Physical or vocal confrontations can result.

Family roles become dysfunctional (Black, 1981; Wegscheider, 1981). Spouses or children take on responsibilities of the addict. Children may take care of parents or each other because parental attention is elsewhere. The family atmosphere becomes tense and fearful as unpredictable behavior continues. Families may live in daily fear, chaos, and acute discomfort. Holidays and special occasions are tense rather than positive experiences (Daley, 1988).

Symptoms of stress may surface in nonaddicted individuals as they try to cope with the behavior of their loved one. Spouses become angry, resentful, and depressed. The focus of the family is centered on the addicted member. Some in the environment seek to control behavior and often try to force solutions. In this attempt to correct the situation, the behaviors of others become unreasonable.

Children become confused and may show symptoms of stress in their school performance or other behaviors, such as their relationships with friends. They may begin to act out their anger and frustration by using substances. Frequently, children turn to peer groups for the acceptance and attention they do not get at home.

Addiction results in high rates of marital separations and divorce. It is estimated that the divorce rate for these couples is seven times higher than in the general population. In addition, sexual abuse also occurs more frequently in these families.

Friendships suffer as addiction progresses. Old friends are dropped in favor of other substance abusers. New friends share the desire to use certain substances, but they lack any other connection to the persons they associate with.

Social Networks

Social networks also change as the individual pursues the substance. This change becomes necessary as friends and acquaintances refuse to put up with the behaviors they experience in the addicted individual. The sense of social connectedness erodes as the individual changes his peer group to accommodate a new life-style. Belonging to groups such as churches and community organizations becomes a hindrance to the time and attention required by the addiction.

Job- and School-Related Problems

As functioning deteriorates in the interpersonal sphere, it also deteriorates in occupational settings. Job performance is hampered by the effects of the substance. For example, a person who is using drugs or alcohol may not be able to think or perform tasks efficiently. Poor attendance at work also hinders performance. Frequent absences before or after a weekend suggest a pattern that alerts supervisors to substance abuse.

Similar functional deterioration occurs in younger people in high school, college, or other training or professional education programs. Lack of ability to perform up to par and poor attendance may alert teachers, or family members, that a problem exists and that the individual is in need of help.

Accidents

Traffic, airplane, occupational, and recreational accidents increase when alcohol or drug abuse is involved (NIAAA, 1987). Urine and blood sample reports show the use of alcohol, marijuana, and other substances to be present in the system of many individuals involved in such accidents.

The likelihood of a motor vehicle accident increases as the blood alcohol level of the driver increases. Drunk driving arrests net thousands of motorists per year, and deaths caused by drunk drivers spurred a national movement called Mothers Against Drunk Driving (MADD). Because of this organization, founded by a woman who had lost a child in a car accident caused by a drunk driver, stiffer penalties for drunk driving have been handed down to those found guilty.

Crimes and Arrests

In recent years, the number of individuals arrested for drunk driving has increased. Not only has the number of arrests increased, but many of those convicted of driving under the influence are receiving more serious sentences for their crimes. Crimes such as negligent homicides carry more serious punishment, usually incarcerations.

Other criminal activity often involves those whose judgment has been impaired by the use of substances. With certain types of addictions, criminal activities may become necessary in order to subsidize the habit. Cocaine or heroin addiction requires large funds to maintain, motivating addicts to engage in criminal behavior to pay for the drug. Antisocial behavior becomes part of the addiction.

SPIRITUAL EFFECTS OF ADDICTION

Addiction has a major impact on spiritual functioning. Many addicts report a feeling of "emptiness." What was important or meaningful in the past no longer matters. As more problems emerge, a sense of being overwhelmed and lost takes over. Hope is replaced by a sense of powerlessness. Positive feelings of love and connectedness are replaced by more negative feelings. Guilt and shame are experienced as the individuals see their behavior and their lives deteriorating. Whereas another individual might alter his or her life to avoid the circumstances that lead to these emotions, the addicted individual escapes them via substance use.

Addicts report that guilt and shame were the most difficult feelings for them to deal with during their addiction. Guilt and shame precipitate intensely uncomfortable feelings from which escape is sought. Some individuals escape into their addiction, where as others become so distraught that suicidal behavior, the "ultimate escape," is chosen as an option. Guilt is the emotion experienced when an individual evaluates his or her behavior. One feels one has done something "bad" or "unacceptable." This can be behavior of "commission," stealing money, hurting family members, losing a job, or relapsing. The addict can also feel guilty about things he or she "omitted" or did not do. Forgetting a mother on Mother's Day, breaking a promise to children and loved ones, failure to attend a child's graduation, or not returning borrowed money are a few common examples. Addicts can also feel guilty for thoughts and feelings (e.g., wishing someone harm or wanting to have sex with someone other than one's spouse).

Shame is self-focused. If guilt tells one that he or she has done something wrong, shame says he or she is a "bad person." It is reported as a feeling of "being defective." It is experienced when the "defect" is publicly exposed and causes embarrassment. It implies difference from others. Shame also brings focus to those involved with the individual. Family may feel ashamed of a parent's addictive behavior. The public nature of the behavior of the "defective individual" reflects on the family members. As with guilt, the "escape" from shame may be intensified involvement in the addiction or other destructive behavior such as suicide.

There are other adverse spiritual effects of addiction, including, but not limited to, the following: loss of one's faith in God, decreased participation in one's religion, a decline of standards and values, a loss of meaning in one's life, and a decrease in the ability to show love toward others (Daley,1988).

CONCLUSION

Considerable evidence exists to substantiate the adverse impact of addictive diseases on addicts, families, and society. Addiction is associated with a multiplicity of medical, interpersonal, psychological, spiritual, and financial problems for the addicted individual. Addicts do not, however, suffer alone. Much pain is often experienced by the family. A proliferation of literature in the past decade has documented adverse effects on young and adult children of addicts, families, and significant others. There is no doubt that all of society pays a heavy price for alcoholism and other forms of drug addiction.

REFERENCES

Ackerman, R. (1982). *Children of alcoholics.* Holmes Beach, FL: Learning Publications.

Ackerman, R. (1987). *Let go and grow.* Hollywood, FL: Health Communications.

Al-Anon faces alcoholism. (1984). (2nd ed.) New York: Al-Anon Family Group Headquarters.

American Psychiatric Association. (1987). Psychoactive substance use disorders. In *Diagnostic and statistical manual of mental disorders.* (DSM III-R) (4th ed., pp. 165-186). Washington, DC: Author.

Anderson, D. (1981). *The psychopathology of denial.* Center City, MN: Hazelden.

Black, C. (1981). *It will never happen to me.* Denver, CO: MAC.

Black, C., Bucky, S., & Wilder-Padilla, S. (1986). The interpersonal and emotional consequences of being an adult child of an alcoholic. *International Journal of the Addictions, 21*(3), 213-231.

Cloninger, C. R. (1987). Neurogenetic adaptive mechanisms in alcoholism. *Science, 236,* 410-416.

Daley, D. (1987). *Family recovery workbook.* Bradenton, FL: Human Services Institute.

Daley, D. (1988). *Surviving addiction.* New York: Gardner.

Daley, D. (1990). Surviving addiction workbook. Holmes Beach, FL: Learning Publications.

Fishel, R., Hamamoto, G., Barbul, A., Jiji. V., & Efron, G. (1985). Cocaine colitis: Is this a new syndrome? *Diseases of the Colon and Rectum, 28*(4), 264-266.

Gawin, F. H., & Kleber, H. D. (1985). Cocaine use in a treatment population: Patterns and diagnostic distinctions. In N. Kozel & E. Adams (Eds.), *Cocaine use in America: Epidemiologic and clinical perspectives* (pp. 182-192). Rockville, MD: National Institute on Drug Abuse.

Goodman, L. S., & Gilman, A. G. (Eds.). (1985). *The pharmacological basis of therapeutics* (7th ed.). New York: Macmillan.

Helzer, J., & Pryzbeck, T. (1988). The co-occurrence of alcoholism with other psychiatric disorders in the general population and its impact on treatment. *Journal of Studies on Alcohol, 29*(3), 219-224.

Hesselbrock, M., Meyer, R., & Keener, J. (1985). Psychopathology in hospitalized alcoholics. *Archives of General Psychiatry, 42,* 1050-1055.

Kaplan, H. I. (1988). *Comprehensive textbook of psychiatry* (5th ed.). Baltimore: Williams & Wilkins.

Kaufman, E., & Kaufmann, P. (1979). *The family therapy of drug and alcohol abuse* . New York: Gardner.

McLellan, A. T., Lubrorsky, L., Cacciola, J., Griffith, J., Evans, F., Barr, H., & O'Brien, C. P. (1985). New data from the Addiction Severity Index. *Journal of Nervous and Mental Disease, 173*(7), 412-423.

Meyer, R. (Ed.). (1986). *Psychpathology and addiction.* New York: Guilford.

Nace, E. (1990). Inpatient treatment of alcoholism. *The psychiatric hospital, 21*(1), 9-13.

Nalbandian, H., Sheth, N., Dietrich, R., & Geogiou, J. (1985). Intestinal ischemia caused by cocaine ingestion. *Surgery, 97*(3), 374-376.

National Institute of Alcohol Abuse and Alcoholism. (1982). *Special population issues.* Alcohol and Health, Monograph no. 4. Rockville, MD: Author.

National Institute of Alcohol Abuse and Alcoholism. (1987). *Alcohol and health.* Rockville, MD: Author.

National Institute on Drug Abuse. (1988). *Drug abuse and drug abuse research*. Rockville, MD: Author.

Pickens, R., & Svikis, D. (1988). Genetic vulnerability to drug abuse. In R. Pickens & D. Svikis (Eds.), *Biological vulnerability to drug abuse* (pp. 1-8). Rockville, MD: NIDA.

Ross, H., Glasen, F., & Germanson, T. (1988). The prevalence of psychiatric disorders in patients with alcohol and other drug problems. *Archives of General Psychiatry, 45*, 1023-1031.

Rubinstein. L., Campbell. F., & Daley, D. (in press). Four perspectives on dual disorders: An overview of treatment issues. *Journal of Chemical Dependency Treatment, 3*(2).

Schuckit, M. (1989). *Drug and alcohol abuse: A clinical guide to diagnosis and treatment*. New York: Plenum.

Seixas, J., & Youcha, G. (1985). *Children of alcoholism: A survivor's manual*. New York: Crown.

Wegscheider, S. (1981). *Another chance: Hope and health for the alcoholic family*. Palo Alto, CA: Science and Behavior Books.

Chapter 4

INTERVENTION: BREAKING THE ADDICTION CYCLE

JOHN D. MASSELLA

It is amazing how far professionals have come in their ability to diagnose and treat chemical dependence. Alcoholism has long been the "whipping boy" of society and the medical profession. It has ranged from being called "the symptom of other psycho-neurotic factors (including but not limited to release of aggression and sexual impulse, the escape to infantile impotence, inferiority, and immaturity) to physiological factors such as hypoglycemia and allergies" (Hunt, 1944, p.1146). There are an estimated 10 to 20 million alcoholics in the United States today (Johnson, 1986). Professionals have become more aware of the emotional, psychological, and physiological symptoms of alcohol and drug dependence. Familial, financial, vocational, and spiritual symptoms of substance dependence enable the chemically dependent person to be identified before gross physical deterioration occurs.

The primary symptom of chemical dependence is denial of the problem, even if the chemically dependent individual has observed gross deterioration in many aspects of personal life due to drinking or drug use. Denial takes many forms. It is not limited to the person who has identified the problem of chemical dependence. Family members often deny or minimize the symptoms of alcohol dependence to assist them in coping with the problem of living with an alcoholic. Health-related professionals, colleagues, coworkers, and other

AUTHOR'S NOTE: Special thanks to my wife Joan, Lori Ward, and Alice Watson.

significant persons deny or minimize the problem because they feel powerless to stop the addictive process. Although there are health professionals and family members who continue to believe that the chemically dependent person must want help before he or she can be treated, many use the approach that was developed approximately 20 years ago by Dr. Vernon Johnson.

Founder of the Johnson Institute and author of the book, *I'll Quit Tomorrow*, Vernon Johnson (1980) identified substance dependence as a chronic illness. He also felt that the symptoms of alcoholism and drug addiction could be described to chemically dependent persons in a way that would force him to identify his own problems with drinking or drug use and to initiate personal change. Johnson called this process "intervention." An intervention process was developed to deal with the symptom of "denial." It is currently used, in varied forms, to facilitate the beginning of treatment for the chemically dependent person, and to help family and friends to contend with the problems involved in coping with the addiction.

This intervention process is described below, and examples from the author's clinical work in a rehabilitation center with chemically dependent persons and their families are cited. A discussion of denial and of "hitting bottom" (a term used to describe the emotional, physical, psychological, and spiritual state of the addict that "forces" him or her to change) is presented. Does the addict or alcohol-dependent person need to hit bottom to get help? Denial and resistance of treatment are also reviewed. Discussion of the intervention process includes gathering a team, rehearsing the intervention, referring to treatment, and following up. Finally, a review of the variety of formal and informal interventions, with emphasis on the role of the health professionals, is presented.

DENIAL

Alcoholism used to be thought of as a psychoneurotic symptom with the function of screening out unsatisfactory external and internal realities (Hunt, 1944). Today, alcoholism is seen as a disease maintained by the psychological defense of denial. Denial allows a person to blot out external and internal realities that would be anxiety-provoking and threatening. Denial is an aspect of the disease that a person goes through before acceptance of illness and final resolution. However, it is unlikely that the chemically dependent person will seek help on his or her own.

HITTING BOTTOM

The time at which the addict turns his or her life around is called "hitting bottom." Other familiar phrases are associated with such change, including "the last straw," "end of the line," "reach my limit," and "that's all I can stand." But, does a person afflicted with an addictive disease have to "hit bottom?" How does this vary for different people, and can the point at which this change occurs be adjusted?

The author has worked with many patients seeking treatment after prompting by family, job, union, physician, or friends. Some patients come after experiencing problems and the realization that their problems stem from drinking and/or drug use. For example, a beautician came to treatment after she could no longer hold her hand steady to put on nail polish; a secretary came because her typing skills dropped 10 words a minute; a physician came after he could not recall performing surgery the previous day; and a pilot came after being unable to recall flying an airplane. Other examples include the drug addict who collapses all the veins in his or her body because of intravenous use and is now injecting into the groin; the alcoholic who is drinking while his body is rejecting his third liver transplant; and the individual who has lost family, job, home, self-worth, mental health, and $100,000 in a six-month period from smoking cocaine. These are the symptoms of addiction.

The chemically dependent person reaches a point where he or she is motivated to seek treatment. Entrance into treatment, however, is not necessarily hitting bottom. Most of the author's patients have come into treatment feeling that their problem with drugs and/or alcohol is minimal or "not that bad." The challenge for the professional is to assist a person in seeing how alcohol or drug use has affected various aspects of his or her life. Treatment can help the patient understand the benefits of a sober existence and acquire the "tools" needed to follow through with recovery.

THE INTERVENTION PROCESS

An intervention is "the process by which the processes of chemical dependency are interrupted and the chemically dependent person is helped to stop using drugs and alcohol and to develop new ways or healthier ways of coping" (Johnson, 1986, p. 61). How does one present reality to an individual who is out of touch with it? In intervention, the chemically dependent person is confronted about his or her alcohol or drug use by family or friends, who also tell their feelings about his or her use. As with any communication or sharing of feelings, one must be tactful but firm. The intervention is no different. Yet, there is a twist to this process. Usually there is a group of caring people involved and all take turns presenting *facts* in a nonjudgmental and caring way. This group, however, may feel guilty intervening. For this reason, clinicians spend time on education about addiction and help families resolve feelings of guilt about intervening with a loved one.

We feel uncomfortable letting people know how we feel, telling what they need to look at or work on, or discussing actions of theirs that we dislike. What about the guilt in telling a person that you believe he or she needs treatment? Family and friends of chemically dependent persons are reluctant to seek intervention. Why do this now? Why me? Why can't he go when he is ready? Am I interfering in his personal life? Am I being sneaky? Does it work? All of these are very common fears. Family and friends must overcome these fears in order to help others change or get well.

When much data have been amassed about someone's drug and alcohol use, a review of these data by family members tends to assure the family that intervention is the best option. At times, the family's own denial of the drug and alcohol problem is more ingrained than that of the person who is chemically dependent. For this reason, it is important that family members and friends of the chemically dependent person receive education on addiction and the enabling process. Education should cover: dispelling myths of chemical dependence, the addiction cycle, denial, the disease concept of addiction, and the continuum of use.

THE STEPS OF INTERVENTION

Step One: Gather the Team

Two or more people should be involved in the confrontation (intervention) with the chemically dependent person. If a health professional is involved in the intervention process, he or she is responsible for gathering the team. If the intervention is being done by a family member or significant other, the person with the highest level of emotional investment and the best understanding of addiction should gather the team. Team members should be individuals who are significant to the chemically dependent person. Therefore, the first step in this process is to make a list of the meaningful people involved in the life of the chemically dependent person. The list is best made by that person who is most significant to the chemically dependent person: the spouse, the employer, the chemically dependent person's parents and/or siblings, children (at least eight years old or older), close friends or neighbors, coworker(s), and/or a member of the clergy. The most important factor in choosing the team is that the people care for the chemically dependent person and/or are involved with him or her regularly. A friend seen infrequently may be as significant as a friend seen daily if he or she is emotionally close to the dependent person.

Experience has shown that a group of three to five is the most effective team. A long list can be reduced by inviting only people who understand addiction and are willing to risk losing their relationship with the chemically dependent person. Team members must understand that the chemically dependent person is extremely delusional because of his or her defense system, and that the person is unable to see his or her behavior clearly. Members should also understand that the addiction is a disease and not a "bad habit." Solid education is the foundation for family and friends to implement a well-structured intervention with minimal guilt.

Step Two: Gather the Data

Two types of data are needed for the intervention—facts about the chemically dependent person's drug and alcohol use and behaviors associated with such use, and information about treatment options. A list should be prepared of the occurrences of drinking or drug use and related behavior of the chemically dependent person. Data must be specific, and one must avoid making general statements like "you're always late or always drunk." Each team member is to list specific times, events, and dates. Examples are:

> Dad, on Tuesday of last week you came home late and you smelled of alcohol and you were staggering. We were to go to my game, as you had promised, but you said you forgot and worked late. I felt very hurt.

> Bill, at our last luncheon meeting you presented some good ideas. Even though you had been drinking, I thought what you said made sense. However, the next day when I asked you about it, you couldn't even remember being at the meeting. That concerned me.

> Sweetheart, when we went to my folks on our anniversary, I asked you not to drink. You said you wouldn't, and that you had your drinking under control. I saw you sneaking booze from the kitchen when everyone was at the dinner table. Later that evening, my parents said you smelled of alcohol. I was ashamed.

These statements focus on facts and firsthand observations. It can be beneficial to share how one "felt" at the time. However, participants in the intervention must avoid such statements as "You made me feel bad." Laying the blame or accusation only causes defensiveness. As Johnson (1986) states, "Each incident should be described in unsparing detail" (p. 73). One family used a camcorder and a tape recorder to collect evidence. This proved to be very effective when they intervened with their addicted member. Such detail is hard for the chemically dependent person to dispute. It allows the family or intervention team members something concrete to present as the basis for concern.

Treatment options need to be explored prior to the actual intervention. "The ultimate goal of the prevention process is to get the chemically dependent person into treatment or some type of continuing care" (Johnson, 1986, p. 74). Treatment options are diverse. If a chemically dependent person is drinking on a daily basis and has difficulty abstaining for more than 24 hours, the appropriate recommendation would be an intensive inpatient rehabilitation program. This type of treatment facility allows the chemically dependent person to lay the foundation for an ongoing recovery process. It is a structured environment in which there are two to four weeks of abstinence and evaluation of other aspects of the chemical dependency. Family members typically are involved in this type of rehabilitation program.

A second option is intensive outpatient rehabilitation. This option is geared for a person who has been abstinent for periods of time but has a compulsion to use alcohol or drugs in spite of deterioration. Intensive outpatient rehabilitation is recommended for a person who has a supportive environment to return to each day. The individual can be maintained on medications that will not allow him or her to drink or use narcotics while involved in rehabilitation. Some treatment facilities will do periodic drug testing to make sure the chemically dependent person is abstinent.

A third option is outpatient counseling with an addictions counselor. Although outpatient counseling can be beneficial, a person who is in a high level of denial will often continue to use alcohol or drugs, and he or she will lie to the outpatient therapist. If outpatient counseling is recommended, the family and significant others need to be included. They are to be contacted if the chemically dependent person decides not to come to counseling or drinks or uses drugs again.

A fourth option is participation in Alcoholics Anonymous (AA) and/or Narcotics Anonymous (NA). AA and NA are support groups that are not affiliated with any private or public organizations established to treat individuals who are chemically dependent. They are comprised of people afflicted with the disease of alcoholism and/or drug addiction who are working on a recovery program. This type of support system can be extremely effective in helping a person to maintain abstinence. Individuals will receive a great deal of support and nurturing from meetings, but they need to give the meetings a chance to work for them.

Denial often presents itself as a problem when a person first begins to go to AA or NA; the chemically dependent person perceives the differences between himself and the other people at AA or NA meetings. Family members and others of the intervention team should attend some type of support group such as Al-Anon or Al-A Teen. These support groups are similar to AA and NA in structure and composition, except that members usually are individuals affected by the chemically dependent person.

There will be some denial by the chemically dependent person no matter where he or she is referred. However, the chemically dependent person is externally motivated, and outside influence is the most effective means of initiating change. The assembled team itself is a very powerful external motivator. The team should not settle for the treatment option the chemically dependent person desires, because he or she is usually not rational and is likely to minimize the severity of the addiction. However, reality dictates that a compromise may be necessary. If the chemically dependent person agrees to go to AA/NA or outpatient counseling and either does not go or fails to maintain abstinence, he or she can agree to inpatient or intensive outpatient rehabilitation.

Treatment facilities can be found in the telephone book. When inpatient treatment is recommended, it is helpful to have a space reserved at the facility for the day of intervention, or the day after if the intervention is conducted in the evening. This gives the treatment program time to gather more data on the chemically dependent person and to familiarize the intervention team with the facility prior to treatment.

Information to obtain about treatment centers includes: philosophy of treatment, recovery rates, aftercare programs, stress management, role of AA or NA, and family services offered. The family frequently needs to feel more comfortable with the treatment facility than the chemically dependent person. Such knowledge helps lessen the feeling of guilt.

Step Three: Rehearsing the Intervention

Practicing the intervention at least once is strongly recommended. Each team member has a role to play and special information to present. It is important that the message given to the addicted person be consistent. The rehearsal also helps each team member feel he or she is not alone. Members are likely to feel less anxious, which lessens the possibility of projecting unclear messages to the chemically dependent person.

According to Johnson (1986), there are six steps involved in the rehearsal. The first step is to choose a designated chairperson. This can be done by vote or volunteer. If a therapist is included, he or she will be the chairperson. The chairperson directs the rehearsals and the intervention itself, and he or she determines the order and timing of each person's presentation of the facts. It is better that a person who has suffered less emotional pain be placed in this role. Not only is he or she likely to be distant but this person can also guide the process with less guilt.

The second step is to review the lists each team member has pre-pared. Reading each item allows the chairperson and the team to weed out messages that may block the chemically dependent person from hearing the true message of concern. Overtones of self-pity and hostil-ity can block progress. Many "secrets" may come out during this process. Usually, there are others on the team who know those same secrets. This can assist in strengthening the commitment to intervene.

The third step is to determine the order in which team members will read the lists. This prevents awkward pauses and minimizes interrup-tions by the chemically dependent person. A person with a close and influential relationship with the chemically dependent person should start the intervention.

The fourth step is choosing a person to play the role of the chemically dependent person during rehearsals. It is best to have two or three members alternate at this. As with any role-play, it is important for a person to be confronted with possible objections. Therapists or clini-cians are often called upon to role-play mock supervisory or therapy treatment sessions, allowing possible problems to be confronted before they occur in the real treatment session. This anticipation of problems is very effective, especially if all group members take a turn at playing the chemically dependent person. Each team member has his or her own view of the chemically dependent person. It is enlightening to see the different personalities that have been exhibited by the patient.

Next, the team members determine what they will say to the chemi-cally dependent person and how they will say it. They must determine what to say if the chemically dependent person refuses treatment. Most importantly, responses must be realistic and firm. Messages that are transmitted with less than genuine feeling will be interpreted as half-hearted threats. For example, if the spouse and children are not prepared to leave, they should not make that threat. If the employer is not prepared to terminate or fire this employee, then the threat should not be made. "Each action on the part of the chemically dependent person must be met with a reaction that is in keeping with the tone and purpose of the intervention" (Johnson, 1986, p. 81).

The ideal rehearsal and intervention should begin with a statement that is concise. For example:

John, we've asked you to come here because we all care about you. We truly feel there has been a number of things happening that we would like to talk to you about. However, we have one specific request: that you sit and listen to us and let each of us tell you exactly how we feel before making any type of comments. As your family and friends, we feel somewhat uncomfortable, as I'm sure you are at this point, and we ask that you help us by promising that you will just listen for now.

Because the chemically dependent person has a passive role in the intervention, the team must help to maintain that role. The most effective way to accomplish this is to remain focused on the plan that was rehearsed. During the rehearsal, each team member will review the information that has been written. Team members should try to present the information as clearly as possible with the same demeanor that they would use with the chemically dependent person. Sometimes, people believe that any emotionality is contrived. Team members will discover how easy it is to adopt their role in the intervention. It is important that the group listen to the information presented. The rehearsal should allow team members to weed out inappropriate comments as well as negative or hostile feelings.

After all the information has been presented, the team can then rehearse presenting the available treatment options to the chemically dependent person. Options need to be presented clearly and concisely. Treatment options that are perceived to be inadequate should not be presented. Some families and friends may wish to present a treatment option that is minimal and that appeases the chemically dependent person. They may believe that allowing the chemically dependent person to choose the treatment option available affords him or her some dignity. However, by the time of intervention, the drug and/or alcohol use has become fairly extreme. For this reason, intensive inpatient or outpatient treatment is usually appropriate. Other options would not be as effective.

The chemically dependent often deny the existence of a problem and the need for treatment (Twerski, 1981). They may feel there is a problem but that going to a few AA meetings or counseling sessions will be sufficiently beneficial. A change in drinking or drug use behavior, however, does not mean that the disease of alcoholism or drug addiction has been eradicated.

Step Four: Finalizing the Details

The team should meet again for the last time before the actual intervention. Issues to be discussed include: when and where will the intervention be conducted? What specific data will be stated? Are all treatment options taken care of and finalized? How will the team members get to the treatment facility? As Johnson (1986) states, "Leave nothing to chance" (p. 85).

TYPES OF INTERVENTION

The model of intervention previously discussed is the traditional model in which a professional guides the intervention. However, there is a number of ways to intervene with a chemically dependent person. Many of these differ due to the means of confrontation or the educational focus. The following sections discuss health care, family, and supervisory interventions.

Health Care and Social Service Interventions

Dr. Abraham Twerski has stated that 30% of general hospital admissions from the emergency room are attributable to problems directly associated with the use of alcohol and/or drugs (Twerski, 1983). Nurses, paramedics, attending physicians, and other specialists all have opportunities to make the patient aware of an alcohol or drug abuse problem. Twerski (1983) cites some resistance by physicians to confront their private patients about substance abuse. As with family members and friends, physicians are either reluctant to label a patient alcoholic or they have a distorted view of chemical dependency.

Physicians and other health professionals need to avoid simplistic approaches to questioning the chemically dependent person about quantity and frequency of usage. The chemically dependent person will not be open and honest about the quantity and frequency of usage. The patient is continuing the use of drugs and/or alcohol despite the negative consequences. Some type of intensive treatment is called for (Pattison & Kaufman, 1982).

If the physician does not wish to confront the patient alone, he or she can incorporate the medical team into this intervention. The medical team may consist of an intake worker or mental health nurse who was involved with the patient in the emergency room; a social worker who has, it is hoped, had contact with the patient and family members while the patient has been in the hospital; and the hospital clergy if the patient has a religious affiliation. These individuals should meet as a formal intervention team and review the information regarding the chemically dependent patient. The team should meet with the patient in the hospital and present the information. The patient must be made aware of their recommendations, and of the fact that they intend to initiate a referral to a treatment program or facility.

Any health professional who suspects a patient of having a problem with drinking and/or drug use should not keep it a secret. The suspicion should be presented to the physician and/or the social service professional, and a drug and alcohol consultation should be requested. This is standard procedure in most hospitals and can usually be done quite easily. After a consultation, the team approach can be used to initiate the patient into treatment. It is extremely effective and beneficial to involve family members. Families have most likely been experiencing the symptoms of the chemically dependent person long before medical problems occurred. Most referrals to intensive rehabilitation programs can be done quite easily, and continuity of care is maintained by transferring a patient from the hospital directly into a rehabilitation program.

Individuals in other social service settings, such as probation officers, have clients that continue to use drugs and/or alcohol. The probation officer has leverage in initiating or motivating treatment. A person on probation may have to submit to periodic urinalysis. If the urinalysis is positive, the probation officer has the option of revoking the probation or parole, or initiating a referral to a drug and alcohol treatment facility for an evaluation. This type of external motivation is an effective means of initiating treatment for chemical dependency. There is probably a higher level of anger associated with mandatory referral for evaluation. However, once the chemically dependent person is in treatment, his or her inability to stop the use of alcohol and/or drugs in the face of positive tests for substance abuse makes clear the power of the addiction.

Finally, the psychotherapist or counselor who works with patients that have psychiatric disorders may also observe alcoholism or drug addiction in their clients. For example, patients with mood disorders who use medications that do not improve the disorder may be abusing alcohol or drugs. The efficacy of medicines such as antidepressants is reduced when patients abuse alcohol or other substances.

Case Example

An outpatient therapist had been working with a 27-year-old single female for approximately three months. The patient came to treatment presenting symptoms of depressed mood, trouble sleeping, decreased appetite, and trouble concentrating. The patient often talked about issues occurring in her life that would prompt anyone to feel depressed, ranging from loss of significant relationships to increased job requirements. The counselor worked diligently to improve the patient's coping skills and even asked her how much alcohol she drank. The patient's response was "not much and not that often." The counselor continued to talk about the patient's inability to cope with stressful situations.

After the initial three months, the patient began to describe problems at work including late arrival on Mondays. This was related to too much "partying" on the weekend. At this point, the counselor became suspicious about the patient's drinking and began to take a more extensive drinking history. Rather than focusing on quantity and frequency of usage, the therapist began to see how the patient's life deteriorated along with her drinking. Also, the therapist saw how the patient often treated her depression with alcohol. After gathering this information, the therapist set very specific limits on the patient's drinking while involved with counseling or therapy. The patient agreed to attend Alcoholics Anonymous meetings and to abstain from alcohol for a period of 30 days. She also stated that if she could not do this, she would enter rehabilitation. This was written in the form of a contract, and both therapist and patient signed this contract. Subsequently, the patient was unable to maintain abstinence for more than one week. The therapist used the contract and the rapport with the patient to initiate referral into rehabilitation.

Health care and social service professionals should gather information on rehabilitation facilities in their area, including the admission and referral processes of these facilities. This information can help maintain the continuity of care for the chemically dependent person. The less continuity of care, the less likely it is for the chemically dependent person to follow through with prescribed treatment. The rehabilitation facility will help the chemically dependent person develop a structured aftercare program (Burgin, 1982).

The referral process is not difficult. With any type of referral, one need only contact a rehabilitation facility or private practitioner. The current situation and feelings about the chemically dependent person, and pertinent symptoms, should be described. The evaluation specialist or therapist will probably have a few questions, and the interested party or family member should be open and honest. The type of intervention will be discussed and a possible admission date will be set at that time. Many facilities also have transportation available directly from the intervention site.

Social service professionals in hospitals or detoxification centers also have opportunity to intervene in the addictive process. Their referral is more direct because they transfer a patient from a hospital or detoxification center into a rehabilitation program. There are also facilities that are not attached to detoxification centers or hospitals that will pick up patients from the hospital. It is more beneficial, however, for family members to transport the chemically dependent person to the rehabilitation center.

In the referral process, general demographic data are given to the admissions staff, who also take the chemical and medical history. Many treatment or rehabilitation facilities are able to accept people who receive financial assistance. Financial information is also given to the admissions staff so that the chemically dependent person cannot argue about the affordability of the treatment. The alcohol- or drug-dependent person cannot afford not to be treated.

Family Intervention Without Professional Input

Family members who for years have felt powerless in face of the chemically dependent person's addiction have discovered new means of changing how they cope with that addiction and their own feelings. There is hope in intervention for both the family and the chemically dependent person, as the following case example illustrates.

Case Example

I woke up and had my usual headache and sour stomach from having drunk Friday night and Saturday night. It was Sunday morning, approximately 10:30 a.m., when my wife came into the bedroom and told me that she and the kids would like to talk to me downstairs. Immediately, my thought was another lecture or hearing of the concerns regarding my drinking. They had tried to make me aware of my drinking being a problem once before. But, I was able to convince them that I would slow down or stop. Still fairly groggy, and before having a cup of coffee,

I walked into the living room and sat down. Sitting there were my two children, 16-year-old John and 18-year-old Kimberly, and my wife, Joan. They had funny looks on their faces. I could not quite place it. It was a look between sorrow and anger, one that I think I have seen before with my family—but not with such intensity.

As I walked into the room, Joan stood up and asked me to sit down. She said that she and the kids had something to tell me, and that they wished I would sit down and merely listen. She went on to say that it was very stressful for her and the kids to tell me what they felt, but they were going to do it because they were concerned and loved me. I agreed and leaned back in my chair. Joan was sitting directly across from me and leaned slightly forward in her chair. John and Kim were sitting off to either side and in front of me, both with hands folded in their laps, also leaning forward. Joan stated that last Friday she was very concerned because when I came in that evening, the car was badly damaged and I did not remember what had happened. She also mentioned two similar incidents on two holidays in the past and talked of how painful and fearful they were for her. At this point, I tried to defend myself but she stopped me and again requested that I just listen to what they had to say. She went on and mentioned a party two months ago where I had promised not to drink and ended up becoming intoxicated and spilling food and beverages on our neighbor's furniture and carpeting, not once, but three times that evening.

John then moved further forward in his chair, his hands now loosened. He looked directly into my eyes and said "Dad, I love you." He went on to say that he had been concerned about my drinking for a long time and that he had wanted me to stop for a long time as well. He said that after his last Friday night football game he came home with his friends to find me passed out on the living room couch. He was embarrassed. He went on to say that he's never forgotten the day that I promised to take him fishing and ended up not taking him because I stayed at a golf outing and drank all day.

Before I had an opportunity to respond, my daughter sat forward and began to cry. At this point, I began to cry as well. She said that she loved me very much and wished I would stop drinking. She also said, as did my son, that she came home three Fridays ago, with her friends, and found me intoxicated and rambling on about cleaning the steps in the basement. The next day, I did not recall the incident. After a pause, she began to talk about the time I took her out to drive with her learner's permit, and I was intoxicated. She was angry at me because I was driving recklessly and she said that she felt I didn't care about her or the family. She again told me that she loved me. My wife then stood up and reached behind the lounge in the den and got a suitcase. She told me that an admission was set up for me at a rehabilitation center, and that they were expecting me there before noon. She ended by saying that she did care a great deal about me and she and the kids could no longer watch me kill myself. She said that if I did not go into treatment, she and the kids were going to leave. Initially, I did not believe her. Then, she walked over to the closet and opened it up to show me that her and the kids' bags were packed. They were very serious.

I reluctantly agreed to go to treatment and believe that it was the best decision that I've ever made in my life. Not only the best decision for me but also for my family.

Family Intervention With Professional Help

Family members can also initiate referrals for evaluation. At times, it is much more difficult to convince a chemically dependent family member than an employee that rehabilitation is needed. However, it might be easier for a family member to motivate the chemically dependent person to talk to a therapist or counselor. Family members can be encouraged to contact a therapist or evaluation specialist (Twerski, 1983). If the goal is to initiate someone into treatment, family members must make the evaluation specialist aware of this goal. They should plan out what they are going to say and give information to the specialist that can be used in the evaluation (Burgin, 1983).

Case Example

A chemically dependent person's wife and daughter called for an evaluation. They expressed concern about the chemically dependent person's drinking and had confronted him a number of times over the past several years. At this point, they became increasingly worried because his blackouts had become more frequent. Information was collected with respect to intoxicated incidences that this particular client had over the years. The wife stated that she was going to confront her husband and ask that he come for an evaluation to please her. She stated that she had asked him approximately one week ago, and he said he'd be willing to talk to someone. A call was received the following day, and it was the chemically dependent person with his wife on the other line. The evaluation was set up for the next day. At that point, bed status was checked at the treatment center and at two other rehabilitation facilities. The possibility of an admission in intensive outpatient rehabilitation was also explored. From the symptoms that were described by the spouse, this patient appeared to need some type of intensive treatment.

On the scheduled day, the patient and his wife and daughter arrived on time for the evaluation. It was asked if the whole family could be present for the evaluation, and the patient felt comfortable with that. The evaluation process was very straightforward. Extremely concrete questions were asked after developing some rapport with the patient and family. At times, when the therapist questioned the chemically dependent person, the family would chime in and give their own impressions and responses. This added reality and gave the patient the opportunity to be slightly more honest about his symptoms.

In this particular case, four different evaluation tools were employed: the MAST (Michigan Alcoholism Screening Test), the SCD (Warning Signs of Chemical Dependency), the CASAS (Craig Analysis of Substance Abuse Syndrome), and the self-report of Alcoholics Anonymous. Each of these evaluation tools, when taken by a person suspected of abusing drugs and/or alcohol, yields a specific score. Each score is then compared to a particular critical value. If the score is above that particular critical value, it is indicative of problematic drug and/or alcohol use. The person evaluated in this particular case scored three to four times the critical value. He was presented with this information. This author has found that the presentation of these scores allows patients to see the severity of their illness. This is particularly true with the CASAS, because patients are compared to an alcohol-dependent population.

This chemically dependent person had been confronted by his employer in the past, and it was suggested by colleagues and coworkers that he seek treatment. He was given the option of being treated at any one of three facilities and was told that all the arrangements would be made and his supervisor informed. It was helpful that the family and the chemically dependent person were able to tour the facility after the evaluation.

The referral process in this case went well. Many rehabilitation facilities or programs conduct interventions. It is one of the more effective means of motivating a person into treatment and taking much pressure and guilt off the family. As stated earlier, families often feel guilty for forcing the patient into treatment. With this evaluation process, the clinician becomes the identified motivator.

Supervisor Intervention

The supervisory referral or intervention model includes monitoring and documenting problematic job performance by an employee. After collecting a certain amount of this documentation, the supervisor conducts a confrontational interview with the employee. In this type of intervention, the employee is presented with his or her job performance over the aforementioned period of time. Positive performance as well as negative is presented. Chemically dependent persons typically have many more negatives than positives in their employee file. Such items include absenteeism, tardiness, scrapped jobs, unexcused absences, absence from job sites, leaving work, and/or returning to work from lunch in a noticeably incoherent or intoxicated state. These are just a few of the items that can be listed. It is important for the employer to have some idea that the person in question has been abusing drugs and/or alcohol, but it is not recommended that employers become the diagnostician.

After presenting the information to the employee in as nonjudgmental a manner as possible, the employer must present the behavior and type of job performance that are desired. It is also important as this time to initiate a referral for either an evaluation or admission directly into treatment.

Referral for an evaluation would come about when deteriorated job performance is the only information that the employer has compiled. Without overt symptoms of alcohol dependence and/or drug abuse (such as smell of alcohol, intoxication at work, drinking at lunch, or positive urinalysis), referral for an evaluation should be general. The employer is making the employee aware that he or she cares about the troubled employee and that the problem is serious enough to take action. At that point, the supervisor, along with the employee with the alcohol or drug problem, will contact a treatment professional or clinic for an evaluation. If, at the time of the confrontation, the employee admits to having a drug and alcohol problem, which is unlikely, a referral can be initiated.

If a person is referred for a general evaluation, it is the task of the evaluation specialist to gather information and symptoms from the employee. The specialist needs to determine the extent of chemical use and motivate the employee to accept treatment if dependence exists. It is beneficial for the supervisor to accompany the employee at the time of the evaluation, The evaluation specialist should get a release of information form signed by the employee prior to talking with the supervisor. Employee records or job performances are key factors in the evaluation process.

Case Example

When Susan arrived at work, Steve, her direct supervisor, called her into his office. He stated that he had been concerned about her getting to work late and had noticed that she had called off several times in the past two months. Her call-offs always followed a weekend. Also, on two occasions last month Steve tried to give Susan an assignment and she was not at her desk. Both times, she came back to her post in about ten minutes stating that she had been in the rest room. Steve stated that this was no problem, but that when she came back to her desk she acted "strange." She was talking rapidly and wiping her nose frequently.

After presenting his concern to Susan, Steve outlined the job performance that he required of her. He did not claim to know what was wrong with Susan, even though he suspected that she was on some type of chemical. He wasn't sure of this. He went on to tell Susan that she had now reached a point with her performance that required a two-day suspension without pay. He wanted her to call a local treatment facility where the company held an Employee Assistance Program for an evaluation.

Susan arrived at her evaluation and was fairly open about her absenteeism and tardiness. When given the evaluation tools mentioned earlier, she scored fairly high on all of them. The therapist also contacted her husband and found that he had been concerned about Susan for two or three years. Susan's husband, Mike, went on to tell the therapist that she had been snorting cocaine and that, in the past 8 to 12 months, she had lied about using it and had been spending money that was to have paid the household bills.

With this intervention, Susan was confronted by the evaluator and finally opened up with respect to abusing cocaine and diverting funds from the family joint account. Susan's admission into treatment was coordinated with the supervisor. Two years later, she is sober.

FOLLOW-UP

After the referral into treatment or rehabilitation, family members, employers, and the intervention specialist or intervening therapist should be in contact with the patient and treatment center throughout the prescribed treatment. This allows for better continuity of care and also shows the patient that he or she has not been forgotten. Family members are extremely significant in the rehabilitation process and must identify problems that they may have developed by living with substance dependence. One cannot stress enough the need for family members to receive education and counseling on addiction and co-dependence.

If an individual is referred to treatment, one should attempt to be in contact with him or her by phone or in person at least three or four times in the intensive rehabilitation process. This also allows one to receive feedback about the referral process and to review techniques that were used in the intervention. It is important to be in contact with the family in case they need to be referred for private counseling or therapy to deal with residual guilt.

SUMMARY

The intervention process is not the answer to all problems of the alcohol- or drug-dependent person. However, alcohol- and drug-dependent persons no longer have to wait to be in the gutter or at "rock bottom" before they seek treatment, rehabilitation, or a life change as an option. Family members do not have to get to the point where they're going to leave the chemically dependent person before feeling they can do something about his or her drinking or drug use. The same is true for employers, colleagues, coworkers, union representatives, medical professionals, and the legal system. If all who know of a person's alcoholism or drug addiction became involved in an intervention process for that person, he or she could not resist going into treatment or changing. The alcohol- or drug-dependent person can resist change or rehabilitation as long as there are only negative options. The intervention process begins to present the chemically dependent person with positive options.

REFERENCES

Burgin, J. E. (1982). *Guide book for the family with alcoholic problems.* Center City, MN: Hazelden.

Hunt, J. M. V. (1944). *Personality and behavior disorders.* New York: Ronald Press.

Johnson, V. E. (1980). *I'll quit tomorrow: A practical guide to alcoholism treatment.* New York: Harper & Row.

Johnson, V. E. (1986). *Intervention: How to help someone who doesn't want help.* Minneapolis, MN: Johnson Institute.

Pattison, M. E., & Kaufman, E. (1982). *Encyclopedic handbook of alcoholism.* New York: Gardner.

Twerski, A. J. (1981). *Caution: Kindness can be dangerous to the alcoholic.* Englewood Cliffs, NJ: Prentice-Hall.

Twerski, A. J. (1983). Early intervention in alcoholism: Confrontational techniques. *Hospital and Community Psychiatry, 34*(11), 1027-1030.

Chapter 5

RECOVERY ISSUES AND TREATMENT RESOURCES

TOD R. MARION
KATHRYN COLEMAN

PRINCIPLES OF RECOVERY

Recovery from addiction is a process of abstinence and change. The problem faced by the alcoholic and addict during addiction must be identified before one can delineate a recovery program. Much research has attempted to develop a classification system for types of alcoholics. Mandell (1983) reports there is no evidence of a relationship between types of alcoholics and the etiology, course, and outcome of the disease. Although there has been less research on other drug addictions it is likely that the same lack of evidence is true for these addictions. Studies support a consistent sequence of symptoms in the development of chemical dependence. This sequence can be reliably divided into phases that reflect the variety and severity of symptoms of chemical dependence. Diagnosis of chemical dependence is based on a clustering of symptoms unique for each individual. Mandell observes that all patients in treatment are not chemically dependent but seek treatment for problems brought on by chemical use. He emphasizes that various levels of functioning and social competency can be found among patients.

A recovery plan, therefore, must take into consideration the diversity of patients and their conditions at the time they enter treatment. Recovery must address the specific problem areas of each person. Defining a recovery program for alcoholism and drug addiction is difficult because of the wide range of symptoms and severity. This diversity requires a plan that addresses problems within all areas of functioning—physical, psychological, social, and spiritual.

Recovery must also consider the potential of each individual, taking into account his or her abilities and skills, as well as any physical, psychological, or social disability.

Recovery is defined ultimately by parameters established by individual drives, ambitions, interests, and motivation. At times, the expectations and the desires of the therapist or significant others for recovery are not shared by the patient. It is well established in psychotherapy that a positive treatment outcome is highly correlated with the patient's motivation to participate in treatment, his or her understanding of the treatment process, and his or her desire for change (Cormier & Cormier, 1985). Consequently, initial efforts in treatment should focus on assessment of the problems and patient characteristics that will influence treatment outcomes. Health care professionals can be effective with chemical dependence cases prior to formal treatment. Interventions include: working with families of dependent individuals to reduce enabling, thus increasing the patient's motivation for treatment; assisting the patient in developing motivation for recovery through education on the disease of addiction, treatment expectations, and the value and hope offered by support groups; and referring patients to specialized treatment programs that meet their individual needs.

The relationship between the therapist and the patient is important. Each therapist has skills and ability to perform with a set group of conditions or clients. No therapist can be effective in all situations or conditions. The therapist must continually evaluate treatment effectiveness and refer patients as required to maximize the clients' motivation and chance for success. In addition, a therapist should recognize that treatment success will be enhanced by a variety of experiences and opportunities. It is unrealistic to expect patients to change solely because of a series of weekly sessions, even with the most talented professional. A variety of recovery issues can be addressed optimally through a combination of professional and self-help approaches.

Finally, it is a mistake to view recovery as a time-limited goal. Life presents a series of conditions to address. The definition of recovery, therefore, encompasses a process involving multiple conditions and continuing struggle to define and maintain balance. Recovery is a lifelong process.

Importance of Abstinence and Change

Recovery is possible when an individual experiences discomfort in his or her current situation and attempts to alleviate it. Increasing discomfort usually promotes greater desire for change. Recovery from addiction involves making many changes—acquiring knowledge, modifying attitudes, and developing behaviors that promote a drug-free life-style.

This process of change can occur only when patients are free from all addictive drugs. Most readers will relate to the concept of craving, "a very strong desire for something." In an addicted individual, this desire often supersedes all other needs, including safety, nutrition, and health care. Abstinence is perceived as impossible by patients who enter treatment because they cannot stop using drugs.

The goal of abstinence in treatment is an accepted approach among professionals and stems from the work of Jellinek in the 1950s. Jellinek hypothesized that the alcoholic's loss of control would turn one drink during recovery into a chain reaction, making the alcoholic unable to prevent further consumption.

The goal of abstinence for alcoholics has been challenged by comparative studies with controlled drinking subjects, most notably the work of Sobell and Sobell (1976). They reported that drinking subjects functioned significantly better in a second-year follow-up study than the control group (those undergoing conventional treatment oriented toward abstinence). Their research supported the development of controlled drinking treatment programs across the country, to the dismay of the general treatment community. During this phase of their research and the research community's interest in controlled drinking, the National Council on Alcoholism and the American Medical Society published a position paper (1974). The paper emphasized that abstinence from alcohol is necessary for recovery from the disease of alcoholism. It called for more research but stated, "in the present state of knowledge, we firmly believe and emphasize that there can be no relaxation from the stated position that no alcoholic may return safely to any use of alcohol." In 1982, research was published by Pendery, Maltzman, and West in an independent follow-up of the same subjects; their research did not substantiate the favorable controlled drinking outcomes reported by Sobell and Sobell.

Abstinence, as a goal in recovery, is supported by another argument. Alcohol and other psychoactive substances are abused in part because they alter consciousness and affect information-processing capabilities. Occasional or frequent use of psychoactive substances alters the analytical processing of data. Continuing drug use precipitates denial or self-delusion. Denial interferes with honest self-analysis, preventing change and recovery. Maintaining drug use requires holding on to old behaviors, attitudes, and a life-style that promotes susceptibility to the illness and relapse.

Miller, Hendrick, and Taylor (1983) report that a remission of life's problems (following a treatment experience) was associated with decreased alcohol consumption. Finney and Moos (1981) studied 131 alcoholics following treatment at residential facilities that were oriented to abstinence. They reported that the work environment of moderate users was more negative than the abstainers. In a two-year follow-up there was a higher relapse rate for those reporting moderate alcohol consumption during the six months following treatment. Finally, as argued by Daley (1988), abstinence in recovery is supported by the knowledge gained by the experience of drug addicts and alcoholics in their attempts to recover. Through AA/NA "leads" and testimonials, alcoholics and drug abusers daily report their inability to recover while using any mood- and mind-altering chemicals. Daley emphasizes that it would be wise for recovering addicts to heed the advice of those who learned the hard way.

Physical Recovery

Alcohol and other addictive drugs adversely affect multiple parts and processes of the human body, including appetite, sleep, the peripheral and central nervous systems, the cardiovascular system, the respiratory system, and the digestive system. These drugs decrease the production of blood cells and promote nutritional deficiencies and liver disease. In addition, they affect skeletal muscles and the skeletal system (causing osteoporosis and increased risk of fractures), and they compromise sexual and reproductive functioning (Ciske, 1983).

Physical recovery comprises two parts. First, the disease agent (alcohol and other drugs) causing the physical illness must be removed. Second, a condition of health must be regained or established, allowing the activities and demands of daily living to be met.

Achieving Abstinence

It makes no sense to treat the symptoms of an illness without attempting to alleviate the cause of those symptoms. It is not appropriate to assume that all symptoms are due to alcohol or other drug use. A thorough assessment is needed to identify the physical problems and to establish a treatment plan to alleviate them. Continued use of the drugs will prevent effective intervention and create new physical symptoms, whether the addictive drugs are the direct cause of the physical problems or a contributing factor. Elimination of drugs from the body can be dangerous and may require the skilled supervision of medical professionals. Abstinence, however, is necessary for recovery to begin. Some patients will accept total abstinence as a goal of treatment whereas others will not. Even patients who accept abstinence may struggle in their attempts to either achieve or maintain it. Initial efforts in treatment often focus on helping patients with this critical issue.

Restoring Physical Health

Recovery from physical injuries can be complicated but is possible with professional support. The physical problems that can be eliminated by professional intervention are only part of recovery. The most difficult aspect of physical recovery involves time, behavioral changes, and the motivation and diligence of the addict to maintain the course of recovery.

Sleep

It is not unusual for erratic and interrupted sleep patterns to develop when one stops using chemicals. Improving sleep leaves one less fatigued and more capable of handling the demands of recovery. A regular pattern of sleep gives the body "recuperative" time to be rested and more prepared and energized to meet the challenge of each day. It is common for individuals to seek medication to alleviate sleep problems that occur in early abstinence. Routine use of sleep medications is usually contraindicated. Only after a thorough medical evaluation should medicine be considered. It is not unusual for sleep patterns in the newly sober person to take weeks or months to normalize, so patients need to be reassured that normalization will occur.

Relaxation

Improving the ability to relax reduces stress and related physical and social disability. Relaxation also can effectively reduce feelings of depression and anxiety that are common during the early stages of recovery and inevitably return throughout life. Routine relaxation refreshes the body, resulting in a feeling of relief and wellness. Successful relaxation efforts will allow the recovering individual to deal better with previously uncontrolled feelings and external pressures.

Diet

Many addicts develop erratic eating habits. Proper diet is often absent—drug use takes precedence over other activities. Chemical ingestion will often interfere with the desire to eat and may interfere with the normal metabolism of vitamins and minerals, inhibiting the effective contribution of even a sporadic diet. Personal energy is decreased, depression occurs, and the ability to deal with injury is reduced. Nutritional deficiencies account for some of the medical difficulties faced by an addict or alcoholic.

Alcoholism will disrupt the blood-sugar balance of the body. Keeping the blood sugar in balance requires a complex chain of events involving the digestive system, pancreas, liver, brain, and endocrine glands. During recovery, as the body seeks to regain its balance, it is important for the recovering individual to maintain a well-balanced diet and to avoid excessive sweets. Regular consumption of sweets disrupts nutritional balance, causing peaks and valleys in blood-sugar levels resulting in cyclical mood swings (Ketcham & Mueller, 1983).

Stimulants such as caffeine, often consumed in excess by recovering individuals, have an adrenalinelike action. Liver damage can cause caffeine to accumulate to toxic levels (Ketcham & Mueller, 1983). Caffeine can directly affect the recovering individual's moods, causing anxiety, nervousness, and irritability, and can often lead to addiction and withdrawal symptoms (Gardner & Beatty, 1988). In addition, poor nutrition during recovery can lead to weight gain or weight loss affecting physical health and self-esteem. Maintaining a well-balanced diet requires diligence, speeds physical recovery of damaged systems, and strengthens the body against reinjury and relapse.

Physical Cravings

Many people report cravings for drugs or alcohol well into their recovery. These cravings, if unchecked, can be very dangerous to a recovering person. There has been much research on craving, illustrated in the workshop titled "Pharmacology of Craving" (1989) supported by the American Medical Society on Alcoholism and other Drug Dependencies. Research presented at the conference showed that craving was a joint phenomenon of physical dependence and withdrawal. Craving is also related to external stimuli (e.g., walking past a tavern can stimulate an unmanageable urge to enter; watching someone using cocaine on TV can stimulate a strong craving). Craving varies by personality type and drug used.

Much of the research on craving seeks to find a chemical intermediary to eliminate or subdue these cravings. In the interim, other proven methods of controlling cravings must be used. One method includes recognizing triggers of cravings and avoiding them where possible. Once cravings occur, it is important to talk through them, attempting to shift one's focus to other thoughts. This can be achieved most easily through the support of another person. However, one has to be able to reach out for help. If it is difficult to ask for help during periods of minor anxiety, it is very unlikely to occur when strong cravings are involved. The development of strong relationships, in which reaching out for help is almost second nature, is a good defense against cravings. Zackon (1986) notes that even a strong commitment to recovery can be eroded by intense drug craving. He emphasizes the need to establish key tasks that reduce craving, including the learning of new pleasures, aided by "steady, sensitive assistance," social integration, and developing a direction in the mainstream of life. A number of practical craving management techniques have been reported by clinicians (Daley, 1986; Washton, 1989). These include both cognitive and behavioral strategies such as talking with others, redirecting activity, journal writing, changing thoughts, talking oneself through the craving, reminding oneself that a craving is only temporary, and avoiding situations in which alcohol or drugs are readily available.

Psychological Recovery

Overcoming Denial

Denial, an unconscious psychological defense, is the major roadblock to recovery. It is considered the "fatal aspect" of addiction (Anderson, 1981). In order for recovery to begin, an addicted individual must face the nature of his or her problem, "the disease of addiction." The person must accept and understand the disease process and its implications for his or her life. Denial impedes progress in recovery by setting in motion innumerable justifications, rationalizations, and excuses. These prevent the addict from accepting addiction as the problem to be faced.

Working through this denial requires a close and detailed examination of the facts of one's addiction. This includes a review of all substances used and the effects of such use on one's life, as well as the impact on one's family. Overcoming denial is best viewed as a process that may be affected by a multiplicity of clinical interventions. Written autobiographies, completion of substance abuse inventories or checklists, the use of bibliotherapy, and participation in psychoeducational groups are a few of the various methods to help patients overcome their denial.

During its early stages, symptoms or consequences of the disease are minor and easier to ignore or cover up. It is often a frightening prospect for addicts to think of life without alcohol or other drugs. They have developed a level of comfort in the addicted life-style; coming to grips with themselves and their lives, drug free, takes them on a journey into the unknown. The analogy is of a doorway behind which one sees nothing but darkness. The addict pictures pain, anxiety, and fear. Recovery requires a leap into the darkness, trusting that the recovery will reduce the pain.

Developing a Desire for Recovery

Sustained recovery requires the addict to have strong motivation. At first, the motivation may come from external pressure exerted by a judge, doctor, employer, or family member. Over time, recovery requires the motivation to come from within the recovering individual. In Alcoholics Anonymous one hears a slogan, "Fake it till you make it."

This is the wisdom of many who have suffered the throes of addiction and felt the hope of recovery. The slogan refers to the fact that many alcoholics do not desire sobriety when they first come to the program of AA or to treatment. It suggests that it is acceptable to fake it as long as you stay involved. *In time* and with perseverance, one will internalize the process. Desire for recovery begins with the awareness that the individual has a problem that he or she can no longer control. This desire is enhanced by being among people who, through their own successful recovery, promote hope for those just starting out.

Self-Assessment

The addict is encouraged to examine the severity of his or her addiction and how it disrupted his or her life. In treatment, patients are asked to discuss the specific details of their chemical-use history—what they have used, their patterns of use, what it does for them, and the impact on their lives. They must be honest. They must evaluate how their thinking processes were altered by their use of drugs and how their self-esteem declined as a result of their behavior. It is not unusual for the addict to have an incorrect perception of reality, his or her thinking clouded and focused on projecting and justifying continued use of the addictive substance. Alcoholics or addicts tend to think they function in a vacuum and harm no one but themselves. This is altered as they assess themselves and recognize the impact of their addiction on others. They can then begin to take responsibility for their behaviors. Addicts must be held accountable for their actions and must become ready to accept the consequences of their choices.

Changing Faulty Thinking

In AA and NA, recovering addicts frequently talk about "stinking thinking." This refers to addictive, distorted, or faulty thinking that can contribute to relapse or dissatisfaction with oneself or one's recovery. For example, an alcoholic may think "recovery is going too slow, things should be a lot better since I'm not drinking any more," or "a few drinks surely wouldn't hurt." Or, a cocaine addict may think that "having fun is impossible without getting high," or that "if I crave cocaine I won't have any control over myself and will have to get high." Identifying and challenging such thinking is essential for recovery to progress. It is not the specific thought or pattern of thinking per se, but how it is interpreted and managed by the addict that determines the ultimate outcome. A variety of cognitive approaches may be used to help addicts change assumptions and beliefs underlying their thinking as well as specific thoughts experienced (Beck & Emergy, 1977; Drilling, 1989; Hafner, 1981; Marlatt & Gordon, 1985; Moorey, 1989).

Changing Behaviors/Handling Emotions

A sober life-style requires an integration into normal life of family, work, self-esteem, intimacy, friendships, socialization, recreation, managing stress, good diet and nutrition, and handling the desire to use drugs. This is a daily endeavor, involving trial and error and requiring adaptions to new drug-free situations.

Recovery, although a positive experience, is also stressful. In rebuilding their lives, addicts experience much anxiety and stress. Sobriety is not a promise of the absence of problems, but a promise of the ability to learn effectively to deal with problems. Learning to deal with stress and negative emotional states is essential. Feelings of depression, anxiety, boredom, or being overwhelmed should not be used as an excuse to return to using drugs. Relaxation techniques and new ways to deal with emotions are part of this learning process. For many, feelings were anesthetized by the addiction, and learning must encompass recognizing, labeling, and communicating feelings in a healthy manner.

New concepts of personal responsibility occur. Learning to face reality becomes the key to making healthy choices, mending old broken relationships, and building a new life-style. Ability to prioritize goals, to form new relationships, and to develop new ways of handling problems are all part of new behaviors essential to recovery.

Improving Self-Esteem

In the downward spiral of addiction, the consistent violation of one's values gradually erodes self-worth. The downward cycle feeds a loss of self-esteem and a loss of control over one's life.

As recovery progresses, clients experience behavior and personality changes that produce rewards and increase belief in themselves and others. Such changes enable successful reintegration into the world drug free, producing a realistic sense of control. As the client experiences more successes and learns properly to evaluate and acknowledge his or her own personal strengths, the new self becomes validated and an increase in self-esteem nourishes an increasing feeling of self-worth.

Changing Character Defects

One of the well-acknowledged areas an addicted person must deal with to accomplish recovery is facing and changing unhealthy personality traits; AA and NA call these character defects. These refer to nonproductive aspects of one's personality that will likely interfere with sobriety. For example, one might have a short fuse and find oneself easily angered; this may be compounded by managing anger ineffectively or inappropriately, lashing-out, or by building resentments. Recovering persons will need to develop more productive ways to manage anger; otherwise, they jeopardize their ability to remain drug free.

It is necessary for the addict in recovery to identify these defects of character and implement ways to change his or her behaviors and attitudes in relationship to them. New ways of relating to self, others, and situations become necessary. For instance, the short-fused person must learn patience; the lashing-out person must learn to verbalize anger or to dissipate hostile energies and diffuse hostile behaviors. Such changes enable sober persons to establish more effective relationships with others and to feel more positive about themselves and more confident in their ability to maintain positive relationships. Two well-tested ways are available for changing character defects. One is found in the 12-Step Program. By taking what AA calls a "personal inventory" the addict does a thorough self-examination and develops a clear picture of his or her strengths and weaknesses. The assets are then used to help change the deficits. This process, usually done in the step-4 level, is then maintained and reevaluated regularly in the step-10 level so that the character deficits remain monitored. The second avenue is found in professional counseling wherein a self-review shared with a clinically objective observer aids in the recognition and reorganization of character defects. With the guidance of a clinician, the recovering person can implement and maintain a process of change.

Family and Social Recovery

Addiction creates problems in significant relationships that need to be addressed in recovery. The addicts must acknowledge those they have hurt and forgive themselves for what they have done. Recovery teaches the addict to accept responsibility for behaviors and, by attempting to face this responsibility, begin to rebuild relationships. With much practice, skills are acquired that allow the recovering person to survive a lifelong process of acknowledging when others are harmed and to deal with it promptly. When possible, the addict must seek to make amends for the harm caused to others as he or she seeks to repair broken relationships and to restructure these into healthy support systems.

Involving the Family

It is the family that is most directly affected by the addiction. Broken promises, violated trust, isolation, verbal abuse, and even emotional and physical abuse are common effects of addiction. Healing these wounds and restoring communication are essential to recovery. Helping the family to understand and recognize how the addiction has affected relationships, as well as beginning to rebuild trust and communication, assists the family in its recovery and builds a supportive environment for the recovering person. This is best achieved by getting the addict's family involved in the recovery process.

Social Networks

The addict must also begin to reorganize his or her social network. His or her primary avenue of socialization has centered around drug-using friends and activities. The addict will need to build a network of support that reinforces a drug-free life-style, to eliminate former drug-oriented relationships, and to seek out new peer support. This task is difficult because the addict's social skills may be at best tenuous. Reinitiating many fractured friendships that were harmed in the addiction process can occur as amends are made. Development of the capacity for trust, intimacy, and enjoyment in shared communication and activities is essential to recovery.

Leisure Interests

New use of leisure time is critical. In the drug-oriented life-style, time is spent in planning drug use, using, and hiding the fact of use. Without drug use, the recovering person finds himself or herself with spare time. Hobbies and interests have been discarded. The addict will need to find opportunities to explore new interests and to be willing to test out new ways to seek enjoyment, fun, and pleasure. Unstructured time can cause boredom and precipitate drug use. Keeping busy and being with others are helpful, but it is equally important to develop the ability to handle "alone" time productively, without resorting to chemical use.

Avoiding Isolation

Fearful of venturing into the new world of recovery, addicts perceive that a "safe" way to avoid use is to have as little interaction as possible beyond the safe limits of home. They do not trust themselves to deal with urges, seeing old friends, or encountering peers. Avoidance behavior as a means of safety is restrictive and ineffective. One cannot survive in isolation. The addict must learn to handle the reactions of others to his or her new recovery status. He or she must learn how confidently to manage potentially troublesome situations. Recovering persons learn to come face to face with the misgivings they have about their ability to build new relationships, and they start to take some risks to address these fears. With time and practice, they begin to reap the benefits of new friendships. The ability to be open to others and to trust soon provides evidence to the addict of the rewards of interpersonal relationships. Building a network of support reinforces recovery efforts and prevents the addict from withdrawing or returning to old habits.

Handling Social Pressure to Use

Our society is uneducated about what it means to be addicted. Often individuals unwittingly reinforce ideas that controlled use is possible and may encourage or pressure the recovering person to use. The recovering person must avoid situations where he or she is likely to be pressured to use. A prime reason for avoiding people, places, and things associated with use is to reduce the pressures to use substances. However, because it is impossible to avoid all social pressures, the addict can develop a response or "dialogue" that he or she can call upon readily to refuse any offers in circumstances where use occurs.

Spiritual Recovery

Spiritual recovery is gaining greater acceptance in treatment. Spirit has been defined as a life force, a vital principle giving life to physical organisms. Many people see this life force as coming from within; others see it as a spiritual being that enters and possesses a physical organism. Many acknowledge the concept of spirit but never fully explore it in their own lives. The concept of spirit gets wrapped up in religious expression, and people run to, or run from, what they understand of this expression without ever coming to grips with the reality of their spirit. Those who actively search for an understanding of their spirit mature, thus allowing themselves to achieve a comfortableness with their life in relationship to others, the world, and the universe. Alcoholics and addicts focus their attention on dealing with crisis after crisis, constantly putting out fires. This process discourages an honest analysis of the spirit; instead, the spirit becomes something to be afraid or ashamed of.

Spiritual recovery is the search for, and understanding of, one's life force. Where did I come from? What purpose do I have? What value am I? Where am I going? Spiritual recovery is an affirmation of life. It is an expression and dedication of life as meaningful, and one that emphasizes that "I" am important.

Shame and Guilt

Alcoholism and drug abuse have personal consequences. These consequences affect one's self-concept by providing negative feedback and producing low self-esteem. Guilt, deriving from the consequences of chemical abuse, progresses with the addiction to a point where the actions of the alcoholic or addict and the related guilt become synonymous with the "spirit" of the individual. Guilt then becomes translated from "something I did" to "who I am". Once guilt is emotionally tied to "who I am" (spirit), it is referred to as shame.

In addition to the active abuse of chemicals, there are other ways people generate guilt and shame. Children growing up in alcoholic families or other dysfunctional situations adapt in a way that often resembles an active substance abuser. In these situations, the child accepts the responsibility and, therefore, the guilt of the dysfunctional situation. Eventually the child emotionally ties guilt with who he or she is. In an attempt to protect themselves from the pain of examining their feelings such children resist direct confrontation with guilt and shame and never come to an understanding of their spirit.

Developing a Relationship with a Higher Power

The addiction spiral maintains a reliance on an unhealthy self. Continuing to rely on one's own strength, and ultimately the drug, results in disease progression. Not until the individual recognizes that he or she has lost control does recovery begin. Accepting this loss of control forces one to reach outside of oneself to a greater source of power. A greater source of power than self can be another person, an organization like Alcoholics Anonymous, a therapy group, a church congregation, or a belief in God. A healthy recovery process challenges individuals to seek more sophisticated higher powers. This process is often one of relationships and one that leads to the development of a relationship with the highest power, God.

Helping Others

In Alcoholics Anonymous and Narcotics Anonymous veterans of recovery reach out to newcomers. By sharing their pain and recovery with the newcomer, they serve as a source of hope for the people new in AA or NA.

Individuals in recovery with at least a year of sobriety assist newcomers by leading meetings, sharing the stories of their own addiction and recovery for insight and inspiration, and by sponsoring them on their road to recovery. A sponsor takes on the responsibility, so to speak, of making himself or herself available to talk on the phone, to meet for coffee, and to assist the newcomers in getting to meetings. The self-help program can assist in the formation of many supportive relationships, from casual as, "Hi Mary, missed you last week. Glad you are back," to more formal sponsorship relationships. Maintaining a variety of relationships within the program will help foster recovery.

TREATMENT RESOURCES

The following section is a brief description of the types of treatment resources available in most communities. Familiarity with both professional and self-help resources is essential in order to establish a network of programs and clinicians to refer patients and families for adequate help.

Many professionals develop an attitude of disgust or hopelessness when faced with a number of patients with active addictions. Professionals are advised to attend "open" AA/NA meetings in order to watch "recovery in action." Lee Grutchfield (1977) identifies a number of personal growth experiences he learned as a "non-AA counselor" at AA meetings. Some of these include: discovering our common humanity, the vicarious experience of alcoholism, free education, experiencing love and fellowship, professional sustenance, and uncovering personal feelings, as well as discovering a source of ideas and speakers.

Generally, treatment seeks to assess the problem as it is expressed within each individual and to prevent further destruction by the disease through the maintenance and the development of skills. Treatment programs, regardless of the type, have similar aims: to educate the patient and significant others, to raise self-awareness, and to assist in the change process.

Detoxification

Detoxification is a medical procedure completed under the care of a physician. It usually requires medication to withdraw safely from the addictive drug. Because withdrawal from drugs, especially alcohol, can be dangerous, detoxification requires close medical supervision. It is not uncommon for other medical conditions to surface during detoxification requiring the attention of trained medical staff. The process of detoxification usually takes a hospital stay of three to seven days. Withdrawing from tranquilizers sometimes requires a longer period of time. However, there are nonmedical facilities, for instance, "social-detox" programs, that are available in some communities to assist the patient through detoxification periods. Some patients can be detoxified on an outpatient basis.

During detoxification, patients also receive education about addictive disease, the need for treatment, and available treatment options. Detoxification is not always referred to as "treatment." This is because of the patient's mental state during detoxification, and because many patients seek it as a haven between drug use episodes, and not as a first step toward rehabilitation. But through detoxification, patients can often be persuaded to get involved in rehabilitation, counseling, and self-help programs. Used to its best advantage, detoxification can be a stepping stone toward effective recovery.

Outpatient Services

While living at home and continuing to maintain a relatively normal existence with work, patients can receive outpatient counseling on an individual and/or group basis. The primary focus of outpatient treatment is on the patient; however, many outpatient clinics also include family education and counseling services.

Outpatient counseling requires the patient to be highly motivated. Especially if in contact with his or her old friends, he or she is likely to be under constant pressure to use drugs.

Outpatient treatment often serves four populations:

1. Patients who require professional care in order to make a commitment to a more intensive recovery effort.
2. Patients who have recently completed a more intense level of rehabilitation and are in need of "aftercare" counseling.
3. Patients who get involved in treatment early in the disease and can work toward treatment goals with minimum structured supervision.
4. Families of addicts regardless of whether or not the addict is in treatment.

Outpatient services usually provide one or more hours of counseling each week, based on specific treatment goals established in the treatment plan. Outpatient treatment may extend from a few months to several years, depending on the patient's motivation and goals for change.

Outpatient programs differ in the types of treatment and requirements for active participation. The most effective program requires that patients stay drug free during treatment. This is sometimes monitored by urinalysis to check for any current drug usage. Attendance at self-help meetings, in addition to counseling sessions, is encouraged by many outpatient clinics or private therapists. Specialized outpatient programs are helpful at times for particular types of patients such as cocaine addicts (Washton, 1989), marijuana abusers (Roffman, Stephens, & Simpson, 1989), or relapsers (Carroll & Ohanesian, 1989).

Intensive Outpatient Rehabilitation

Some patients require more extensive treatment, which can be provided in an intensive outpatient program. These programs vary from 10 to 30 hours of treatment per week, and they provide medical supervision and multifaceted programming such as family therapy, individual and group counseling, educational groups, and occupational and recreational therapy. Intensive outpatient programs typically have an identified length of involvement in terms of the number of days/hours per week and the total number of weeks. Patients who do not succeed in standard outpatient treatment are often moved into this level of care for closer monitoring.

Patients who start in an intensive outpatient program frequently move to a standard outpatient program for continuing care and follow-up. Intensive outpatient rehabilitation is serviced by a multidisciplinary team of professionals. It is a nonresidential program with patients returning daily to their living environments.

Inpatient Treatment

Inpatient rehabilitation patients receive treatment from a multidisciplinary team of professionals within a highly structured milieu where they reside 24 hours a day. As in intensive outpatient programs, the length of stay is time-imited. Depending on the nature of the program, the stay may vary from 14 to 45 days. Skilled treatment services such as psychotherapy, family therapy, individual and group counseling, educational programming, and occupational and recreational therapy are provided. Inpatient facilities may be freestanding residential facilities or hospital-based with a chemical dependency treatment unit. Levels of monitoring of physical health problems and other comorbidity (e.g., psychiatric illness) will be more specialized in the hospital-based programs. Inpatient programs are highly structured. They are often designed to deal effectively with greater degrees of severity of addiction and with patients more resistant to treatment or those more entrenched in denial.

Inpatient care provides a complete therapeutic milieu, involving a controlled environment with a very structured approach to treatment, and a more regimented set of rules, regulations, and expectations. It is a safe, behaviorally-oriented environment in which the patient begins to look at what addiction has done to his or her life. The whole treatment community—staff, patients, and visiting family—is active in treatment.

Specialty Programs and Tracts

Treatment specialists recognize that individuals require different treatment approaches related to their unique needs. Treatment programs have sprung up across the county in an effort to address or meet needs of special populations. These include specialty programs for adolescents, the elderly, pregnant women, and relapsers, to name just a few. In addition, there are culturally sensitive programs targeting African-American populations, native Americans, and Spanish-speaking Americans. Other populations requiring specialized treatment efforts include patients with learning or hearing difficulties, and those with addiction and related psychiatric illness. With many treatment programs, resources are not available to provide a total array of required specialized programs. It is not uncommon to find programs adjusting to individualized needs by introducing treatment tracks or specialized groups to accommodate smaller populations. These tracks or groups require fewer resources and can be adapted to fluctuations in patient populations.

Halfway Houses and Therapeutic Communities

Halfway houses initially evolved as a buffer system for mental health patients leaving the hospital setting and emerging into society (Chafetz, 1983). They were later adapted for drug addicts and alcoholics. The halfway house provides a supportive environment, encouraging continued sobriety while gradually promoting social reintegration.

Lewis Yablonsky (1989) offers four basic factors that must exist for halfway houses or other settings to be defined as a true therapeutic community: (1) voluntary entrance, (2) use of various group methods, (3) use of recovering addicts as cotherapists, and (4) an open-ended social structure allowing for movement up the status ladder of the organization into increasingly responsible positions.

Many alcoholics and addicts have severed previous relationships during their addiction or are forced to make radical changes to maintain their sobriety. Halfway houses or therapeutic communities provide safety and a base from which recovering alcoholics and addicts can slowly rebuild their lives. They continue in outpatient and vocational counseling in these environments and develop other supports as needed. A therapeutic environment, nutritious meals, a built-in socialization process, and an integration into Alcoholics Anonymous, Narcotics Anonymous, or other self-help groups are provided to encourage recovery.

The length of stay in halfway houses varies for each person, usually progressing through stages as identified by DeLeon (1987). Phase 1 is the Induction Phase (1 - 30 days), which includes orientation to concepts, rules, and resources as well as strengthening motivation to continue. Phase 2 is the Primary Treatment Phase (2 - 12 months), in which clients engage in educational seminars, encounter groups, tutorial sessions, and proceed through role and responsibility changes. Phase 3 is the Re-Entry Phase (13 - 24 months), in which focus is on readjustment to work, social life, and family outside the supportive environment. Some patients have been unable to maintain sobriety outside the halfway house and have resided there on a long-term basis.

Personal Care Homes

Persons with greater physical and cognitive damage resulting from drug and alcohol use may require the services of a Personal Care Home. Unlike other programs, these homes do not house only one diagnostic group—a focus of counseling or treatment is less likely to be found. Attention is given to assisting persons in their activities of daily living but not in resocialization.

Mutual Self-Help Groups

Alcoholics Anonymous (AA), Narcotics Anonymous (NA), Cocaine Anonymous (CA), and other self-help programs, although not considered formal treatment, are one of the first available levels of assistance. There are no professionals and no fee for service is required. This has been the initial avenue many have used for recovery. There are no formal diagnostic determinations needed at this level. The groups are available to any person who wishes to stop drinking or using drugs. The programs are conducted by persons actively recovering from addiction and are based entirely on the premise that addicts and alcoholics can help one another. AA and NA clearly recognize that addiction/alcoholism is a disease process affecting body, mind, and spirit. All aspects of the self-help program address these areas to accomplish recovery.

Fellowship

One of the many sources of help provided by self-help programs is based on the idea of fellowship—one addict helping another based on the common bond of their addiction. The fellowship is extended to anyone in need, whether in their home area or in other parts of the country. Geography is not a deterrent, and the mutually caring relationships are offered unconditionally, 24 hours a day, based solely on the desire to help and to change.

12-Step Philosophy

The self-help programs involve the 12 steps that are suggested for a drug addict or alcoholic to take to achieve and maintain recovery. These steps offer guidelines for the necessary changes a person will need to make in order to support abstinence from chemicals and a sober life-style. Fundamental to the steps is the realization that more than abstinence from chemicals is necessary. In addition to being free of chemicals, the individual must be willing to make attitudinal and behavioral changes in his or her life-style to support an ongoing process of recovery. Having integrated these steps, addicts in recovery will then reach out to others still suffering from the disease in an effort to offer the benefits and rewards of recovery to them. The 12 steps offer a focus on the body, mind, and spirit and effectively suggest practical guidelines that ensure recovery on a "one day at a time" basis.

Meetings

Involvement in the self-help programs will include attendance at meetings. Meetings are often identified as "open" or "closed" meetings. Open meetings are available to the public and encourage attendance by those who are learning about addiction, but are not sure whether the meetings apply to them, and by those who recognize they have a problem with chemicals. Most open meetings are speaker meetings, where a recovering person will share the experience of his or her addiction and recovery with others. Telling how it was, what happened, and how it is today is mutually beneficial for both speaker and listener. The narration of the struggles encountered and the successes in dealing with these provides valuable insight and inspiration to continue daily efforts in recovery. Family, friends, and helping professionals can learn much from attending these meetings.

Closed meetings are normally held for those individuals who are identified as chemically dependent and are seeking support. There are two types of meetings for this purpose. (1) Discussion meetings in which addicts and alcoholics meet to discuss issues essential to recovery (i.e., changing attitudes, surrendering, spirituality), common problems encountered in recovery (i.e., relationships, intimacy, relapse), the 12 steps, and the promises and traditions of the program. Addicts share their feelings, thoughts, and experiences in these meetings as a mechanism for support. (2) Specialty meetings are held for small subgroups (e.g., professionals such as doctors, nurses, and lawyers). Their premise is that a shared professional's identity or common interest can help the alcoholic and addict.

Sponsorship/Home Groups

In the effort to help one another, seasoned members will become advisors or "sponsors" for the program. The sponsor will share the strength, experience, and hope of recovery with the new person. He or she will help by taking the newcomer to meetings, introducing him or her to others, and acquainting him or her with the principles and 12 steps of the program. A sponsor also offers personal availability for the one-to-one talks or phone discussions when needed. The offer of help is beneficial to both the helper and the person being helped.

In addition to a sponsor, the newcomer is asked to find a home group, a sort of AA home where he or she establishes regular attendance and becomes involved in the daily routine of keeping the meetings and its membership vital and functioning. He or she may serve as an officer for the group (treasurer, secretary) and assist in the organization and direction of group activities.

In addition to the regular meetings, groups often sponsor special events, including conferences, dinners, dances, and other social activities. These are offered generally in conjunction with a meeting and provide an opportunity for education, affirmation of the program, and socialization with others in recovery. Retreats are also offered to "recharge one's battery." An active role in these home group activities helps to form a bond with the program and to ensure the development of self-esteem.

Slogans/Literature

In an effort to keep a clear focus, the AA/NA programs use key slogans that are handy "rules of thumb" to guide the recovering person. "Take It Easy," "Keep It Simple," "One Day at a Time," and "Let Go and Let God" are a few examples of the slogans that, if practiced, help make ongoing recovery more manageable.

In addition to the slogans, literature is available in the form of books and pamphlets to help members increase their knowledge of the self-help program, addiction, and recovery. Practical advice in the slogans and the literature will help the recovering addict learn how to deal with many of the problems he or she will face when sober. The AA "Big Book" *Alcoholics Anonymous,* the NA "Basic Text" *Narcotics Anonymous,* the *Twelve Steps and Twelve Traditions,* the *Twenty-Four Hours a Day* book, and many others offer the recovering person hope, inspiration, practical guidelines, and support for recovery.

It would be inaccurate to say that everyone needs AA or NA to recover. It is generally agreed, however, that the help provided by these programs will significantly increase the recovery rate and decrease the relapse rate. A successful approach or combination of approaches will depend on the severity of the addiction and on the motivation of the alcoholic or addict to change.

Recovery Clubs

There are resources available in some areas in the form of recovery clubs. These normally offer AA/NA and other recovery meetings, social activities, and a place for people to go to when they need to be in an environment that totally supports recovery. For many, these clubs are life sources as they provide a place to go when there seems to be no one else available for help or support. They are a place to network with other recovering people, build solid support systems, and have fun in an environment free of chemicals. Activities such as dancing provide the opportunity to learn to enjoy oneself while sober.

Renewal Centers

Renewal centers are a relatively new concept in recovery and serve much the same purpose as retreats. These centers recognize that healthy recovery requires a lifetime commitment and a great deal of effort and energy, but that there is also a need to stop periodically for rest and reflection. It may be because one has hit a plateau and needs a boost, or because one is at a decision crossroads and needs to consider options, or that one is tired and needs a rest. There is a need for a place to rest and take time for one's self in order to rejuvenate. The stay can be long or short and can be tailored to meet the needs of the person. One can travel a solo trail or join with others in this time away. These centers normally offer an environment of hospitality and serenity, as well as make available a variety of activities and opportunities for reflection, discovery, and sharing of recovery experiences. One can participate in as much or as little as may seem beneficial. Activities include group discussions on the 12 steps and recovery issues; personal one-to-one direction; and quiet reflective time alone. Lectures, movies, literature, conversation, and community meetings are also part of the program.

The experience provides the recovering person opportunities to explore personal concerns, to benefit from the relaxed atmosphere of the center, to rejuvenate one's commitment to, and appreciation of, the 12-step program, and to renew one's feeling of purpose and belonging in the fellowship of the program.

Pharmacological Adjuncts

Some patients may need the extra help of prescribed medicines to prevent relapse to alcohol or drug addiction. The dosage of these drugs is carefully monitored by medical staff, and patients are not permitted to use any alcohol or addictive drugs while receiving this type of therapy. These prescribed drugs are not a "cure" for alcoholism or other drug addiction. They are used solely to help the patient stop drinking or using opiate drugs. They include naltrexone for opiate addicts and disulfiram (Antabuse) for alcoholics.

Naltrexone

Unlike methadone—actually a substitute for opiate street drugs— naltrexone prevents the body from experiencing the effects of opiate drugs. When used with naltrexone, heroin, morphine, or any other opiate no longer gives pleasurable feelings. After all opiates are removed from the patient's body, usually through inpatient detoxification, naltrexone is administered. Then, if an opiate drug is used, no "high" is experienced. Without this feeling, the addict eventually learns to stop using opiates. As with methadone, patients must consistently use naltrexone, receive counseling on a regular basis, and use no addictive drugs.

Disulfiram

Disulfiram (Antabuse) is used to help sober alcoholics not drink. This medicine stays in the system for up to two weeks following the last dose, providing an "insurance period" for the alcoholic. If a patient drinks alcohol while taking Antabuse, nausea and vomiting result. The undesirable physical symptoms help the patient attach negative feelings to drinking alcohol. During this reprieve, he or she can learn more positive coping behaviors, as the desire to drink may simply leave. Antabuse does not solve alcoholics' problems, it just helps them to stay drug free while they work on their problems. There is no guarantee that the patient will ever develop the skills necessary to stop drinking. Antabuse can cause serious reactions if the patient drinks while it is in his or her system. It is best used as an adjunct for motivated patients and for patients who are not impulsive.

Methadone Maintenance

Methadone maintenance is a treatment only for opiate addicts who have demonstrated an inability to stay clean despite participation in professional treatment. In addition to counseling, methadone is substituted for the opiate street drug that the addicted person is illegally using. These programs provide daily doses of methadone to attract drug abusers to a treatment facility. They provide clean drugs under supervision in the hopes of exposing a drug abuser who normally does not seek help to education and a life-style free from drug use. A patient in this setting is not permitted to use any other drugs, and the dosage of methadone is carefully monitored and gradually reduced until the patient is drug free. Unannounced urine screenings reveal the patient's use of any drug other than methadone. As with other types of treatment, counseling, behavior modification, and involvement in self-help programs are important elements.

Other Medications

In addition to the above drugs used to help in achieving sobriety, there are other medications that can be beneficial for some patients in recovery. As mentioned early in this chapter, addiction can be associated with psychiatric symptoms. Some patients have psychiatric symptoms prior to alcohol or other drug abuse. If, after a period of abstinence, psychiatric symptoms remain or are aggravated, they need to be managed for recovery.

Continued unmanaged psychiatric illness will interfere with any gains made by sobriety. Poor physical health will also impede the progress of recovery. Under such conditions it may become necessary to use other medications to manage other health care problems. The addictive potential or abuse potential of all treatments for "recovering" patients should be considered, for addiction is a primary, progressive disease sustained by mood- and mind-altering chemicals.

SUMMARY

This discussion reviewed major issues regarding recovery from addiction. Recovery is a multifaceted process addressing the whole person: physical, psychological, emotional, social, family, and spiritual. Recovery requires first a commitment to change and an attempt at abstinence, but it is much more that this, involving major attitudinal and behavioral changes to support a sober life-style.

Multiple levels of treatment exist. In order to determine the appropriate level of care, one must take a close look at the readiness, motivation, severity of illness, and damage created in significant life areas to determine an appropriate plan for each treatment. Each recovery journey is unique, reflecting these individual needs.

Physical recovery requires detoxification in a medically safe way and treatment of medical problems related to use. In addition, aspects of nutrition, diet, exercise, relaxation, cravings, and stress management must be addressed.

Psychological recovery addresses denial, faulty thinking patterns, motivation, and skills through which change in thoughts, feelings, behaviors, and self-esteem can occur.

Social recovery involves one's social networks, recognizing the need to change and to include the family and peer system. Building new relationships that support a drug-free life-style is imperative.

Spiritual recovery addresses purpose and value in life, relationship with a higher power, and guilt and shame. It may also involve reaching out to others suffering from addiction.

Options available for treatment include outpatient, intensive outpatient, and inpatient programs. Specialty tracks are available to service specialized needs (e.g., elderly, relapse, adolescents, women), and many residential programs and therapeutic communities are also available for addicts who require longer-term, more structured recovery environments.

In addition to formal treatment programs, most communities offer self-help groups. These self-help programs, such as AA/NA, are essential adjuncts to treatment and offer lifelong support to the recovering addict through the 12-step program, fellowship, and mutual support among addicts.

As helpers we must recognize our own strengths and weaknesses, knowing when to stay with an issue and when to seek the advice of others. It is important to remember that alcoholics and addicts do best with a multidimensional treatment experience that includes professional and self-help involvement. Addiction continues to remain a baffling disease. Denial prevents many from ever experiencing recovery, while others try or are offered treatment experiences without success. Despite our limited scientific knowledge about prognosis, we still have the obligation to work for the achievement of sobriety for the clients we serve.

REFERENCES

Alcoholics anonymous (3rd ed). (1976). New York: AA World Services

American Psychiatric Association. (1987). *Diagnostic and statistical manual of mental disorders* (3rd ed.). Washington, DC: Author.

Anderson, D. (1981). *The psychopathology of denial.* Center City, MN: Hazelden.

Beck, A., & Emergy, G. (1977). *Cognitive therapy for substance abusers.* Philadelphia, PA: Center for Cognitive Therapy.

Carroll, J. & Ohanesian, S. (1989). Relapse prevention in a drug free therapeutic community. *Journal of Chemical Dependency Treatment, 2*(2), 193-208.

Chafetz, M. (1983). *The alcoholic patient: Diagnosis and management.* Ordell, NJ: Medical Economics.

Ciske, S. J. (1983). Assessment and management of physical consequences. In G. Bennett, C. Vourakis, & D. Woolf (Eds.), *Substance abuse* (pp. 313-327). New York: John Wiley.

Cormier, W. H., & Cormier, L. S. (1985). *Interviewing strategies for helpers* (2nd ed.). Belmont, CA: Brooks/Cole.

Daley, D. (1986). *Relapse prevention workbook.* Holmes Beach, FL: Learning Publications.

Daley, D. (1988). *Surviving addiction.* New York: Gardner.

DeLeon, G. (1987, October). Therapeutic communities: Perspective, effectiveness, and application as a general model. *Community as teacher and healer,* Fourth Ind. G. S. symposium on community and mental health, Bangalore, India.

Drilling, E. (1989). *Anxiety and worry: Thoughts, feelings, actions.* Center City, MN: Hazelden.

Finney, J. W., & Moos, R. H. (1981). Characteristics and prognosis of alcoholics who become moderate drinkers and abstainers after treatment. *Journal of Studies on Alcohol, 42*(1), 4-105.

Gardner, D. C., & Beatty, G. J. (1988) *Never to be tired again.* New York: MacMillan.

Grutchfield, L. A. (1977, December). What AA meetings taught a non-AA counselor. *AA Grapevine,* pp. 1-5.

Hafner, A. (1981). *It's not as bad as you think.* Center City, MN: Hazelden.

Jellinek, E. M. (1960). *The disease concept of alcoholism.* New Brunswick, NJ: Hollhouse.

Kethcham, K., & Mueller, L. A. (1983). *Eating right to live sober.* Seattle, WA: Madrona.

Ludwig, A. M. (1986). The mystery of craving. *Alcohol Health and Research World, 11*(1), 12-17.

Mandell, W. (1983). Types and phases of alcohol dependence illness. In M. Galanter (Ed.), *Recent developments in alcoholism* (pp. 415-447). New York: Plenum.

Marlatt, G. & Gordon, J. (Eds.). (1985). *Relapse prevention: Maintainance strategies in the treatment of addictive behaviors.* New York: Guilford.

Mello, N. K. (1971). A quantitative analysis of drinking patterns of alcoholics. *Archives of General Psychiatry, 25,* 527-539.

Miller, W. R., Hendrick, K. E., & Taylor, C. A. (1983). Addictive behaviors and life problems before and after behavioral treatment of problem drinkers. *Addictive Behaviors, 8,* 403-412.

Moorey, S. (1989). Drug abusers. In J. Scott, J. Williams, & A. Beck (Eds.), *Cognitive therapy in clinical practice* (pp. 157-182). New York: Routledge.

Narcotics anonymous. (1988). Van Nuys, CA: World Service Office.

National Council on Alcoholism/American Medical Society. (1974, September 16). *Abstinence.* New York: Author.

Pendery, M. L., Maltzman, T. M., & West, L. S. (1982). Controlled drinking by alcoholics? New findings and a reevaluation of a major affirmative study. *Science, 217*(4555), 169-175.

Pharmacology of craving. (1989, April). American Medical Society on Alcoholism and Other Drug Dependencies, Twentieth Annual Medical-Scientific Conference, Atlanta, GA. Tape recording by Infomedix, Garden Grove, CA.

Roffman, R., Stephens, R., & Simpson, E. (1989). Relapse prevention with adult chronic marijuana smokers. *Journal of Chemical Dependency Treatment, 2*(2), 241-257.

Sobell, M. B., & Sobell, L. C. (1976). Second year treatment outcome of alcoholics treated by individualized behavior therapy results. *Behavior Research & Therapy, 14,* 195-215.

Twelve steps and twelve traditions. (1978, November). New York: Alcoholics Anonymous World Services.

Twenty-four hours a day. (1975). Center City, MN: Hazelden.

Washton, A. (1989). *Cocaine addiction.* New York: W. W. Norton.

Yablonsky, L. (1989). *The therapeutic community.* New York: Gardner.

Zackon, M. (1986). Lifestyle rehabilitation. *Alcohol Health and Research World, 11*(1), 18-70.

Chapter 6

RELAPSE PREVENTION AND TREATMENT EFFECTIVENESS STUDIES

DENNIS C. DALEY
MIRIAM S. RASKIN

This chapter will discuss relapse in addiction from five perspectives: (1) the professional who may encounter a relapsed client or his family members, (2) the alcoholic or drug-dependent client, (3) the family, (4) the treatment system or agency providing services to addicted clients and their families, and (5) other systems—legal, work, and medical. Definitions of relapse will first be provided, several conceptual issues related to relapse and methodological problems related to studying treatment effectiveness will be addressed, and relapse will be reviewed. An overview of general approaches to treatment and four specific approaches to relapse prevention also will be provided.

DEFINITION OF RELAPSE

According to Webster's New Collegiate Dictionary, *relapse* is "a recurrence of symptoms of a disease after a period of improvement," or "the act or an instance of backsliding, worsening, or subsiding" (1986). The first of these definitions implies an illness or disease model in which symptoms return. The second definition implies that relapse is a behavior (i.e., an action) evidencing a regression in one's condition. Daley (1987a) states that "relapse refers to the 'event' of resumption of substance use after a period of abstinence or the 'process' of returning to substance use (that is, manifesting behaviors or attitudes which indicate a person is likely to resume substance use unless interventive measures are taken" (p. 138). Alcholics in AA, for example, refer to the relapse process as a "dry drunk syndrome" (Solberg, 1978, 1982).

These approaches assume that an addicted individual could be in relapse before using a substance. It is extremely difficult, however, to quantify the "process" of relapse. Gorski and Miller (1982) define relapse as a "process that occurs within a patient. It manifests itself in a progressive pattern of behavior that reactivates the symptoms of a disease or creates related debilitating conditions in a patient who has previously experienced remission" (pp. 21-22). This view acknowledges the role of behavior (i.e., "progressive pattern of behavior") in reactivating the "disease" state of alcoholism. Marlatt (1985b) refers to relapse as "a breakdown or setback in a person's attempt to change or modify any target behavior" (p. 3). This definition would be applicable to a multiplicity of behaviors, including drug or alcohol addiction.

CONCEPTUAL AND
METHODOLOGICAL PROBLEMS

Studies of treatment effectiveness discuss relapse in terms of the resumption of (1) substance use, (2) an abusive pattern of substance use, or (3) substance use that causes problems in functioning. Lack of uniformity in discussing relapse raises several conceptual problems. For example, does any substance use represent a relapse, or is relapse limited to an individual's primary addiction? Is an alcoholic who uses marijuana a relapser? Is a heroin addict who drinks alcohol or uses tranquilizers a relapser? Unfortunately, much of the literature on relapse does not adequately address these questions, and some outcome studies are limited to the primary substance used.

A second issue involves "improvement" of an addicted client. Is it possible, for example, for a client to continue using substances following treatment and evidence improvement in psychological, social, or occupational functioning? Several studies on the effectiveness of drug abuse treatment, published by the National Institute of Drug Abuse (NIDA), indicate that many clients experience improvement in occupational or social functioning (e.g., reduction of criminal behavior, increased employment, and increased productivity) despite some continued drug use (NIDA 1981a, 1981). Literature on alcoholism treatment effectiveness documents reduced alcohol consumption and enhanced social or occupational functioning for many clients (Miller & Hester, 1980; Emrick, 1974, 1976, 1982).

A third issue relates to diagnosis and/or the nature of the substance use problem. For example, should relapse apply equally to a person physically and psychologically addicted to heroin who uses substantial quantities on a daily basis (i.e., meets DSM-III-R criteria for "dependence") and to a person who has an episodic pattern of marijuana abuse (i.e., meets DSM-III-R criteria for "abuse")? There is no agreement in the literature on terminology. Many terms such as alcoholic, substance abuser, addict, and chemically dependent are used. Although DSM-III-R differentiates "abuse" from "dependence," outcome studies do not draw this distinction. One study found no significant differences in functioning between patients diagnosed as "alcohol abusers" and those diagnosed as "alcohol dependent" (Schuckit, Zisook, & Mortola, 1985).

A fourth issue deals with the concept of "relapse." Relapse is an "all or nothing" phenomenon. As Marlatt (1985) points out, this dichotomous view of relapse implies "one is either 'cured' (or the symptoms are in remission) or one has relapsed (recidivism)" (p. 31). All replases would be counted similarly, whether they involved one episode of substance use with no adverse consequences or a several-month binge with multiple adverse consequences.

A final conceptual issue concerns relapse and client motivation. Should a client who completes a treatment program but uses substances because he or she had no intention of abstaining be considered a relapser? Does one have to be in "remission" or "wellness" (and, if so, for how long) before one can be considered to have relapsed? An alcoholic gets intoxicated the day he is discharged after completing a 28-day residential program. Gorski and Miller (1982) state that "a patient cannot relapse until he has initiated a recovery process. The patient who has not accepted his alcoholism and initiated a recovery program is not relapsing; he is merely continuing to use alcohol in accordance with the dictates of his disease" (p. 2).

In addition to conceptual problems, treatment effectiveness studies have methodological problems. In a major report of outcome evaluation studies in the areas of alcohol and drug abuse, reported in 50 major journals between 1969 and 1979, Goldstein, Surber, and Wilner (1984) found numerous design problems. These included methodological deficiencies, such as minimal use of randomized or matched control groups, lack of prospective research designs, inadequate outcome measures, and inadequate follow-up data. Methodological issues in evaluating the effectiveness of alcoholism treatment were also pointed out by Saxe, Dougherty, Esty, and Fine (1983) in a report prepared for Congress, which summarized the literature. They reported problems in treatment design, research design, sampling design, and outcome measures (pp. 35-39). They stated that

> much of the existing literature on the effectiveness of alcoholism treatment is not of very good methodological quality. Scientific research on the effectiveness of alcoholism treatment is difficult to conduct, in part because of the complexity of the alcoholism problem. Ethical and practical problems have hindered the implementation of randomized clinical trials and other controlled research. Furthermore, the assessment of individual treatments is difficult because treatments for alcoholism are often provided in combination. Measuring treatment outcomes is problematic, as well, because there is intense diagreement in the alcoholism field about what the outcome of treatment should or must be—i.e., total abstinence from alcohol or some other outcome such as controlled drinking. The reliability and validity of outcome measures are also at issue. Finally, the interpretation of the studies that are available is hindered because particular types of patients tend to receive certain treatments and not others. (p. 4)

These conceptual and methodological issues are noted in order to point out the complexities of the concept of relapse and the difficulties in studying treatment effectiveness. Despite the incidence of relapse, there is sufficient evidence, however, that treatment of alcohol and drug problems can be effective.

RELAPSE RATES
AND TREATMENT OUTCOME

Relapse rates across the various addictions are high (Marlatt & Gordon, 1985; Cummings, Marlatt, & Gordon, 1980). In one of the first outcome studies for alcoholics, smokers, and heroin addicts, Hunt, Barnett, and Branch (1971) reported that almost 70% relapsed within one year of treatment. The majority of these relapses occurred within the first 90 days. Shiffman and colleagues (1985) report that 75% to 80% of smokers relapse within six months of stopping smoking

(p. 472). Caution is required in evaluating success or failure rates; a particular cohort with a high percentage of relapsers does not give an accurate long-range picture. Many addicts, for example, will eventually become sober or clean as a result of the cumulative effects of multiple treatment attempts over time.

Alcoholism Outcome Studies and AA Survey

After reviewing over 500 alcoholism treatment outcome studies of problem drinkers or alcoholics, Miller and Hester concluded that "data from studies with longer follow-up suggest that, on the average, only 26 percent of those treated remain abstinent or improved after one year" (1980, p. 104). Emrick's major reviews of the alcoholism literature (1974, 1976) showed that, although many treated patients were considered "improved," rates of relapse were high. Other systematic reviews by Costello (1982) similarly report that the majority of alcoholics treated relapsed. In a Rand Corporation study of over 700 alcoholics treated in a variety of programs, it was found that over 90% of the subjects relapsed within two years of treatment (Armor, Polich, & Stambul, 1978). Another Rand study reported that 96% of the subjects had relapsed four years after treatment (Polich, Armor, & Braiker, 1981). According to Gorski and Miller (1982), over 60% of alcoholics relapse. Many of these experience a pattern of chronic relapse.

A major survey of almost 25,000 members of Alcoholics Anonymous (AA) found that over half of the new members dropped out within the first three months. This AA survey ("Analysis," 1984) showed that approximately 41% of the remaining newcomers were sober and active in AA one year later. It is probable that many of the dropouts relapsed. Studies of clients who have good social support systems (i.e., employment and intact families) show lower rates of relapse (Hoffman & Harrison, 1986).

Drug Abuse Treatment Effectiveness Studies

High rates of relapse are also documented in studies of drug abuse treatment effectiveness. A recent study, published by the National Institute on Drug Abuse, on opiate addicts who participated in a "Recovery Training Program" indicates that 32% of the experimental group were classified as abstinent or "rare use" compared to 18% of controls at the end of the first year (Zackon, McAuliffe, & Ch'ien, 1985). The combined relapse rate for these opiate addicts was over 76% at one year follow-up. In a report entitled *Effectiveness of Drug Abuse Treatment Programs,* issued by the National Institute of Drug Abuse (1981b), a review of many studies reported high rates of relapse. For example, two studies from the 1950s and early 1960s (with samples of 1,900 and 453 opiate addicts, respectively) reported over 90% "readdiction" rates (p. 3). More recent studies reported better outcome rates in terms of reduced illicit drug use, lower crime, and improved productivity. A study of 50 patients originally hospitalized for primary sedative-hypnotic dependence found that 84% had resumed these drugs during the 4 to 6 year follow-up period (Allgulander, Borg, & Vikander, 1984).

Self-Help Literature

The problem of relapse is also discussed in the self-help literature. *Narcotics Anonymous,* the "basic text" of NA, devotes an entire chapter to relapse and states that "as an incurable disease, drug addiction is subject to relapse" (p. 73). Although relapse rates are not quantified, the basic text discusses addicts who "eventually returned to active addiction" (p. 72). In *Alcoholics Anonymous,* the "Big Book" of AA, reference is made to those "who do not recover" (p. 58). In a chapter titled "How It [AA] Works," the person who does not recover is viewed as incapable of being honest. In all likelihood, this was written for the chronic relapser unable to maintain sobriety, or for the alcoholic with a comorbid psychiatric illness.

Treatment outcome studies, the AA survey, and clinical and self-help literature document the problem of relapse in addiction. The professional, however, should not become too pessimistic, for it is apparent that many clients with addictive disorders improve with treatment, even if they relapse. Treatment can be viewed as a journey, and part of this journey for many clients will be relapse. Although relapse has negative consequences, it may also be therapeutic and help the client in his or her long-term recovery.

THE PROFESSIONAL'S PERSPECTIVE ON RELAPSE

Attitudes, perceptions, and feelings regarding both relapse and the client who relapses are critical in working with an addicted client. The professional frequently views the client who relapses as a "treatment failure." In answers to open-ended questions of professionals, one typically hears "the client isn't motivated," "he hasn't hit bottom yet," or "he's a treatment failure." These responses are negative and attribute relapse solely to the client and to his or her "lack of motivation." In a recent article, Daley (1987b) reviews several erroneous beliefs and myths concerning relapse. These include: (1) the substance abuser is "not motivated" or uses the substances because he or she "wants to," (2) the person relapsed because treatment was not used properly, (3) the person hasn't "hit bottom" yet, (4) relapse doesn't occur until the person uses substances, (5) one substance use episode will lead to "loss of control" of all substance use, and (6) chronic relapsers cannot be helped. Daley posits that these beliefs and myths about relapse may interfere with a professional's ability to help relapsers. Understanding and challenging these beliefs and myths should enable the professional to improve his ability to work with relapsed clients and families. For example, if the clinician learns to identify warning signs that commonly precede relapse, he or she will be able to help a client identify these signs and develop appropriate coping responses.

THE ADDICT'S PERSPECTIVE
ON RELAPSE

Case History

Beth is a 39-year-old divorced nurse with a 14-year history of alcoholism and multiple drug abuse. Following a confrontation with her employer four years ago, Beth sought treatment for her problem. She attended outpatient counseling for 14 months, followed by a recovering womens' support group for one year. Beth also became involved in the AA program at the advice of her counselor. Approximately seven months after Beth stopped using substances and entered treatment, she experienced thoughts of "social drinking" and began questioning whether she was "really an alcoholic." She reduced her AA attendance and felt increasingly "bored" on weekends because she no longer socialized at the local club where she used to do much of her drinking. At this time, she also began accepting the invitations of several cowork-ers to attend parties where drugs were plentiful. Beth went to several parties, but she did not drink alcohol or use drugs. After struggling for several weeks with a strong desire to get high, Beth finally talked to her outpatient counselor and several AA friends about her conflict. With their help, Beth devised a plan to help her prevent a relapse. This plan included: not accepting invitations to parties where she knew the main purpose of the party was to get high on substances; talking about her desires to use with her counselor and AA friends; planning enjoyable recreational and social activities during the weekends to help reduce feelings of boredom; attending AA meetings on weekends; reminding herself that she still is an alcoholic and drug abuser by reviewing her long history of substance use and its impact on her life; and challenging any thoughts of "social alcohol or drug use." Beth was able to maintain her sobriety during this difficult period by following her plan.

About one year ago, following the third anniverary of her sobriety date, Beth became depressed. She wasn't happy with her job, had broken off her relationship with her boyfriend of 18 months, and missed a married couple whom she was fond of but who had moved to another state. During this time, she began to think that a few drinks or joints would improve her spirits. She thought perhaps she could handle it now; after all, she'd been sober for over three years. Beth made a decision to purchase wine and marijuana during the upcoming weekend.

The day after making this decision, Beth had second thoughts. She began to remember all that she had learned during her involvement in counseling and AA, although she had only been minimally involved during the past year. Beth reminded herself that she had done an excellent job of putting her life back together following extreme difficulties with her addiction. She carefully weighed the benefits of using alcohol and marijuana against the risks, and listed these on a sheet of paper. Beth was able to talk herself out of buying the wine and marijuana. Because she still felt vulnerable to relapse, Beth called a close friend and shared her conflict. After an open and honest discussion, Beth took the advice of her friend to resume involvement in AA. Beth is still sober today.

The case of Beth is very typical in several respects. Most, if not all, recovering substance-dependent persons are likely to experience stressful events, feelings, or thoughts that could contribute to a relapse if the person is not cognizant of them and does not take constructive action. Also, a recovering person may experience relapse warning signs similar to Beth's at any time, after relatively brief periods of recovery, or following years of sobriety. Warning signs may be readily noticable or subtle. The critical task facing recovering addicts is to utilize methods to prevent a relapse from occuring when warning signs appear or when they experience stressful life events.

In this section, relapse from two critical client perspectives will be examined: (1) before the relapse—understanding and managing factors that commonly contribute to relapse, and (2) after a relapse—intervening in a relapse to minimize detrimental effects. Special attention will be focused on the initial "slip" or lapse (the first substance use episode following a period of abstinence and recovery). It is the response to this slip that often dictates whether a full-blown relapse will occur.

Recent clinical literature on relapse in addiction has identified a number of high-risk factors that commonly precede relapse (Chaney & Roszell, 1982; Daley, 1989b; Gorski & Miller, 1982; Litman, Stapleton, Oppenheim, Peleg, & Jackson, 1983; Marlatt & Gordon, 1985). Although separated for purposes of discussion, these factors often overlap. Suggestions to the clinician will be provided on how to help a client vis-à-vis these relapse determinants. For purposes of this discussion, the following major factors have been identified that may contribute to a relapse: affective, behavioral, cognitive, environmental and relationship, physiological, psychological, and spiritual variables.

Affective Variables

Negative and positive mood states have been associated with relapse episodes across a wide spectrum of addictions (Cummings, Gordon, & Marlatt, 1980). Anger, anxiety, boredom, depression, and loneliness are often identified by addicts as emotional states leading to relapse (Daley, 1987a). Pickens, Hasukami, Spicer, and Svikis (1985) reported that 31% of relapsers stated that a depressed or anxious mood preceded their relapse. Depression was also identified by Hatsukami, Pickens, and Svikis, as a major factor in relapses (1981). In AA the acronym *HALT* is used frequently to alert members to the connection between hunger, anger, loneliness, tiredness—and relapse.

These negative emotional states may result from a variety of problems encountered by a recovering person in day-to-day living, adjusting to losses resulting from addiction (financial, relationship, self-esteem, etc.), or as a consequence of losing the active addiction, often the equivalent of a loss of a life-style (Daley, 1988b). In some instances, the client may have an affective disorder requiring treatment. Because of the effects of both substances and abstinence on mood states, it is sometimes difficult to determine if an affective disorder exists until the client has been substance free for several weeks or longer.

The professional can help the addict by informing him or her of the emotions associated with relapse and early recovery (e.g., depression and anxiety), and by helping the client develop coping skills. In cases where a possible underlying psychiatric disorder exists, help can be provided by identifying the specific symptoms according to the DSM-III-R criteria for affective disorders. Professionals who are not trained in identifying these disorders can refer the client for a psychological or psychiatric evaluation to determine proper diagnosis and treatment needs.

Positive emotional states have been associated with a small percentage of relapse (Cummings, Gordon, & Marlatt, 1980; Litman, Stapleton, Oppenheim, Peleg, & Jackson, 1987). In relapse prevention groups conducted by one of the authors, a small percentage of clients consistently report that they are more likely to relapse when experiencing positive affective states than negative affective states. Abraham Twerski has written that the exhilaration of self-discovery commonly experienced in the early stages of recovery may obscure the problems that the alcoholic still needs to confront. He believes that the alcoholic is at high risk for relapse when the "novelty" of self-discovery loses its glamour and a "sudden letdown" occurs. Some alcoholics' feelings of enthusiasm lead them to believe they may recover on their own. They then fall away from AA and resume drinking (Twerski, 1984).

Behavioral Variables (Coping Skills)

Lack of coping skills or personal competencies also impacts on relapse. Marlatt (1985a) emphasizes the need to teach clients alternative coping skills in order to increase their ability to manage high-risk relapse situations. Marlatt makes an excellent case for the need to go beyond helping an addicted client identify high-risk situations. The client must be taught specific coping skills to handle these situations. These skills may include problem-solving, relaxation, meditation, lifestyle balancing, cognitive restructuring, and substitution of "positive" addictions. In a study of posttreatment functioning of alcoholics, Cronkite and Moos (1980) found that "the use of positive coping responses is related to better . . . outcome" (p. 311). Many studies document the effectiveness of skills training with alcoholics and its implications for relapse prevention (Catalano & Hawkins, 1985; Chaney & O'Leary, 1978; Foy, Miller, Eisler, & O'Toole, 1976; Jones & Lanyon, 1981;). As Donovan and Chaney (1985) state, "The individual likely to relapse views more situations as threatening to sobriety and has fewer effective ways of dealing with these situations" (p. 374). Interventions that help addicted clients learn effectively to manage stress, plan leisure time activities, and refuse substance use are some examples of behavior skills useful in recovery.

Cognitive Variables

An addicted client's knowledge of addiction and recovery, beliefs, attitudes, expectancies, and level of cognitive functioning will affect the relapse process. The literature documents the association "between long-term heavy drinking and the deterioration and atrophy of brain tissue . . . reflected in defective cognitive functioning" (Abbot & Gregson, 1981, pp. 230-231). Several studies show that patients with poorer cognitive functioning, as determined by neuropsychological tests, experience more relapses and shorter periods of abstinence than patients with higher levels of cognitive functioning (Abbot & Gregson, 1981; O'Leary, Donovan, Chaney, & Walker, 1979).

A critical treatment goal is to help the addicted client increase his or her knowledge of addiction and recovery in terms of physical, psychological, social, familial, and spiritual components. The client must be able to apply this knowledge to his or her own unique situation (e.g., to identify symptoms and behaviors of his or her addictive pattern of substance use, and to identify ways in which his or her use has affected family members or significant others). Another goal is to increase knowledge of common relapse signs, both for clients in treatment for the first time and for relapsers (Daley, 1989a; Gorski & Miller, 1982). Relapsed clients will benefit from a review of their experiences in order to personalize this learning and use it in developing relapse prevention plans. Marlatt (1985e, p. 78) employs the following open-ended questions to help clients identify possible determinants of their relapse:

1. What would you say was the main reason for taking that first drink (cigarette, etc.)?
2. Describe any inner thoughts or emotional feelings (things within you as a person) that triggered your need or desire to take the first drink at that time.

3. Describe any particular circumstances or set of events or things that happened to you in the outside world that triggered your need or desire to take that first drink. (p. 78)

Daley (1986, p. 3) asks relapsed alcoholic and drug-addicted clients to read a review of the relapse process, which provides examples of common "relapse clues" and a "case example" of an actual relapse. The relapser is then asked to answer the following questions:

1. What specific clues or warning signs preceded your relapse?
2. How much time elapsed between the emergence of your relapse clues and the actual use of alcohol or drugs?
3. If these were to occur with you again, what specific steps could you take to try to prevent a relapse?

The client may benefit from reviewing common beliefs held by recovering individuals, particularly in the first several months of recovery. Typical beliefs or "negative thoughts" regarding relapse are (1) "it (relapse) will never happen to me," (2) "I can control my (substance) use," (3) "recovery isn't happening fast enough," (4) "I need alcohol or drugs in order to have fun," (5) "my problem is cured"—this last belief typically occurs after an initial period of recovery, usually several months to a year or more (Daley, 1987b, pp. 12-15). The client can be taught to challenge these beliefs. For example, after telling himself or herself "I can control my use," he or she may be instructed to state instead: "I am feeling as though I would like to use alcohol or drugs, and I wish I could control my use. However, I know from my past experience that I eventually lose control, even if I'm able to limit use for a while. I have too much to lose by returning to substance use."

Clients can also benefit by keeping journals in which they record both their conflicting thoughts about relapse and counterstatements. This enables the client to continue working at recovery and gives him or her greater responsibility as an "active" participant in treatment.

Marlatt (1985d) reviews four major cognitive factors that have an interactive effect on relapse: self-efficacy, outcome expectancy, attributions, and decision making.

Self-efficacy refers to the individual's perception of his or her ability to cope with prospective high-risk situations. Successful coping with a

> variety of high-risk situations increases one's sense of self-efficacy and decreases the probability of relapse, whereas failure has the opposite effect. To the extent that one's inability to cope with a high-risk situation is associated with a perception of decreased efficacy, the attraction to the old "coping crutch" or addictive substance will increase. (p. 128)

For example, if a recovering drug addict believes he or she is competent enough to refuse offers of drugs, there is a greater likelihood that he or she will successfully do so. Success in refusing an offer increases self-efficacy. On the other hand, if an alcoholic believes that he or she "can't say no to an offer of alcohol," he or she is likely to give in and relapse. This decreases self-efficacy. Outcome expectancy is the second cognitive factor in this relapse sequence. This refers to the anticipated effects of engaging in a particular behavior (e.g., alcohol or drug use). Positive expectancies about the effects (physical, psychological, or behavioral) of substances increase the likelihood of relapse in a given individual. According to Marlatt (1985d), positive outcome expectancies arise from a variety of sources, "including conditioned stimuli associated with prior drug experiences, physical dependency, the influence of personal and cultural beliefs about drug effects, and situational-environmental factors" (p. 138).

When an individual actually engages in the activity considered taboo (in this instance, alcohol or drug use), the third cognitive process, attribution of causality, will determine whether the initial lapse ends in a full-blown relapse. The reaction to the first slip "will be determined in part by whether the individual attributes the 'cause' of the slip to internal (self-related) or external (situational) factors" (p. 128). Marlatt observes that an Abstinence Violation Effect (AVE) or a cognitive-affective reaction occurs when a person initially engages in the taboo activity. This AVE "influences the probability that the lapse will be followed by an increased use of the substance or activity . . . . The greater the AVE, the greater the probability of relapse or an exacerbation effect following the initial lapse" (p. 179).

Marlatt also emphasizes the influence of decisionmaking as an important component in the chain of events that precedes and follows the initial lapse. He focuses on decision making as it relates to "covert planning or setting up of a relapse" (p. 186). A key concept is the Apparently Irrelevant Decision (AID). This describes the "mini-decisions that lead the individual closer to the brink of relapse" (p. 192). An example of an AID is an alcoholic who went to a tavern for a steak dinner in order to celebrate the award of a lucrative contract. Once in the tavern, the alcoholic experienced "social pressure" to drink and was unprepared to cope effectively. Alcoholics and addicts report many common AIDs such as going into bars or taverns to buy cigarettes or to conduct business.

Environmental and Relationship Variables

Social networks and support systems are critical variables in addiction relapse. Good progress is associated with social stability and marital adjustment (Baekeland, 1977; Saxe, Dougherty, Esty, & Fine, 1983). Many addicted clients are part of broader social networks in which others misuse substances, or they are involved in a primary relationship in which the partner misuses or is addicted to substances. Reviewing the client's social network and determining the persons with whom he can maintain contact will help him reduce social pressures to use alcohol and/or drugs (Daley, 1987; Zackon, McAuliffe, & Ch'ien, 1985).

Clinicians are all too familiar with the relationship between lack of family involvement in treatment and the addict's relapse. A critical task of the professional is to engage family members in the treatment process. Equally important, however, is helping the family assess its role in the perpetuation of the addiction (e.g., enabling) and in recovery. Spouses indicate they often play a major role (consciously and unconsciously) in sabotaging the recovery of the alcoholic or drug addict. For example, the wife of an alcoholic, when angry at her husband, might say, "Why don't you go out and get drunk?" Some spouses have indicated they prefer their mate to use substances actively. In a videotape presentation entitled "Spousaholics," Dr. Douglas Talbot (1977) cites a case of a relapse that occurred after an alcoholic's wife gave him a fifth of his favorite liquor to celebrate his first year of sobriety. She had immense difficulty during her husband's recovery and apparently preferred him to be drinking.

There are addicted clients who have few or no supportive family members and no significant interpersonal relationships. A recent report states, "one of the most significant and prevalent differences in women who relapse, as compared to men, is their lack of support from family members or significant others" (Cusack, 1984, p. 12). Poorer outcome is related to the absence of a strong, prosocial interpersonal network (Catalano & Hawkins, 1985).

Clients benefit from halfway-house programs in which they can slowly build a social network supportive of recovery efforts. If the professional's assessment of the client's social network is negative, discussing the option of a halfway-house program as a context in which to build a sober social network will aid the client. Because this option may be totally new to the client, a brief visit by the client to the program or its clear explanation by the worker is very important.

A study of the precipitants of relapse identified social pressure as a major factor in 20% of relapse for a range of addictive behaviors (Cummings, Gordon, & Marlatt, 1980). For heroin addicts, social pressures were a factor in 36% of relapses. Clients should review specific social pressures in their lives, and how these pressures affect thoughts, feelings, and actions. For example, clients often discover that being offered substances is attractive and triggers an underlying desire to use or become intoxicated. The professional can help the addicted client by teaching him or her ways to refuse offers of substances, discussing how to inform significant others that an addiction exists (to reduce social pressures), helping him or her learn avoidance strategies, such as staying out of bars and away from drug use parties, and advising him or her to restructure his or her life around activities without the use of substances (Daley, 1987a). Assertiveness training or the use of role plays can help the client build skills in refusing offers of substances (Foy, Miller, Eisler, & O'Toole, 1976).

Major life changes or stresses may mediate relapse. Research has been conducted on the relationship between major life events and stress. Marlatt (1985c) cites studies that support the relationship between stress and changes in physical/mental health and personal effectiveness and that show negative or mixed results in terms of major stressful life events and the frequency of alcohol-related problems. In order to reduce stress associated with major changes, the professional should discourage the newly recovering person from making major life changes or decisions in the early phases of recovery. In a guide written for recovering persons on relapse prevention, Daley (1987a) advises addicted clients "to minimize major changes during the early months of recovery unless these are related to helping . . . sobriety" (p. 31). There are, however, some major life changes over which the client has no control, such as unexpected unemployment or the untimely death of a loved one.

Other studies cited by Marlatt report that "daily hassles" have been associated with psychological and physical symptoms. Positive life experiences or "uplifts" may also affect relapse, although research to date has not been conducted on this relationship (Marlatt, 1985e).

Gorski and Miller (1982) observe that situational life problems and life-transition periods can increase anxiety for the alcoholic and "can trigger a relapse dynamic" (p. 86). Cronkite and Moos (1980) review several studies and report that patients who experienced more post-treatment stressors or negative life changes showed poorer treatment outcomes.

In a review of posttreatment factors that appear to be related to relapse following treatment for either drug or alcohol abuse, Catalano and Hawkins (1985) identified the following: isolation, lack of productive work or school roles, and lack of involvement in active leisure or recreational interests. Other factors related to cultural and sexuality issues may contribute to relapse. For example, a male homosexual alcoholic whose primary place of socializing is a gay bar would be at higher risk for relapse. He would need help in exploring alternatives less threatening to his sobriety.

Physiological Variables

Cravings, cue responsivity, brain chemistry, degree of addiction, diet, and physical illness or pain are physiological factors that may contribute to a relapse. Physiological factors often have cognitive, behavioral, and social components.

Several reports in the literature discuss the role of cravings in relapse (Ludwig & Wikler, 1974; Ludwig, Wikler, & Stark, 1974). Cravings may occur in response to internal and external stimuli. Several studies report that "cues" associated with substance use (e.g., sight or smell of substance of choice, or environmental cues associated with use) or withdrawal may elicit conditioned responses (Cooney, Baker, Pomerleau, & Josephy, 1984; Cooney, Gillespie, Baker, & Kaplan, 1987; Pomerleau, Fertig, Baker, & Cooney, 1983). These responses may have physical components, such as mild withdrawal symptoms, or cognitive components, such as increased thoughts of using the substance. Clients in treatment have reported the following stimuli as triggering off cravings to use substances: "finding a bag of pot in my dresser"; "viewing an ad of my favorite beer on TV"; "running into my old 'partner'" (person with whom the client frequently used drugs); "seeing baby powder spilled on a coffee table" (reminding the cocaine addict of his or her favorite drug); "hearing an old rock and roll song I often listened to when getting loaded"; and "throwing up when I was sick with the flu" (reminding a heroin addict of past drug use). Although there are often obvious stimuli associated with substance use (e.g., bars and ads for liquor), the "cues" may be more subtle.

Professionals can help recovering clients by educating them about cravings or urges. Clients should be taught that cravings or urges are to be expected, particularly in the early months of recovery, and should be informed of the internal and external stimuli commonly associated with cravings. In addition, clients should be taught to recognize the physiological and cognitive signs of cravings. They can then be taught to utilize practical coping strategies, such as talking about cravings with others, redirecting activity, changing thoughts, and avoiding threatening situations that may increase the risk of giving in to a craving (Daley, 1986). Another effective strategy is to alert clients that cravings or urges typically decrease in frequency and intensity as recovery progresses. Education and counseling are particularly important because many clients are apt to interpret cravings as a negative sign (i.e., they are not motivated to stop if they still experience cravings to use substances).

Gorski and Miller (1982) believe that an alcoholic may be predisposed to relapse in the first several months of recovery as a result of "post acute withdrawal syndrome (PAW)." They believe that alcohol actually has a normalizing effect on the body for many alcoholics. When the alcoholic stops drinking, PAW symptoms are produced and may last up to three months. As with other physiological formulations of addiction and relapse, Gorski and Miller also believe that cognitive, phychological, behavioral, and social factors affect the extent and nature of the relapse. Educating clients about the PAW phenomenon, and helping them develop recovery plans that recognize that the first three months of sobriety are the most difficult, are helpful strategies for the professional.

Wallace (1985) reviews research that discusses the relationship between addiction and brain chemistry. He reports that the neurotransmitter noradrenaline may play a role in addiction to opiates, "since the level of this chemical is very high during narcotic withdrawal," and "it is entirely possible that alcoholics also have noradrenaline surges in their brains during withdrawal and that these chemical surges set up craving for more alcohol" (pp. 19-20). This research suggests that opiate addicts and alcoholics going through withdrawal may be more susceptible to relapse. Clients often report extremely strong cravings to use substances during the initial period of withdrawal. Many clients report that the craving or need was so intense that they felt compelled to resume substance use. Providing basic education on the role of brain chemistry in addiction and recovery may facilitate the client's recovery.

Donovan and Chaney review models and methods of relapse prevention and intervention with alcoholics and report that the "severity of dependence may also contribute to relapse" (1985, p. 363). The severity of dependence relates to the pattern of substance use (quantity, frequency, and length of addiction), tolerance, withdrawal symptoms, and physical problems caused or exacerbated by the addiction.

Several reports discuss the importance of diet or "postaddiction nutrition" in recovery (Hindin, 1984; Stouder, 1984). A proper diet is seen as one of the physical components of recovery that may reduce the likelihood of relapse with alcoholics. Educating clients on the importance of a proper diet and arranging for nutritional assessments and counseling will help recovery efforts.

Complications related to physical illness or pain can also contribute to relapse. According to Gorski and Miller, "acute illnesses produce high levels of stress that can reactivate post acute withdrawal" (1982, p. 80). Many alcoholics have other chronic illnesses that contribute to stress or restrict the person from participating in alcoholism treatment activities. "Negative physical states" were identified as a factor in 3% of alcoholic relapses and 9% of heroin addicts' relapses (Cummings, Gordon, & Marlatt, 1980).

The use of mood-altering medications contributes to relapse for some alcoholics and drug addicts (Daley, 1987a; Gorski & Miller, 1982). For example, a client recovering from alcoholism and multiple drug addiction, who had been abstinent over two years, reported that he received small dosages of pain medications for five days following surgery. As a result, he experienced physical withdrawal symptoms and subjective craving for substances. Fortunately, he had a very strong recovery program and utilized appropriate supports to prevent himself from relapsing. Another alcoholic relapsed after using pain medications following dental work. Addicted individuals receiving treatment for medical or dental conditions requiring medication should be instructed to alert the physician or dentist to the addiction so that medication is used cautiously and monitored appropriately. There are many cases of "inadvertent" relapse occurring following the prescription of a drug. The body cannot differentiate between a substance taken for the "high" and one taken for medical purposes.

Potential difficulties with an addict or alcoholic using any mood-altering drugs are mentioned in several of the classic recovery books used in the self-help programs of AA and NA. In *Living Sober: Some Methods AA Members Have Used for Not Drinking* (1975), a chapter is devoted to "avoiding all chemical mood-changers." This chapter also discusses the use of other chemicals by alcholics:

> And thousands of us used other chemicals, too. We discovered pep pills . . . sedatives and tranquilizers . . . bromides and non-prescription pills and elixirs.
>
> Evidently the strong desire . . . for such psychoactive mood-changers can become embedded root-deep in anybody who is much of a drinker.
>
> Even if . . . a drug is not a physiologically addicting one, we can easily get habituated to it and dependent on it, we have repeatedly found. It's as if "addiction proneness" was a condition inside us, not a quality of the drug itself . . . . So we go to great lengths to avoid pot, cocaine, hash, hallucinogens, downers, uppers, and even over-the-counter pills and nostrums aimed at the central nervous system . . . . They seem to reawaken the old craving for "oral magic" or some kind of high. (pp. 53-54)

The "Basic Text" also discusses difficulties addicts have with any use of substances. In the opening chapter it states that "we could not successfully use any mind-altering or mood-changing substance" (1983, p. 2). The need to justify "legal prescriptions" is also mentioned. These statements by NA and AA members imply that great caution must be taken if an addict or alcoholic uses any mood-altering substance; otherwise, he or she is at higher risk of relapse.

The professional can help recovering persons by developing a network of physicians knowledgeable about addiction and recovery that can be used when referrals for medical or psychiatric services are needed. He or she can also advise clients to inform medical practitioners of their recovery from addiction.

Psychological and Psychiatric Variables

Alcohol- and drug-dependent individuals often evidence a multiplicity of psychological or psychiatric symptoms that may complicate their recovery. The pharmacological effects of substance use and withdrawal can lead to these symptoms, or symptoms may result from losses associated with the addiction (loss of self-esteem, finances, relationships, or a job). Symptoms such as depression often remit, however, with continued abstinence from substances.

A significant percentage of substance-dependent individuals also have psychiatric disorders. The Epidemiologic Catchment Area (ECA) survey of 20,000 adults in the United States conducted by the National Institute of Mental Health found that alcoholism and drug abuse/dependence were two of the three most common disorders. Among the alcoholics in this survey, 47% had an additional psychiatric diagnosis. All psychiatric disorders were more common among alcoholics than among nonalcoholics in this survey (Helzer & Pwyzbeck, 1988). Rates of psychiatric illness among substance abusers in clinical populations is even higher. Numerous reports indicate the rates of dual disorders to be as high as 80% among some substance-abuse populations (*Alcohol and Health,* 1984; Carroll & Sobel, 1986; Hesselbrock, Meyer & Keener, 1985; McLellan, Luborsky, Woody, O'Brien, & Druley, 1983; Rubinstein, Campbell, & Daley, in press). There are many possible relationships between substance abuse and psychiatric illness (Meyer, 1986). As a result, it is sometimes difficult to determine if psychopathology is the cause or the result of addiction. In many instances, the individual will have to be substance free for several weeks or longer in order to determine if a psychiatric disorder exists and related treatment is needed.

In some cases, the addicted client will need stabilization in a psychiatric hospital before receiving treatment for a substance-abuse problem. For example, a client with a bipolar disorder, and in a manic phase or severely depressed, would need to have his or her symptoms under control. A schizophrenic who is decompensating and experiencing hallucinations would need to be in a reasonable state of remission to benefit from specialized treatment for substance dependence. Cases of addiction with psychiatric comorbidity may require the use of psychotropic medications. There will be cases of dual diagnosis in which the client relapses following cessation of medications and a return of psychiatric symptomatology (Daley, Moss, & Campbell, 1987).

A significant number of substance-dependent individuals also experience other addictive or compulsive disorders that have implications for relapse. These include compulsive gambling, and sexual and eating disorders. For example, an alcoholic relapsed following a gambling binge during which he lost the family's expense money for the month.

He felt guilty and angry at himself for this action and rationalized that "I might as well get drunk. I lost everything else, so what's the difference?"

Recent literature has addressed other psychological problems of substance-dependent individuals, including posttraumatic stress disorders, difficulties associated with being an adult child of an alcoholic/ addict, and traumatic experiences such as rape or parental violence (Anderson, 1985; Black, Bucky, & Wilder-Padilla, 1986; Jelinek & Williams, 1984; Schnitt & Nocks, 1984; Van Kampen, Watson, Tilleskjor, Kusala, & Vassar, 1986). *Women and Relapse* (Cusack, 1984) identifies the role of "unresolved problems" in relapse for female alcoholics. These problems may relate to a range of experiences, including unresolved anger and resentment toward one's mother, incest, sexuality conflicts, and "unmentionable" experiences common with female addicts, such as abortion, miscarriages, giving up children, children being taken away, and disliking motherhood (Cusack, 1984, p. 30-32). The affective components of memories related to traumatic experiences are often intensive with addicted individuals. These painful memories can be experienced as "intrusive thoughts" over which the person feels no control and that are triggered by a multiplicity of factors (e.g., contact with the parent or viewing a movie that portrays the traumatic experience).

Another critical psychological variable affecting relapse is the individual's motivation. Ambivalence is common with alcoholics and drug addicts, particularly in the early months of recovery (Daley, 1990). Most maintain fantasies of "controlled use" and want to have the "option" to use. It is helpful to get the client to discuss his or her ambivalence and to accept it as a normal reaction to recovery. Discussion will aid the client in resolving his or her ambivalence. When the issue is evaded, however, the risk of relapse may increase.

Spiritual Variables

As discussed in an earlier chapter, guilt and shame are common characteristics of substance dependency (Kurtz, 1982). Failure on the part of the alcoholic or drug addict to confront his or her guilt and shame in recovery will increase the possibility of relapse.

Early recovery often gives the addict a sense of emptiness or a "void," a powerful motivator to return to substance abuse (Daley,

1988b). Zackon (1989) refers to this as a state of unhappiness, as "joylessness," and contends that it "often drains energies and threatens abstinence for many months" (p. 73).

The variable of faith is important in recovery from addiction. The addicted person's chances of avoiding relapse increase if he or she has faith that: (1) recovery is possible, (2) a benevolent "higher power" desires this for the person (although this higher power can be anyone or anything, most choose God), (3) this higher power will help the person achieve and maintain sobriety, (4) recovery programs work and will help the person improve his or her life, and (5) individuals with the AA and NA fellowship will also help.

The self-help programs place a great emphasis on "spirituality" in recovery. One study found that the spiritual component of treatment was perceived as very important to ongoing sobriety (Laundergan, 1982). The "fellowhip" of the self-help programs helps reduce the person's feeling of being alone, provides an opportunity to experience love and caring from others who want to help and assist the addict in utilizing the 12-step program. More importantly, the fellowship offers the newly recovering person hope that he or she can overcome the addiction. All of this can help reduce shame and guilt and develop a sense of meaning or joy in life.

RELAPSE INTERVENTION

Case Histories

Roberta is a 52-year-old married mother of three adult children and two grandchildren. She has an episodic pattern of alcohol abuse over the past 20 years with several periods of abstinence up to four months. However, these periods decreased significantly over the past seven years, and her family recently demanded she seek treatment. Seven months ago, Roberta completed a four-week nonresidential treatment program and continued involvement in a women's aftercare group and AA. Following an argument with her husband a month ago, she became angry and had three drinks. She immediately told herself that she made a mistake and should stop drinking. Roberta expressed her guilt and fears to her husband and asked for his help in stopping. She admitted making a mistake and acknowledged she could not safely continue drinking alcohol. In addition to talking about this experience with her husband, Roberta shared her mistake with her support group and gained additional ideas on ways to prevent herself from having a full-blown relapse. She is still sober today.

Jack is a 32-year-old single, self-employed contractor with a five-year history of cocaine addiction. Following detoxification in a medical hospital two and one-half years ago, Jack attended NA meetings and outpatient counseling. He remained clean for 28 months. About nine weeks ago, he encountered several friends with whom he was previously high. He impulsively gave in to their offers to snort coke with them. Jack enjoyed the high, despite some feelings of guilt, and he was reminded of his early years of drug use when he wasn't addicted. Following his initial episode of use, Jack told himself, "I blew my recovery and lost my 28 months of clean time. I might as well continue using." He then decided to limit his cocaine use to weekends. This worked for three weeks. Then, Jack began more frequent use and eventually began using on a daily basis. He quickly became readdicted and began to experience health and job problems. Although he at times wanted to not use, he felt he had to, particularly to help him get out of his depression states following heavy cocaine binges. Jack couldn't stop on his own or with the help of NA friends he called upon for advice. Following the recommendation of a close friend, Jack decided to seek detoxification so that he could receive medical help in stopping his relapse. After he was detoxified, Jack completed a residential treatment program and then resumed NA involvement and outpatient counseling. He is now clean from drugs.

These two cases illustrate that relapses will differ among individuals in terms of their length, severity, and consequences. Relapse intervention approaches will also vary. In some instances, relapse will prove helpful to an individual's long-term recovery; in other cases, a relapse will have severe, or even fatal, effects.

Response to an Initial Lapse

The cognitive and affective responses to initial substance use after a period of abstinence largely determine if a full-blown relapse will occur. Clients often label themselves as "failures" following an initial lapse. This self-criticism typically triggers negative affective states such as self-anger, depression, and negative cognitions such as "I blew my recovery, so why should I continue trying," or "I took a drink (or drug), I might as well get drunk." This is the Abstinence Violation Effect (AVE) discussed earlier.

The client's response to an initial lapse affects the cessation or continuation of substance use. Professionals can intervene by informing clients about the critical role of affective and cognitive responses to initial substance use following a period of self-imposed abstinence. Marlatt's AVE concept is easily operationalized by experiences of clients who have relapsed. Clients can be taught to expect negative affective responses unless positive actions are taken to stop the relapse. They can also be taught to challenge cognitions that are likely to precipitate a full-blown relapse. In addition to strategies aimed at early relapse intervention, such as talking oneself out of continued substance use or talking about an initial lapse with a concerned person (family member, friend, counselor, AA or NA sponsor), clients can be shown other steps to take should a full-blown relapse occur. An addicted client must understand the importance of utilizing professional services such as detoxification, rehabilitiation, or counseling to interrupt a relapse. Cases in which physical readdiction occurs, for example, may very well require medically supervised detoxification, because other strategies can be ineffective.

Clients and families who intervene early in lapse or relapse episodes can minimize damage. For example, in the 15 most recent relapse cases in which one of the authors was involved, 12 relapses were stopped within one to seven days of the initial substance use.

Because rates are high, it is crucially important for professionals to teach clients and families methods to interrupt relapses. Education and counseling approaches about relapse intervention enhance the client's and family's hope and give them control over what can be done following an initial lapse.

THE FAMILY'S PERSPECTIVE
ON RELAPSE

"Family relapse" has recently been discussed in the literature. This refers to a family member's return to dysfunctional behaviors (usually defined as a return to "codependency") following participation in recovery. The relapse cases cited below illustrate this phenomenon.

Case Histories

Joan was very happy when her husband Paul entered treatment and got sober. She thought things would improve at home. As Paul progressed in his sobriety, however, Joan began resenting him, and she did not like the changes that occurred in the family. Although she didn't say so, it bothered her that she had to adjust so much to Paul's sobriety. And, all the sympathy she had received from others for putting up with Paul when he was drunk stopped! Although she attended some meetings to learn about addiction and recovery for the family, she insisted that "it's his problem, not mine." For Christmas, which just happened to coincide with Paul's first year of sobriety, she bought him a fifth of his favorite liquor.

Len was a typical spouse of an alcoholic. He tried to control his wife's drinking. Finally, she entered treatment and was sober. This delighted him. He also entered treatment, although he didn't agree with the notion that he had a problem in his relationship with his alcoholic wife. Len stopped participating in recovery after two months. After the inital "honeymoon effect" of recovery, Len resumed his old ways. He often reminded Fran of how much pain she brought to the family. He told her of his distrust toward her and how he always checked to see if she had been drinking. He also began to nag her about her cigarette smoking. Len couldn't adjust to his wife's sobriety and modify his behavior. In order to avoid a complete relapse into destructive, co-dependent behaviors, Len had to seek help. He was then able to understand and change his negative feelings and reactions to his wife's recovery from alcoholism (Daley, 1988b, pp. 109-110).

The family plays a critical role in either the recovery or the relapse of the substance-dependent individual. Chalmers and Wallace note, for example, that "there is evidence to indicate that longer-term sobriety in the alcoholic is just as strongly related to life change and attitude change of the spouse as it is to his own change" (1985, p. 382). Family members can contribute to relapses of addicted individuals. In general, families that do not maintain involvement in treatment activities (e.g., educational programs, counseling, and self-help programs) are more prone to act in ways that contribute to, or exacerbate, a relapse than are families who are active in treatment services. Families and significant persons in the alcoholic's or drug addict's life can benefit from education and counseling. For example, families participating in recovery can be taught to identify common relapse warning signs, to present these warning signs to the addicted member, and to support this member's effort at abstinence. Family involvement in relapse prevention and intervention significantly affects its ability to help the addicted member and to manage its own negative response to a relapse. Previous responses to relapses, such as "He is hopeless" or "She isn't motivated to stop drinking," are modified, giving the family a feeling of control over what occurs. Family members learn that they do not have to sit helplessly and watch a loved one deteriorate following a relapse. The family perceives its joint involvement with the alcoholic member in recovery.

Gorski and Miller (1984a, 1984b) have described relapse of co-alcoholics, family relapse warning signs, and family relapse prevention planning. In a guide on addiction and recovery written for alcoholics, drug addicts, and families, Daley (1988b) includes a section on relapse of the family member and provides numerous examples of family relapse (pp. 115-117).

TREATMENT AGENCY'S PERSPECTIVE ON RELAPSE

There is a variety of factors within a particular treatment agency that may contribute to a relapse of a client. These factors may relate to an individual staff member or to the agency's practices and policies in service delivery.

Staff Member Variables

As mentioned in an earlier section, attitudes regarding relapsers, and knowledge and skills in working with addicted individuals and their families, can affect the nature and duration of a relapse. The professional who utilizes creative methods to engage an alcoholic's resistant family in treatment will provide a more useful service than one who passively accepts a family's lack of involvement. Gorski and Miller (1982) believe that "many therapists contribute directly to relapse by failing to thoroughly educate their patients about the relapse process and ways to avoid it" (p. 89). A professional who is cognizant of common relapse warning signs and skilled in educating and counseling a client and his or her family in identifying early warning signs and developing prevention plans will aid recovery efforts.

Agency and Organizational Variables

In a study of relapse among recovering substance abuse (RSA) counselors, William White (1978) found that several of the RSAs were placed in counseling positions without proper education or training. Agencies erroneously assumed that because an alcoholic or drug addict had experienced recovery, he or she would be able to counsel other addicted individuals.

White's study of RSAs who relapsed focused on "burnout" from an interactional perspective of the RSA (knowledge, skills, coping abilities), the work environment, staff interactions, and the organizational structure. He provides case examples of relapse that illustrate that the relapse of several counselors could be attributed to intrapersonal and agency-related factors. For example, one of the ten "role stressors" associated with relapse of RSAs was a "role/person mismatch." Recovering persons were placed in counseling positions without any specialized education or training and with limited periods of recovery (less than one year in some cases). Role/person mismatch also found the RSA in a stressful role that he or she was unprepared to handle. These mismatches resulted in the RSA's relapse. For example, a heroin addict in a therapeutic community was hired to work in a youth agency with young drug abusers. No adequate assessment was made of the addict's ability to sustain himself emotionally in an isolated area, and no training was provided to him. His job performance decreased, his alcohol use increased, and he isolated himself from other staff. Yet, there was no supervisory intervention. Tragically, this RSA died from an overdose of heroin taken after he had been drinking (White, 1978, pp. 20-24).

Waiting lists at outpatient agencies may inadvertently contribute to relapse. A client who completes a primary rehabilitation program for 28 days typically will experience a variety of stresses and adjustments common in early recovery. He or she may be at greater risk for relapse if he or she has to wait several weeks or more for an outpatient appointment.

Agencies that do not properly address long-term treatment needs may influence relapse. Many agencies appear successful at helping clients achieve initial sobriety and short-term sobriety, but have more difficulty with longer-term sobriety. An alcoholic of 15 years who has suffered multiple problems from his or her addiction cannot be expected to recover in a few months. Helping clients to maintain long-term involvement is a critical task facing the professional. This may take the form of counseling, self-help meetings, or referral to other services. Helping addicted individuals understand the long-term nature of recovery and become familiar with community resources can facilitate an individual client's recovery.

Many relapses occur following detoxification and/or rehabilitation services when not followed by halfway house, self-help, or outpatient services. It is very common for alcoholics and drug addicts detoxified in general medical or psychiatric wards of hospitals to convince staff that they will stop substance use on their own. Often the professional will expend considerable time, energy, and resources in discharge planning for an addicted client who has no intention of staying sober. The worker may help the client obtain housing, benefits, employment, or meet other needs. Merely providing supportive services, however, will not decrease the chances of relapse. Treatment for the addiction is of primary importance.

A professional in a hospital setting may contribute to the recovery of an addicted individual by a diagnostic confrontation (discussed in the chapter on intervention methods) and/or referral for follow-up services. Involving the family or significant others will normally increase the effectiveness of such a confrontation or referral. Programs that do not adequately provide services to families or significant others may contribute to relapse of the alcoholic or addict. A previous chapter has outlined the recovery needs of the family. Professionals who take into consideration the needs of families for services will also be helping the addicted individual. Some agencies give inadequate attention to the importance of family involvement in treatment services. Professionals may help alleviate this inadequacy by advocating services for families of addicts, and by developing educational, treatment, and referral services.

Legal, educational, occupational, religious, mental health, or medical systems can directly or indirectly influence a relapse. For example, recovering addicts who are treated for dental, medical, or psychiatric problems can relapse from using medications. In some instances, these relapses are planned by the addict; in other instances, they are not and take the person by surprise. Clients should be made aware of the possibility of inadvertent readdiction or transference of addiction to a different substance. They can also be advised to discuss their addiction with any medical professional who may need to treat a problem with a mood-altering medication.

One young alcoholic was mandated to participate in treatment as a condition of his parole. He successfully completed a 28-day rehabilitation program, and his counselor recommended to the parole officer that he continue participation in AA and outpatient counseling. The client did not follow through with these recommendations, and his parole officer did not monitor him to ensure this. The client believed that he could recover without any further help. Three months later, he relapsed.

A professional involved in direct treatment of a client may help minimize the chances of an inadvertent relapse by collaborating with other systems in which the client is involved. This helps ensure that specific treatment recommendations are shared with others and assist in collaborative monitoring of a client's participation and progress in treatment.

MODELS OF RELAPSE PREVENTION

General Treatment Approaches

All treatment for addictive disorders generally aims at prevention of relapse and improvement in client functioning. A variety of approaches has been used with clients such as multimodal treatment, cognitive therapy, behavioral therapy, problem solving, assertiveness training, family therapy, aversion therapy, and the 12-step programs of AA and NA. However, in recent years, there has been an increase in educational, counseling, and self-management models specific to relapse prevention (Daley, 1988a, 1989b).

In this section, selected aspects of four models of relapse prevention (RP) are reviewed. Although there are differences among these models in terms of theoretical perspective or clinical application, there is a number of commonalities. These include providing the client with information, enhancing self-awareness, and helping him or her develop coping skills. All approaches review: (1) teaching clients about relapse as a process, (2) helping clients identify high-risk relapse situations and develop coping strategies, (3) exposing clients to common relapse risk factors (such as drug cravings and social pressure to use) and coping strategies, and (4) helping clients develop lapse and relapse intervention strategies.

Cognitive-Behavioral Model

The most comprehensive theoretical and clinical model of relapse prevention was developed by Marlatt and his colleagues and is described in a large number of publications and several books. According to Marlatt (1985a), relapse prevention (RP) is a "self-management program designed to enhance the maintenance stage of the habit-change process. The goal of RP is to teach individuals who are trying to change their behavior how to anticipate and cope with the problem of relapse" (p. 3). This model is applicable to alcohol and drug addictions, eating disorders, compulsive gambling, other impulse-control problems (e.g., sexual disorders such as exhibitionism or pedophilia), and impulsive aggressive acts (e.g., child abuse and rape). This model is theoretically useful for a wide range of problematic behaviors that are addictive or compulsive in nature. It is most appropriate for individuals who have made a commitment to change rather than for those who are in treatment as a result of external pressures.

Marlatt (p. 21) views recovery as a "learning task," and his RP model is based on three major assumptions about treatment and behavior change:

1. The etiology of an addictive habit and the process of behavior change "may be governed by different factors or principles of learning."
2. "The process of changing a habit involves at least three separate stages"—commitment and motivation; implementation of change; and long-term maintenance of behavior change.
3. The maintenance stage of behavior change "accounts for the greatest proportion of variance associated with long-term treatment outcomes."

According to Marlatt, relapse is viewed as a "transitional process, a series of events that may or may not be followed by a return to baseline levels of the target behavior." A lapse (of substance use) is viewed "as a fork in the road, with one path returning to the former problem level . . . and the other continuing in the direction of positive change" (pp. 32-33).

If the individual develops effective cognitive or behavioral coping responses to deal with high-risk relapse situations, the probability of relapse decreases significantly. Marlatt emphasizes the importance of helping clients learn new coping mechanisms or skills. Self-monitoring procedures, stress management, relaxation training, skill training, cognitive restructuring, and the use of clinical aids such as relapse fantasies, a decision matrix, or a programmed relapse are examples of cognitive or behavioral interventions that are helpful in treatment of addicted clients (pp. 53-59).

Marlatt states that teaching clients specific skills and cognitive strategies to cope with high-risk situations is not enough to prevent relapse, and other global, self-control strategies such as positive addictions, substitute indulgences, and a balanced daily life-style are needed (pp. 59-65).

This model emphasizes the importance of "life-style modification." The addicted client may reduce his or her chances of relapse if specific life-style changes are made. Exercise, relaxation, meditation, biofeedback, and self-hypnosis are several examples of specific interventions that will aid an individual client in modifying his or her life (Marlatt, 1985c).

Dr. Helen Annis of the Addiction Research Foundation in Canada has developed a variation of Marlatt's Cognitive-Behavioral RP model. She has devised several instruments such as the Inventory of Alcohol (or Drug) Taking Situations, and Alcohol (or Drug) Taking Confidence questionnaires, which can help the clinician identify high-risk situations and assess the client's confidence to deal with these situations. This information can then be incoporated in a relapse prevention plan (Annis, 1986).

Neurological Impairment Model

This model was developed from Gorski's survey of 118 alcoholics who completed a 21- or 28-day inpatient program for alcoholism and made a commitment to ongoing sobriety by participating in AA and counseling, but who returned to uncontrolled drinking. The approach of Gorski and Miller (1982) to relapse prevention planning (RPP) is viewed as "an adjunct to alcoholism treatment, not a substitute. RPP is a method of constructing a fence between the alcoholic and his or her first drink" (p. 1).

This approach views alcoholism as a disease with two cutting edges: One occurs when the person is actively drinking, and the other occurs when the person is sober. Gorski and Miller discuss "sobriety-based symptoms" of alcoholism and believe these may trigger the relapse dynamic, which is viewed as a freestanding syndrome. In other words, abstinence from alcohol use produces symptoms that may result in relapse if RPP measures are not initiated.

Gorski and Miller state that relapse manifests itself in a progressive pattern of behavior and allows the symptoms of alcoholism to become reactivated or causes other debilitating symptoms (p. 22). Because they view alcoholism as a chronic disease and the possibility of relapse is high, they believe recovery is a long-term process involving changes in physical, psychological, behavioral, and social habits. They present a developmental model of recovery with several phases, each of which has specific tasks to be accomplished.

Gorski and Miller describe a relapse prevention plan as a "protocol designed to reduce the risk of relapse in the alcoholic through a process of education, self-exploration, and action planning that involves the alcoholic and those people significant in his life" (p. 90). They believe that RPP will only work if the patient believes he or she is an alcoholic and can no longer use alcohol. RPP works most effectively with patients who have been treated for alcoholism and failed to maintain long-term sobriety. Gorski and Miller state that RPP "should become an integral part of treatment for any alcoholic who has attempted previous sobriety and failed" (p. 91). RPP for relapsed alcoholics involves nine steps:

1. *Stabilization.* The alcoholic is stabilized in order to help stop alcohol use. This often requires detoxification.
2. *Assessment.* Presenting problems of the alcoholic, the current relapse dynamic, relapse history, stage or level of treatment, and the patient's personality style are all evaluated.
3. *Patient Education.* The relapsed alcoholic is provided with information on the recovery process, sobriety-based symptoms of alcoholism, factors complicating recovery, personality style contributing to relapse or recovery, the relapse dynamic and relapse warning signs, and the RPP process.
4. *Warning Sign Identification.* This involves reviewing relapse warning signs, selecting priority signs, constructing summary titles and descriptive statements of these warning signs, assigning accuracy ratings, experientially processing these signs, and clarifying and correcting warning signs.
5. *Review of the Recovery Program.* This step entails reviewing the sobriety plan, developing new aspects of the plan based on the relapse, structuring reinforcement for working the recovery plan, and monitoring the plan until it becomes habitual.

6. *Inventory Training.* A daily inventory to help determine if the person is in recovery or relapse is completed. This inventory is integrated into AA and counseling.
7. *Interruption of the Relapse Dynamic.* Problems that occur as a result of relapse warning signs are solved.
8. *Involvement of Significant Others.* Significant others (e.g., family, friends, AA sponsor) are identified who will form an intervention network to assist the alcoholic in recognizing relapse warning signs or in interrupting a relapse, should it occur.
9. *Follow-Up and Reinforcement.* RPP is integrated with other forms of treatment such as AA and family counseling.

As a result of difficulties encountered with families refusing to participate in treatment or participating in counterproductive ways, Gorski and Miller reformulated the RPP in 1983 to include the need for treatment of co-alcoholism in family members (Gorski & Miller, 1984b). A Family Relapse Prevention Planning model was developed, which comprises the nine-step process outlined above but also includes helping improve the communication skills of the family.

Psychoeducational Model

The psychoeducational model was developed in an inpatient treatment program for alcoholics and drug addicts (Daley, 1989a). It was designed by reviewing the literature on relapse and working with hundreds of relapsed clients. Although initially employed in large groups of patients (up to 40) in a 30-day residential program, the model has also been used with individual clients, small groups, and families, in residential and nonresidential treatment settings (e.g., outpatient counseling). This approach to relapse education is used with relapsed clients and those in treatment for the first time. A written workbook (Daley, 1986) with specific tasks is used by the client with a counselor, other recovering person, family member, or independently. This model is one part of a multimodal treatment program involving individual, group, and family therapy; patient education; and self-help groups. Specific relapse issues are reinforced or explored in depth in other aspects of the treatment program, including individual or group therapy.

The general goals of this model are to challenge common erroneous beliefs of relapse held by patients; reinforce the expectation that recovery is an ongoing process requiring active involvement of the addicted individual; provide information on a wide range of topics relevant to

likely to experience boredom, identify leisure activities that were given up as a result of the addiction, and begin to think about new, constructive leisure activities to pursue during recovery.

8. *Building a long-term sobriety plan.* This session reinforces the notion that recovery from an addiction is a long-term problem. The client must identify specific steps to maintain sobriety and acknowledge the changes in life-style to support this sobriety and the resources (counseling, self-help, etc.) required to achieve these changes. The importance of family involvement, when appropriate, is also emphasized.

Several days prior to completion of the program each client reviews his or her written sobriety plan with a staff member and small group of patients.

9. *What to do if a relapse occurs.* The importance of being prepared for the actual relapse is emphasized. Clients are assigned to task-oriented groups, each with the task of reviewing a common relapse situation and imagining they are actually in this situation. Clients are taught to identify thoughts, feelings, and behaviors following an initial lapse. Each group is asked to write a concrete relapse intervention plan.

The small group presents its relapse situation and plan to the entire client group. The main goals are to get clients to challenge the faulty notion that one alcohol- or drug-use episode always leads to a total loss of control. Clients are taught to view an initial lapse as a mistake, rather than a process of throwing away an entire period of recovery, and to understand how to make decisions after an initial lapse to prevent a full-blown relapse.

10. *Emergency sobriety card, daily relapse prevention inventory.* Clients learn the importance of devising an emergency sobriety card, which lists names and phone numbers of at least 5 to 10 people who can be relied on. Clients are taught to accept help in the recovery journey.

Addicted clients are also instructed to watch for relapse clues and high-risk factors. They are to ask two questions: (1) Were there any clues present indicating they were building up to alcohol/drug use, and (2) did they experience any high-risk situations during the day, which could trigger a relapse (if ignored)?

Verbal feedback and written evaluations from over 500 clients indicate that the relapse prevention groups and the relapse prevention workbook are preceived as beneficial. The groups and workbook provide clients useful information and coping strategies on relapse prevention and intervention.

Addict Aftercare: Recovery Training and Self-Help Model

The aftercare model was developed for opiate addicts to facilitate life-style change and to prevent relapse following treatment. The objectives of this model are to: (1) adapt treatment techniques used in Hong Kong with opiate addicts to American addicts, (2) further develop methods to prevent relapse by changing life-styles, and (3) evaluate the efficacy of a particular treatment approach using a classical experimental design (Zackon, McAuliffe, & Ch'ien, 1985).

This model views addiction as "not only a disease . . . but also a way of life within a distinct subculture. Recovery is not just the cessation of drug use; usually it also demands adjustment to a new way of life within the culture of the larger community" (p. 5). In order to adjust to a new way of living addicts need to have guidance, acquire new skills, and make new interpersonal contacts.

Specific aftercare training sessions were developed to meet the following challenges of recovery:

1. Handling drug cravings.
2. Developing a new social network and social skills to facilitate socializing in new ways.
3. Learning to adjust to drug-free activities and satisfaction.
4. Learning to cope with physical pain and stress without resorting to drug use.
5. Learning to initiate and sustain relationships in order to meet needs for interpersonal intimacy.
6. Learning to refuse drug-use offers.
7. Learning to respond to a "slip" (initial period of substance use) in order to prevent a full-blown relapse (pp. 5-6).

The addict aftercare model consists of four components: recovery training sessions, fellowship meetings, drug-free social and community activities, and networks of "senior" ex-addicts. Each of these components is reviewed below.

1. *Recovery training*(RT). Professionally led workshops focus on specific recovery topics. Twenty-three weekly RT group sessions are conducted, each with a format designed to facilitate the attainment of specific objectives. Written information is provided that requires participants to complete related tasks. The RT session attempts to utilize

real-life experiences of recovering addicts and current research on pertinent recovery issues.

Specific RT sessions were devised to complement each other; however, most can stand alone without reference to the others. Each RT session relates to one of several broad categories.

- Being Clean. These sessions deal with the most direct threats to abstinence and issues of drug use. Topics for RT sessions include readdiction and craving, dangerous situations, and coping with pain and prescription medication.
- Highs and Lows. Help is offered in these sessions with stressful events and the search for new pleasures common in the first year or two of abstinence. Specific RT sessions emphasize having good times without drugs and preparing for stressful situations.
- Social Relations. These sessions review social problems confronting most recovering addicts. Examples of topics include assessing one's social life, making a new friend, and relating to active drug users.
- Work and Growth. Issues are reviewed relating to performing certain roles in a straight world and how these affect recovery. Examples include presenting one's past to employers; handling on-the-job problems; and looking ahead at plans, goals, and dreams.
- Recovery Stories of Senior Ex-Addicts. These sessions expose group members to recovered ex-addicts who can provide information about issues in recovery and serve as role models (pp. 21-31).

2. *Fellowship meetings.* Weekly self-help group meetings are held that aim to meet common needs of addicts in a supportive environment. Group members discuss personal issues and plans, get help with problems or current crises, receive praise for gains, see how others are doing in their recoveries, and gain perspective from those who are doing well in recovery.

Fellowship meetings also stimulate new recreational interests and friendships among group members. Although meetings are informal, they follow general procedures. Selected examples include:

- Having a Standard Meeting Agenda. Meetings generally include brief reports from members on the past week, group business, discussion of personal issues, and social and recreational plans.
- Encouraging Socializing. Social gatherings are planned as adjuncts to other meetings.

• Supporting the "Doers." Members who follow through on plans and take healthy risks are acknowledged.

3. *Drug-free social and community activities*. This program component attempts to help recovering addicts develop new social and recreational activities. Opportunities are provided for members to plan and carry out a diversity of social and recreational activities in nondrug environments. An interesting norm developed from this model is the rule that alcohol use is not condoned by members at group social activities.

4. *Network of senior ex-addicts*. The addict aftercare model utilizes recovering addicts in the recovery training sessions, fellowship meetings, and social activities. Former addicts offer experience and guidance to others and provide models of success. The ex-addicts in this program are people who have a minimum of five years' "clean" experience without their primary drugs; present no current drug problems in any form from any substance (half reported light to moderate use of alcohol or marijuana); have learned methods of avoiding dangerous situations; have developed social networks, straight friendships and intimate interpersonal relationships; have healthy recreational interests; are gainfully employed; have a philosophy of life integrating new, positive values; have developed key activities or interests in their lives; and have accepted their past. Overall, the senior ex-addicts are viewed as well-adjusted people with normal life-styles.

A comparison of experimental groups of those who participated in the addict aftercare training model with control groups found that 32% of the experimental group was abstinent or rarely used illicit opiates (less than once per month) after one year, and 18% of the controls reported abstinence or rare use (p. 2).

CONCLUSIONS

Clinical experience and review of the literature suggest that relapse is best understood as a complex process resulting from an interaction of multiple variables. These variables include intrapsychic and biologic factors of the alcoholic or drug addict; social and cultural factors; attitudes, knowledge, and skills of professionals; treatment systems factors; and other system-related factors. Conceptual frameworks that rely on one set of variables to discuss relapse, particularly client variables, are incomplete. Addicted clients and families can be better prepared for the challenges of recovery if they are provided education and counseling on relapse prevention and relapse intervention. Because high relapse rates are well documented, special attention should focus on relapse intervention so that damage occurring from a relapse may be minimized.

Outcomes vary widely among individuals and their families undergoing relapse. Although some experience detrimental effects, others are able to learn from a relapse and improve efforts as a result.

In the past several years the literature on relapse prevention has grown and more workshops are being offered to professionals. As a result, more professionals and treatment programs are utilizing relapse prevention approaches. Addicted clients and their families are receiving better education and counseling. It remains a challenge for professionals to continue to provide effective treatment and to develop new and improved treatment approaches.

REFERENCES

Abbot, M., & Gregson, R. (1981). Cognitive dysfunction in the prediction of relapse in alcoholics. *Journal of Studies on Alcohol, 42,* 230-243.

Alcohol and Health. (1984). Fifth special report to the U. S. Congress. Rockville, MD: NIAAA.

Alcohol and Health. (1987). Sixth special report to the U. S. Congress. Rockville, MD: NIAAA.

Alcoholics Anonymous (3rd ed.). (1976). New York: AA World Services.

Allgulander, C., Borg, S., & Vikander, B. (1984). Four-to-six-year follow-up of 50 patients with primary dependence on sedative and hypnotic drugs. *American Journal of Psychiatry, 141*(12), 1580-1582.

Analysis of the 1980 survey of the membership of AA. (1984). New York: AA World Services.

Anderson, S. (1985). Early recovery for the chemically addicted co-dependent. *Focus on Family and Chemical Dependency.*

Annis, H. (1986). A relapse prevention model for treatment of alcoholics. In W. Miller & N. Heather (Eds.), *Treating addictive behaviors: Process of change.* (pp. 407-434) New York: Plenum.

Armor, D., Polich, J., & Stambul, H. (1978). *Alcoholism and treatment.* New York: John Wiley.

Baekeland, F. (1977). Evaluation of treatment methods in chronic alcoholism. In B. Kissin & H. Begleiter (Eds.), *Treatment and rehabilitation of the chronic alcoholic.* New York: Plenum.

Black, C., Bucky, S., & Wilder-Padilla, S. (1986). The interpersonal and emotional consequences of being an adult child of an alcoholic. *International Journal of the Addictions, 21*(2), 213-231.

Carroll, J., & Sobel, B. (1986). Integrating mental health personnel and practices into a therapeutic community. In G. DeLeon & J. Ziegenfugy, Jr. (Eds.), *Therapeutic communities for addictions: Readings in theory, research, and practice* (pp. 209-226). Chicago: Charles C Thomas.

Catalano, R., & Hawkins, J. (1985). Project skills: Preliminary results from a theoretically based aftercare experiment. *Progress in the development of cost-effective treatment for drug abusers,* Research Monograph no. 58, 157-181. Rockville, MD: NIDA.

Chalmers, D., & Wallace, J. (1985). Evaluation of patient progress. In N. Zimberg, J. Wallace, & S. Blume (Eds.), *Practical approaches to alcoholism psychotherapy* (2nd ed.) New York: Plenum.

Chaney, E., & O'Leary, M. (1978). Skill training with alcoholics. *Journal of Consulting and Clinical Psychology, 46*(5), 1092-1104.

Chaney, E., & Roszell, D. (1982). Relapse in opiate addicts: A behavioral analysis. *Addictive Behaviors, 7*(3), 291-297.

Cooney, N., Baker, L., Pomerleau, O., & Josephy, B. (1984). Salivation to drinking cues in alcohol abusers: Toward the validation of a physiological measure of craving. *Addictive Behaviors, 9*(1), 91-94.

Cooney, N., Gillespie, R., Baker, L., & Kaplan, R. (1987). Cognitive changes after alcohol cue exposure. *Journal of Consulting and Clinical Psychology, 55*(2), 150-155.

Costello, R. (1982). Evaluation of alcoholism treatment programs. In E. M. Pattison & E. Kaufman (Eds.), *Encyclopedic handbook of alcoholism* New York: Gardner.

Cronkite, R., Cummings, C., Marlatt, G., & Gordon, J. (1980). Relapse: Prevention and prediction. In W. Miller (Ed.), *Addictive behaviors: Treatment of alcoholism, drug abuse, smoking and obesity.* Elmsford, NY: Pergamon.

Cusack, S. (1984). *Women and relapse.* Center City, MN: Hazelden.

Daley, D. (1986). *Relapse prevention workbook for recovering alcoholics and drug dependent persons.* Holmes Beach, FL: Learning Publications.

Daley, D. (1987a). *Relapse: A guide to successful recovery.* Bradenton, FL: Human Services Institute.

Daley, D. (1987b). Relapse prevention with substance abusers: Clinical issues and myths. *Social Work, 45*(2), 38-42.

Daley, D. (1988a). *Relapse prevention: Treatment alternatives and counseling aids.* Bradenton, FL: Human Services Institute.

Daley, D. (1988b). *Surviving addiction: A guide for alcoholics, drug addicts and their families.* New York: Gardner.

Daley, D. (1989a). A psychoeducational approach to relapse prevention. *Journal of Chemical Dependency Treatment, 2*(2), 105-124.

Daley, D. (Ed.). (1989b). *Relapse: Conceptual, research and clinical perspectives.* New York: Haworth.

Daley, D. (1990). *Surviving addiction workbook.* Holmes Beach, FL: Learning Publications.

Daley, D., & Moss, H. (1987). Preventing and limiting relapse. *NIDA Notes, 2*(3), 10-11.

Daley, D., Moss, H., & Campbell, F. (1987). *Dual disorders: Counseling clients with chemical dependency and mental illness.* Center City, MN: Hazelden.

Donovan, D., & Chaney, E. (1985). Alcoholic relapse prevention and intervention: Models and methods. In G. A. Marlatt & J. Gordon (Eds.), *Relapse prevention: Maintenance strategies in the treatment of addictive behaviors* (pp. 251-416). New York: Guilford.

Emrick, C. (1974). A review of psychologically oriented treatment of alcoholism, I: The use and interrelationship of outcome criteria and drinking behavior following treatment. *Quarterly Journal of Studies on Alcohol, 36* 88-108.

Emrick, C. (1982). Evaluation of alcoholism therapy methods. In E. M. Pattison & E. Kaufman (Eds.), *Encyclopedic handbook of alcoholism* (1152-1169). New York: Gardner.

Foy, D., Miller, P., Eisler, R., & O'Toole, D. (1976). Social skills training to teach alcoholics to refuse drinks effectively. *Journal of Studies on Alcohol, 37* 1340-1345.

Goldstein, M., Surber, M., & Wilner, D. (1984). Outcome evaluations in substance abuse: A comparison of alcoholism, drug abuse, and other mental health interventions. *International Journal of the Addictions, 19*(5), 479-502.

Gorski, T., & Miller, M. (1982). *Counseling for relapse prevention.* Independence, MI: Independence Press.

Gorski, T., & Miller, M. (1984a) Relapse—the family's involvement: Part II—co-alcoholism factors. In *Alcoholism: A family matter* (pp. 27-32). Hollywood, FL: Health Communications.

Gorski, T., & Miller, M. (1984b). Relapse—the family's involvement: Part III—protocol for long term recovery. In *Alcoholism: A family matter* (pp. 33-39). Hollywood, FL: Health Communications.

Gorski, T., & Miller, M. (1986). *Staying sober: A guide to preventing relapse.* Independence, MI: Independence Press.

Gorski, T., & Miller, M. (1988). *Staying sober workbook.* Independence, MI: Independence Press.

Hatsukami, D., Pickens, R., & Svikis, D. (1981). Post-treatment depressive symptoms and relapse to drug use in different age groups of an alcohol and other drug abuse population. *Drug and Alcohol Dependence, 8*(4), 271-277.

Helzer, J., & Pryzbeck, T. (1988). The co-occurrence of alcoholism with other psychiatric disorders in the general population and its impact on treatment. *Journal of Studies on Alcohol, 49*(3), 219-224.

Hesselbrock, M., Meyer, R., & Keener, J. (1985). Psychopathology in hospitalized alcoholics. *Archives of General Psychiatry, 42,* 1050-1055.

Hindin, T. (1984). Eating right: Lowering the risk, preventing alcoholic relapse. *Focus on Family and Chemical Dependency, 7*(4), 17-19.

Hoffman, N., & Harrison, P. (1986). *CATOR 1986 report: Findings two years after treatment.* St. Paul, MN: Ramsey Clinic.

Hunt, W., Barnett, L., & Branch, L. (1971). Relapse rates in addiction programs. *Journal of Clinical Psychology, 27,* 455-456.

Jelinek, J. M., & Williams, T. (1984). Post-traumatic stress disorder and substance abuse in Vietnam combat veterans: Treatment problems, strategies and recommendations. *Journal of Substance Abuse Treatment, 1,* 87-97.

Jones, S., & Lanyon, R. (1981). Relationship between adaptive skills and outcome in alcoholism treatment. *Journal of Studies on Alcohol, 42,* 521-525.

Kuritz, E. (1982). *Shame and guilt.* Center City, MN: Hazelden.

Laundergan, J. (1982). *Easy does it: Alcoholism treatment outcomes, Hazelden and the Minnesota model.* Center City, MN: Hazelden.

Litman, G., Stapleton, J., Oppenheim, A., Peleg, M., & Jackson, P. (1983). Situations related to alcoholism relapse. *British Journal of Addictions, 78,* 381-389.

Living sober: Some methods AA members have used for not drinking. (1975). New York: AA World Services.

Ludwig, A., & Wikler, A. (1974). Craving and relapse to drink. *Quarterly Journal of Studies on Alcohol, 35,* 108-130.

Ludwig, A., Wikler, A., & Stark, L. (1974). The first drink: Psychobiological aspects of craving. *Archives of General Psychiatry, 30,* 539-547.

Marlatt, G. A. (1985a). Relapse prevention: Theoretical rationale and overview of the model. In G. A. Marlatt & J. Gordon (Eds.), *Relapse prevention: A self-control strategy for the maintenance of behavior change* (pp. 3-70).

Marlatt, G. A. (1985b) Cognitive assessment and intervention procedures for relapse prevention. In G. A. Marlatt & J. Gordon (Eds.), *Relapse prevention: A self-control strategy for the maintenance of behavior change* (pp. 201-279).

Marlatt, G. A. (1985c). Lifestyle modification. In G. A. Marlatt & J. Gordon (Eds.), *Relapse prevention: A self-control strategy for the maintenance of behavior change* (pp. 280-350).

Marlatt, G. A. (1985d). Cognitive factors in the relapse process. In G. A. Marlatt & J. Gordon (Eds.), *Relapse prevention: A self-control strategy for the maintenance of behavior change* (pp. 128-200).

Marlatt, G. A. (1985e). Situational determinance of relapse and skill-training interventions. In G. A. Marlatt & J. Gordon (Eds.), *Relapse prevention: A self-control strategy for the maintenance of behavior change* (pp. 71-127).

Marlatt, G. A. & Gordon, J. (Eds.). (1985). *Relapse prevention: A self-control strategy for the maintenance of behavior change.* New York: Guilford.

McLellan, A., Luborsky, L., Woody, G., O'Brien, C., & Druley, K. (1983). Predicting response to alcohol and drug abuse treatments: Role of psychiatric severity. *Archives of General Psychiatry,* 40, 620-625.

Meyer, R. (Ed.). (1986). *Psychopathology and addictive disorders.* New York: Guilford.

Miller, W., & Hester, R. (1980). Treating the problem drinker: Modern approaches. In *The addictive behaviors: Treatment of alcoholism, drug abuse, smoking and obesity.* Elmsford, NY: Pergamon.

Narcotics Anonymous. (1983). Van Nuys, CA: NA World Services.

National Institute on Drug Abuse. (1981a). *Comparative effectiveness of drug abuse treatment modalities.* S. Sells, R. Demaree, & C. Hornick (Eds.), DHHS Pub. No. (ADM) 81-1067. Rockville, MD: Author.

National Institute on Drug Abuse. (1981b). *Effectiveness of drug abuse treatment programs.* DHHS Pub. No. (ADM) 81-1143. Rockville, MD: Author.

O'Leary, M., Donovan, D., Chaney, E., & Walker, R. (1979). Cognitive impairment and treatment outcome with alcoholics: Preliminary findings. *Journal of Clinical Psychiatry, 40,* 397-398.

Pickens, R., Hatsukami, D., Spicer, J., & Svikis, D. (1985). Relapse by alcohol abusers. *Alcoholism: Clinical and Experimental Research, 9*(3), 244-247.

Polich, J., Armort, D., & Braiker, H. (1981). *The course of alcoholism: Four years after treatment.* New York: John Wiley.

Pomerleau, O., Fertig, J., Baker, L., & Cooney, N. (1983). Reactivity to alcohol cues in alcoholics and non-alcoholics: Implications for a stimulus control analysis of drinking. *Addictive Behaviors, 8,* 1-10.

Rubinstein, L., Campbell, F., & Daley, D. (in press). Four perspectives on dual disorders. *Journal of Chemical Dependency Treatment, 3*(2).

Saxe, L., Dougherty, D., Esty, J., & Fine, M. (1983). *The effectiveness and costs of alcoholism treatment.* Health Technology Case Study 22. Washington, DC: Office of Technology Assessment.

Schnitt, J., & Nocks, J. (1984). Alcoholism treatment of Vietnam veterans with post-traumatic stress disorder. *Journal of Substance Abuse Treatment, 1*, 179-189.

Schuckit, M., Zisook, S., & Mortola, J. (1985). Clinical implications of DSM-III diagnoses of alcohol abuse and alcohol dependence. *American Journal of Psychiatry, 142* 1403-1408.

Shiffman, S. (1982). Relapse following smoking cessation: A situational analysis. *Journal of Consulting and Clinical Psychology, 50,* 71-86.

Shiffman, S., Read, L., Maltese, J., Rapkin, D., & Jarvite, M. (1985). Preventing relapse in ex-smokers: A self-management approach. In G. A. Marlatt & J. Gordon (Eds.), *Relapse prevention* (pp. 472-520). New York: Guilford.

Solberg, R. (1978). *The dry drunk.* Center City, MN: Hazelden.

Solberg, R. (1982). *The dry drunk revisited.* Center City, MN: Hazelden.

Stouder, L. (1984). Post-addiction nutrition: Diet, vitamins, mineral supplements and bio-individuality. *Focus on Family and Chemical Dependency, 7*(4), 19-21.

Talbot, D. (1977). *Spousaholics.* [Videotape]. Georgia: Fortune.

Twerski, A. (1984). *Self-discovery in recovery.* Center City, MN: Hazelden.

Van Kampen, M., Watson, C., Tilleskjor, C., Kusala, T., Vassar, P. (1986). The definition of posttraumatic stress disorder in alcoholic Vietnam veterans. *The Journal of Nervous and Mental Disease, 174*(3), 137-144.

Wallace, J. (1985). *Alcoholism: New light on the disease.* Newport, RI: Edgehill.

White, W. (1978). *Relapse as a phenomenon of staff burn out among recovering substance abusers.* Rockville, MD: HCS.

Zackon, F. (1989). Relapse and "re-joyment": Observations and reflections. *Journal of Chemical Dependency Treatment, 2*(2), 81-104.

Zackon, F., McAuliffe, W., & Ch'ien, J. (1985). *Addict aftercare: Recovery training and self-help.* DHHS Pub. No. (ADM)85-1341. Rockville, MD: NIDA.

Chapter 7

EFFECTS OF ADDICTION ON THE FAMILY

RUTH ANN SEILHAMER

Over the past 100 years, there have been several shifts in popular attitudes toward the families of alcoholics. In the early twentieth century, alcoholism was viewed primarily as a moral shortcoming, and the alcoholic was considered a willful participant in his or her "sinfulness." The predominant stereotype of the alcoholic also depicted him or her as a loner with few social ties. When spouses and children were considered, they were usually perceived as pitiful victims entrapped in a situation over which they had little influence. With the advances of medical science, alcoholism was reconceptualized as a disease, and, in this context, the alcoholic was considered as much a victim as other family members. The "disease model" persists today with the diagnosis of alcoholism relying heavily on physiological criteria, such as tolerance to consume increasing amounts of alcohol and the occurrence of withdrawal effects when drinking ceases.

A repercussion of the "disease model" or "addiction model" was that alcoholism continued to be defined and studied as an individual problem. As a result, family approaches were minimized; this de-emphasis was furthered by clinicians who considered the addiction process so complicated that it could only be dealt with on an individual basis. Reluctance to involve families in the treatment process was also based on the concern that this would intensify the drinker's guilt feelings (Bosma, 1972; Whitfield, 1981). As a result, separate literature and treatment paradigms evolved that focused on the alcoholic *or* the spouse *or* the children. By comparison, there was little information on how alcohol abuse affected the family as a unit. Moreover, the existing information on families of alcoholics was criticized for a preponderance of impressionistic reports and a lack of information based on programmatic studies using rigorous scientific methods.

Within the past 15 years, however, there has been an increasing amount of research, as well as treatment and prevention efforts, based on a family systems approach to alcoholism. As clinicians began to note that patients frequently relapsed when they returned to their family settings, attention turned to the role of the family in the onset and perpetuation of the disordered behavior. In this context, alcoholism shifted from being perceived as an individual problem, and researchers and clinicians moved from discussing the "family of the alcoholic" to describing the "alcoholic family." No longer was the spotlight on the alcohol-abusing family member; rather, the focus was on the family as a unit that consisted of members in interdependent relationships. Within this framework, the alcoholic family was studied in several ways: (1) in terms of the way it changed and developed across the family life span, (2) in terms of the bidirectional effects of family interactional behaviors and problem drinking, and (3) in reference to the "supporting roles" of family members, who became labeled as "enablers," "codependents," or "coalcoholics."

This chapter will first summarize approaches that focus on individual members, namely, the spouse and the children of the alcoholics. Second, the literature dealing with the family as a system will be discussed in light of several theoretical models that have been proposed. Last, various methods of family assessment will be discussed.

IMPACT ON SPOUSES

Marital discord has been reported so consistently by alcoholics and their spouses that questions about marital problems are usually included in screening procedures and diagnostic criteria for substance abuse. Common complaints are poor communication, a lack of trust, financial irresponsibility, role reversals, sexual problems, conflict, and aggressive behavior. Given these reports, it is not surprising that the marriages of alcoholics are characterized by high rates of divorce and separation. Despite reports about the negative impact of abusive drinking upon marital relationships, the majority of marital studies have focused on the spouse of the alcoholic rather than the relationship per se. Moreover, wives of male alcoholics have received the most attention; relatively little is known about husbands of female alcoholics.

"Disturbed Personality" Versus "Stress" Theories

There have been two major hypotheses about wives of alcoholics. The earlier hypothesis developed from clinical impressions of therapists working within a psychodynamic framework. Often called the "disturbed personality" hypothesis, this proposition suggested that a woman of a particular personality type selected an alcoholic (or potential alcoholic) as a mate to satisfy her own unconscious needs. Furthermore, if her spouse displayed any remission of his alcoholism, the wife supposedly would decompensate or manifest psychiatric symptoms of depression, anxiety, or somatic disorders (Kalashian, 1959; Macdonald, 1958). Also, this hypothesis inferred that the wife would sabotage any improvement in her husband's drinking problem.

As more became known about the effects of living in a stressful environment, the wife of the alcoholic was recast as a respondent to the cumulative crises in her life situation. Labeled "stress theories," this redefinition of alcoholics' wives did not receive much attention until the mid-1950s with Jackson's (1954) description of the adjustment of the family to the problem drinking of the husband/father. On the basis of a three-year study of accounts of Al-Anon wives, Jackson proposed a seven-stage process of disorganization and reorganization as the family adapted to living with an alcoholic. Those stages were:

1. *Attempts to avoid and deny the problem:* During this stage the husband and wife minimize or ignore the increasingly frequent drinking episodes.
2. *Attempts to eliminate the problem:* This stage is marked by social withdrawal and isolation from friends, community, and extended family. Attempts to curb the husband's drinking fail.
3. *Family disorganization:* During this phase hostility and resentment erupt. Children, confused and often torn in loyalties, exhibit behavioral problems. The husband is often arrested; family life becomes more chaotic; the wife avoids sexual contact with the husband.
4. *Attempts to reorganize:* The wife gradually assumes control of the family finances and discipline of the children, and she eases her husband out of his family role. There is somewhat more stability, but less security as finances dwindle and the father often exhibits bizarre or violent behavior.

5. *Efforts to escape the problem:* This stage is marked by separation and even divorce, depending on how much independence the wife has achieved, as well as emotional distance from her husband.
6. *Reorganization of part of the family:* The wife and children reorganize without the father.
7. *Recovery and reorganization with the father:* This stage is dependent on the father's sobriety, and the initial period of reconciliation is marked by apprehension of a resumption of drinking and hesitancy of the wife to relinquish control of family administration.

Although written over 35 years ago, Jackson's representation of alcoholic families continues to be cited as relevant for today's families that have a substance-abusing member. Most importantly, Jackson redefined the wife's behavior as a response to real-life stresses, rather than the result of an aberrant personality.

Both "disturbed personality" theories and "stress" theories propose that wives of alcoholics are psychologically distressed. This profile arose primarily from clinical impressions of wives who either initiated help-seeking or came to the attention of professionals because of their spouses' involvement in health or judicial systems. Concerns about the typicality of these samples prompted researchers to assess wives of alcoholics in more systematic ways. Generally, these studies, utilizing personality inventories, found that wives' responses fell within normal limits, with no clearly distinguishable response patterns that typified wives of alcoholics (Corder, Hendricks, & Corder, 1964; Kogan, Fordyce, & Jackson, 1963; Paolino, McCrady, Diamond, & Longabaugh, 1976; Rae & Forbes, 1966; Tarter, 1976). Also, studies that compared wives whose husbands were active or relapsed drinkers with wives whose husbands maintained sobriety found that wives of recovered alcoholics exhibited less psychological and somatic symptoms (Bailey, Haberman, & Alksne, 1962; Kogan & Jackson, 1965: Moos, Finney, & Gamble, 1982). In a rare example of a longitudinal study, Paolino, McCrady, and Kogan (1978) assessed wives at six weeks and at six months after their husbands were discharged from hospitalization and found that reports of anxiety and depression significantly decreased over time. In summary, the majority of empirical studies have reported that wives' psychological distress is alleviated as their husbands recover from alcohol abuse.

How Do Wives Cope?

As it became more generally accepted that wives' psychological complaints resulted from their difficult life situations, attention turned to understanding how these women coped. Several studies found that wives used a variety of coping styles that often increased in intensity and frequency as their spouses' drinking problems progressed.

Orford and Guthie (1976) analyzed the responses of 80 wives to questions about coping behavior and found that wives coped using both defensive and direct strategies. Defensive coping involved denying or ignoring the problem, or caretaking behaviors such as seeking to make the husband comfortable, nursing him during hangovers, avoiding conflicts, or retrieving him from bars or police detention. Direct strategies involved assuming financial responsibilities, keeping children out of the husband's way, and taking over tasks usually performed by the husband. Other direct styles included the "acting out"response, which involved efforts to berate or ridicule the husband or to make him jealous, or even getting intoxicated herself. The "attack" style included locking him out of the house, calling police, or seeking separation or divorce. Other studies have described similar categorizations of coping behaviors that generally fell into confrontational or avoidant response patterns.

Wiseman (1980) described the coping strategies of wives as a sort of quasi-therapy. Drawing on interviews with 76 wives of alcoholics, Wiseman cataloged the methods that wives used to deal with "their husband's problem drinking in the privacy of their homes when they first became aware that he may be an alcoholic" (p. 542). This "home treatment" involved an aggregate of trial-and-error efforts. Initially believing that their spouses' drinking could be controlled voluntarily, wives typically used direct approaches first. Starting with "logical persuasion," wives made casual suggestions for more moderate drinking, which then escalated to "case-making"—arguments that presented the adverse effects of continued drinking. Frustrated by the failure of these efforts, wives became increasingly critical and nagging, behaviors that then converted to "emotional pleading and threats to leave."

When these direct approaches failed, wives resorted to indirect moves, "strategies which they hoped would help the husband cut down on his drinking without his being aware of the fact that his wife was trying to change his behavior" (p. 545). According to Wiseman, this switch from direct to indirect strategies occurred when the wife began to view her spouse's drinking as compulsive and involuntary. "Acting normal" was an initial indirect approach that other writers have described as the "making-husband-comfortable" or "protection" approach. Although intended to reduce stress, this method led to a pretense of normalcy and "stilted" interactions.

Wiseman described the next endeavor, the "taking over" strategy, as a further effort to reduce demands on the alcoholic. This strategy involved manipulative behaviors, such as the selection of temporary companions, managing available finances, controlling the liquor supply, and creating tasks to divert the spouse from drinking to constructive activity (the "industrial therapy" approach). Repeated failure at these and other indirect approaches, such as drinking along with her spouse or withholding sex, finally led to a "hands-off" approach, a disengagement that signaled acceptance of her inability to stem her husband's alcoholic degeneration.

One of the hallmarks of alcoholic marriages is what Orford, Guthrie, Nicholls, Oppenheimer, Egert, and Hensman (1975) described as "withdrawal or disengagement from the marital bond" (p. 1265). Jackson's seven stages of adjustment, described above, tell how families splinter, with wives and children reorganizing as a group that is disengaged from husband. An example of disengagement can be found in this account given by the wife of an alcoholic: "He is cut off from the family and refuses to have anything to do with us. . . . We keep our feelings to ourselves, and I try to stay out of his way. . . . I am more content without him."

Another wife described her disengagement this way: "My husband ignores me, and I totally steer clear of him and voice no opinion, so we don't argue. . . . We pretend each other doesn't exist." And another wife said: "My children and I are a family. Their father has made himself obsolete. . . . He no longer associates with the family. . . . There is very little communication. My children and I participate in activities alone with each other. My daughter wants me to divorce, and my son is now beginning to say the same thing."

Divorce or separation may be viewed as an ultimate "disengagement," and the high rate of marital dissolution among alcoholics indicates that it is a frequent occurrence (Nace, 1982; Paolino & McCrady, 1977). For some wives, however, this may not be a feasible alternative. Wiseman (1975), in a report on 75 alcoholics' wives in Finland (where social factors deter divorce or separation), described how some wives achieved independence that was both tangible and psychological. Independence, which is conceptually analogous to "disengagement," was defined as: (1) the development of skills and/or a career, (2) spatial and temporal independence, where spouses arrange schedules and residential space to allow minimal contact, (3) the development of separate friends and social spheres, and (4) disregard for the husband in the making and execution of plans. Wiseman suggested that marriages in which the wife has attained independence may face greater adjustment difficulties when the husband attempts sobriety.

Other studies have also noted that successful recovery is associated with how well the couple was able to maintain some degree of cohesiveness and communication. For example, Schaffer and Tyler (1979) reported that a critical variable in the outcome of alcoholism recovery is the "safety of the atmosphere" between husband and wife. If the wife was able to convey her feelings of frustration to her spouse in a way that he perceived as nonthreatening, attempts at sobriety were more successful. Orford, Oppenheimer, Egert, Hensman, and Guthrie (1976) compared 28 "good outcome" with 29 "bad outcome" cases based upon husband-and-wife reports of affectional exchanges, perceptions of spouse, husband participation in family tasks, and pooled opinions about the future of the marriage. Generally, high levels of cohesion contributed to better recovery outcomes. Similarly, in a comparison of family functioning in relapsed alcoholics, recovered alcoholics, and community controls, Moos and Moos (1984) found that relapsed alcoholics' families were characterized by less cohesion and expressiveness as measured by the Family Environment Scale.

These reports and observations suggest that a major task facing clinicians who are working with married alcoholics attempting recovery is the "re-engagement" of both spouses in their relationship. Improving communications, realigning family roles and responsibilities, and creating an atmosphere of optimism are vital to preserving the marriage and increasing the likelihood of continued abstinence.

Conclusion

The major problem with the literature on spouses of alcoholics is that much information is based on small, biased samples, most often women in clinical settings or support groups such as Al-Anon; non-help-seeking wives are largely unrepresented. Also, assessments of wives are often obtained at times of acute stress, such as at the hospital admission of their alcoholic spouses or involvement with police or the courts. Additionally, there is need for better evaluation of other ongoing stressors, such as poverty, unemployment, critical life events, and family violence. Also, the majority is based on interviews or questionnaires, and inaccuracies caused by difficulty in recall or discomfort with disclosure limit the interpretability of results. Furthermore, studies fail to specify treatment variables (type, duration, number of contacts, spouse involvement) that may have accounted for variation in coping styles among wives or individual changes in coping strategies over time.

Although there is some consistency among writers in their descriptions of coping styles, clinicians must guard against generalizations based on these reports. The responses likely to be exhibited by wives with different personality characteristics at various stages of their husbands' drinking have not been well established by systematic research studies. However, the literature suggests that marriages in which wives maintain involvement with their spouses, as opposed to marriages in which wives "disengage," are likely to have better outcomes. Also, seeking professional help early in the course of their mate's substance abuse would help prevent further frustration and disintegration of the marital relationship.

IMPACT ON CHILDREN

The deluge of reports on children of alcoholics during the past 10 to 15 years gives the impression that these children are a recently discovered cause for concern. Actually, interest in children of alcoholics extends to early Greek and Hebrew writings that warn against drinking during conception and pregnancy. The moral leaders of temperance movements in England and the United States during the 1700s and 1800s expounded upon these early religious proscriptions and bolstered their arguments with physicians' observations of the mental and physical deficiencies of the children whose parents consumed alcohol (Warner & Rosett, 1975).

In the past century, research and clinical attention to children of alcoholics has been impeded by a number of factors, including a concentration on the more obvious problems of the alcoholic parent, the social stigma attached to alcoholism, and social sanctions about family privacy. The recent renewal of interest in these children comes after the prodding of several writers in the 1960s and 1970s who described them as "forgotten," "neglected," and "hidden" (Bosma, 1972; Cork, 1969; Sloboda, 1974).

Similar to the literature about the spouses of alcoholics, reports about children of alcoholics have been problem oriented, focusing on a wide variety of biological, psychological, and social difficulties. Additionally, much of the literature is based on descriptive accounts, and research reports are characterized by limitations in theory and methods. As with spouses, much of the available information about children is based on those involved with mental health or judicial systems. Some writers have challenged popular assumptions that children of alcoholics are impaired, stressing the wide variability among offspring of alcoholics. Some of these children have been labeled "invulnerables" or "superkids" because of their high level of functioning (el-Guebaly & Offord, 1980). Population estimates that run as high as 29 million children of alcoholics in the United States would also suggest considerable variability among offspring (Woodside, 1988). Nevertheless, there is a general consensus that children of alcoholics are more likely to experience a host of psychosocial difficulties, as well as an increased risk for adult mental health problems, such as depression, substance abuse, and antisocial behavior. The eventual outcome for any individual child of an alcoholic, however, is determined by a complex interplay of many factors.

Generally, the literature on children of alcoholics falls into two main categories: (1) that which describes the effects, direct and indirect, of parental drinking upon the child, and (2) that which discusses "buffering" influences that temper the impact of parental drinking upon a child's adjustment.

Impact of Parental Drinking

Seilhamer and Jacob (1990) discuss three major effects of parental alcohol abuse upon offspring. First, there are the effects attributable to the ingestion of ethanol (the chemical name for pure alcohol found in beer, wine, and liquor). Ethanol changes the way in which an individual thinks, feels, and behaves. The following comments were made by children of alcoholics about their ethanol-intoxicated fathers:

He acts strange.
He is out of it.

He gets mad and . . . hits the walls.
He fights with the family.
If I move, I get yelled at.

Mood changes, memory "blackouts," and aggressive behaviors such as these often occur during drunkenness and impair the parent's ability to provide a consistent, dependable relationship. Furthermore, the withdrawal and self-centeredness of the alcoholic during drinking bouts renders him or her unavailable and unable to provide emotional support to offspring. As the alcoholic moves from intoxicated to sober states, the child must adapt different response patterns to the unpredictable moods and behaviors of the drinking parent. One mother gave these observations of the father-child interactions in her family: "He yells a lot of the time at them; other times he lets them get away with things he punishes another time. . . . My children never know how to act toward him." Such "chameleon" behavior likely leads to the difficulty, often described as characteristic of adult children of alcoholics, in identifying and labeling their own emotional states. That is, these children become so adept at responding according to how they think others want them to be that they ignore or repress their own feelings.

In addition to the immediate impact of intoxication, the physiological effects of long-term drinking "aggravate a host of medical problems, which in turn may compound financial problems, create absences due to hospitalization, and lead to chronic illnesses that further hamper parenting functions" (Seilhamer & Jacob, 1990, p. 176).

The second major effect of abusive drinking is the stress upon the family caused by financial hardship, marital conflict, social isolation, and changes in family roles, routines, and interactions. There is a broad literature that sympathetically describes the chaotic home situation of children of alcoholics. Role instability and a lack of regularity are cited as common phenomena. According to these reports, the child's need to structure his or her environment in a consistent framework is frustrated when the nonalcoholic parent, the child, or a sibling assumes the role responsibilities of the alcoholic. Also, when the home environment fails to provide safety and security in the form of rules, discipline, and regular family schedules, children do not develop adequate confidence and an internal sense of control. Prewitt, Spence, and Chaknis (1981) suggest that as a result of having a sense of no control over their environment, children of alcoholics are more likely than children of nonalcoholics to attribute effective action or success to external factors rather than to personal competency.

Social isolation is another common stressor in descriptions of children of alcoholics. Feelings of loyalty bent on maintaining the family "secret," and feelings of stigmatization, lead these children to withdraw from peer relationships. Additionally, the family retreats from contact with extended family and community, and children are thus further deprived of sources of support. These responses were given by children of alcoholics who were asked how their father's drinking affected relationships outside the family:

> It is embarrassing if anyone finds out.
> Our family tries to keep outsiders out.
> My father doesn't like other people around the house.
> We have no friends who visit us.

The third main effect of abusive drinking is that it provides a poor example of how to cope with one's problems. To the extent that parents use alcohol to relieve tension, regulate the expression of emotions, or avoid issues, drinking becomes a model for problem solving. Although other social influences also affect the acquisition of drinking behavior, the family provides the earliest and most salient information about acceptable drinking practices.

In summary, abusive drinking, either by chemically altering the moods, thought processes, and behavior of the drinker, or by generating multiple family stressors, seriously affects the provision of adequate parenting. In addition to creating this void, excessive consumption provides a poor model of coping behavior. These effects "interact to produce a family environment characterized by varying degrees of deficiencies in organization, cohesiveness, predictability, discipline, emotional sustenance, and training in basic life skills" (Seilhamer & Jacob, 1990, p. 177).

Fetal Alcohol Syndrome (FAS)

Children of alcoholics usually attain this distinction on the basis of their father's or mother's current drinking. When their impairments are described in research or clinically oriented reports, there is seldom mention of whether a critical confounding risk factor was considered: the risks associated with maternal drinking during pregnancy. The biological effects of maternal drinking during pregnancy have been called "fetal alcohol syndrome" (FAS), a condition characterized by physical abnormalities and mental impairments including pre- and postnatal growth retardation, neurological deficits, and facial anomalies. Some newborns of drinking mothers may exhibit only partial expression of FAS; in some cases, developmental delays may not be evident until the child is one to two years old or until learning difficulties emerge at school age.

The research findings about FAS must be tempered by several criticisms, namely: retrospective reports of consumption; inconsistent diagnostic criteria; and a lack of control of interacting influences such as other drug use, nutritional deficits, and emotional stress. A full discussion of FAS can be found in several reviews (Ernhart, Wolf, & Linn, 1985; Rosett & Weiner, 1982; Steinhauser, Nester, & Spohr, 1982). Fetal alcohol syndrome is mentioned here to alert clinicians that a complete assessment of dysfunctional children should consider any possible effects of maternal drinking during pregnancy.

Buffering Influences

The overriding emphasis on the negative aspects of life with an alcoholic has generated an impression that their children are destined to have serious adjustment problems. This assumption has been challenged by several studies that reported on the adequate to superior functioning of many children (Clair & Genest, 1987; Jacob & Leonard, 1986; Werner, 1986). The following profiles of three adolescent children of alcoholics are based on questionnaire and interview data gathered from father, mother, and the child. These examples show the variability that exists among these children:

John is 13 years old, the youngest of three children. He reports a variety of frequent somatic complaints such as headaches, stomachaches, and "feeling tired." His parents describe him as a "quiet, moody kid," a description that coincides with his self-report as an unhappy, nervous, and tense individual who worries a lot and "can't get my mind off family problems."

David is a 14-year-old with serious behavior problems. He acts aggressively toward his three younger siblings, is disobedient at home and at school, and makes poor grades. He is already abusing alcohol; he reported frequently sharing a bottle of wine or six-pack of beer with "some older kids." His scores on a measure of self-concept indicate a low level of self-esteem. He also has a history of deliberate self-inflicted injuries.

Susan is a 14-year-old "only child" with an outstanding academic performance, including winning an exhibition in a state science fair. Although she is involved in many social activities, Susan complains of feeling lonely. Her mother describes her as an "ideal child," although "somewhat competitive and perfectionistic."

Although factors that distinguish those children who fare poorly from those who fare well are not clearly understood, several influences have been proposed as moderators, or "buffers," of child outcome. Some of those influences are related to the child's personal characteristics, or what have been called "constitutional moderators" (Seilhamer & Jacob, 1990). These include the child's sex, age, intellectual level, temperament, and genetic risk. For example, the effects of parental substance abuse may vary with the age of the child when problem drinking first occurred. A child born into a family system already adapted to abusive consumption may perceive his or her parent's drinking as "normal" behavior. On the other hand, if parental alcohol abuse began abruptly during a child's adolescence—essentially sending a shock wave through the family—that child may have different reactions. Age differences are not well investigated, but clinicians need to be aware that children of alcoholics may have very different attitudes and responses, depending upon their developmental stage when the substance abuse emerged in the family.

Other factors are environmentally related and include family variables as well as characteristics of the larger social network. Peer influences, cultural attitudes, and supportive resources found in community, educational, or religious institutions are examples of environmental moderators that can buffer the effects of a negative home environment.

Heritability Risk

Although the overall psychosocial adjustment of children of alcoholics has been a topic of concern, most attention has been given to their increased risk for developing a substance abuse problem themselves. Both clinical observations and research studies have clearly established that alcoholism runs in families. However, as Goodwin (1976) pointed out, speaking Chinese and voting Republican also runs in families, but that does not mean that these behaviors are determined by one's genes. The transmission of alcoholism from one generation to another may be attributable to a genetic risk or to social influences, or both.

Nevertheless, many studies have offered compelling evidence for a genetic influence in the development of alcoholism. Among such studies are those that report a higher concordance for alcoholism in identical twins (who share 100% of the same genes) than in fraternal twins (who share 50% of the same genes). Other studies have found that compared to adopted children whose biological parents were not alcoholics, adopted children whose biological parents were alcoholics have a higher risk of alcoholism. Also, other researchers claim that the variation in rates of alcoholism among different ethnic groups supports a genetic hypothesis.

Genetic studies, however, are not completely explanatory; they do not clarify why alcoholism is not found in both members of 40% to 50% of identical-twin pairs with an alcoholic member. Also, the majority of alcoholics have no parental history of alcoholism, and most children of alcoholics do not develop a substance-abuse problem. Obviously, a genetic risk is not the sole determinant of whether one develops alcoholism. There are many interacting, nongenetic influences that serve to encourage or discourage the development of substance abuse in vulnerable offspring.

An example of a social influence in the heritability of alcoholism comes from studies of family rituals by Wolin and Bennett and their colleagues (Wolin, Bennett, & Noonan, 1979; Wolin, Bennett, Noonan, & Teitelbaum, 1980). Family rituals are the ways that a family conducts day-to-day activities (such as meals), the way it marks transitional events (births, deaths, graduations, marriages), and celebrates special occasions (birthdays, holidays). These researchers found that if a family maintained its rituals despite a parent's alcoholism, the children were less likely to develop problem drinking in adulthood. On the other hand, if a parent's abusive drinking disrupted the observance of a family's rituals, the children had an increased risk for alcohol problems.

Conclusion

Inheriting a genetic vulnerability for alcoholism or exposure to maternal drinking *in utero* are risk factors that are fixed early in a child's development. The impact of social exposure to drinking, however, can be quite variable. The age of the child when parental drinking began, the behavior of the parent when intoxicated, the degree to which family life is disrupted, and the psychological state of the nonalcoholic parent are examples of influences that can moderate whatever genetic risk (if any) the child may have inherited. Given the wide diversity of family and social factors that may buffer or intensify the maladjustment of offspring, it is not surprising that children of alcoholics are a diverse group.

Some writers emphasize the resiliency of these children and refute claims that they are irreparably damaged by their experience. Other writers, most often those who see children of alcoholics in clinical or judicial systems, claim that these offspring cannot escape unscathed from the effects of parental alcoholism. The critical issue, however, is that we need to know more about what factors serve to moderate the adverse impact of living in an alcoholic home so that better methods of treatment and prevention can be developed. In this respect, each child of an alcoholic, regardless of his or her capacity for resiliency, can contribute to our understanding of this complex issue.

IMPACT ON THE FAMILY

Much of the literature on families of alcoholics has been inferred from the reports of individual family members. For example, Jackson's seven stage theory of adaptation was based on wives' reports, and the ritual theory of Wolin and his colleagues was based on individual interviews of adult children of alcoholics. These reports provide rich insights into the lives of alcoholic families. However, whenever the alcoholic family is observed or studied as a unit, other family phenomena are revealed that are not readily apparent in approaches focusing on individual family members.

A major contribution to a family perspective in this area has been the work of Peter Steinglass and his associates (1971, 1977, 1987). Their research was based on observations of family units in two different situations, when the alcoholic was sober and when he or she was intoxicated. Striking differences in family behavior were found in sober and intoxicated states. Moreover, it appeared that these changes in behavior provided a temporary solution to a problem in the family. For example, one couple became more expressive and affectionate, whereas another couple became more assertive when sobriety gave way to intoxication. Another couple found it easier to express previously suppressed anger and frustration when drinking occurred.

On the basis of these observations, Steinglass proposed that the cycling between sober and intoxicated states was perpetuated because it served an adaptive, problem-solving function for the family. According to this "alcohol maintenance" theory, the family comes to depend on the drinker's intoxicated state to function as a "pressure valve" that restores stability when tensions in the family system become intolerable. Thus reliance on alcohol reinforces its continued use.

In direct observations of alcoholic families as they interacted in their own homes, Steinglass (1981, p. 300) found that

> in some families, equilibrium is restored by increasing interactional distance (the drinker goes off to drink in the basement), or diminishing physical contact (the nonalcoholic spouse refuses to have sex with someone who is drunk) . . . whereas in other families alcohol might be associated with closer interactional distance (the nonalcoholic makes contact by fighting after the alcoholic spouse has been drinking), disinhibition (the use of alcohol permits ritualized sexual behavior), or maintaining distance from the social environment (the alcoholic fights with the neighbors when drunk).

From a clinical perspective, Steinglass's theory would suggest that treatment of alcoholics should include a careful assessment of how family interactions change when the drinker is intoxicated. Removing alcohol from a family system whose stability depends on a parent's drinking cycles may create a void. If not replaced by more effective ways to resolve tension, this void would increase the risk of relapse.

In another series of studies of alcoholic families, Jacob and his colleagues (1989) analyzed videotaped family discussions when alcohol was present and when it was absent. These researchers also found differences between drinking and nondrinking conditions. Some families exhibited more positive behaviors and better problem-solving skill in the presence of alcohol, whereas other families displayed more hostile, negative behavior and less problem-solving effort. Of particular interest, the research of these investigators suggests differences in family interactions between "binge" drinkers and "steady" drinkers (who consume fairly regular day-to-day amounts of alcohol). Alcohol appeared to facilitate problem-solving and the expression of positive emotions in families of steady drinkers. An opposite effect was found in the interactions of binge drinkers. These findings suggest that intoxication may serve different functions in families of binge versus steady drinkers. However, the important issue is that alcohol abuse *serves a function* and, in so doing, increases the likelihood of continued use.

Although problem drinking may serve as a temporary solution to an immediate strain in the family, its long-term effects are detrimental. This is the key concept of Steinglass's "life history model," which focused on drinking cycles over extended periods of family life. In contrast to the "alcohol maintenance" theory, which focuses on day-to-day cycles of sober and intoxicated states, the life history model looks at longer phases of drinking and nondrinking. According to this broader framework, some families may have many dry and wet periods (with transitional phases). Other families may have only one wet phase, which is resolved only when permanent abstinence is achieved or when death or divorce alters the family structure. The major implication of the life history model is that as alcoholic families progress through natural stages of family development, they are unable to adapt to change in a growth-enhancing way. Rather, stage-related issues (e.g., the independence-seeking behavior of adolescent children) is constricted and distorted by alcoholism.

The Smith and Jones families (pseudonyms for real families) provide illustrations of how family interaction patterns and abusive drinking patterns are associated:

Case History 1

At initial assessment, Mr. Smith was a 52-year-old factory worker with a 30-year history of problematic drinking. He reported high levels of somatic and psychiatric symptoms, particularly complaints of depression. He reported that he drank to relax and forget his troubles and that drinking made him more "sociable" and "tolerant." His perception was that his family accepted his drinking and that his wife "didn't mind" and "never mentioned it." He drank almost every day, starting with a beer in the morning. Most of his drinking occurred in the evening hours at home when he typically drank 10 to 12 beers.

Mrs. Smith was a 45-year-old receptionist who reported feeling moderately depressed. She described her family life as tense and unhappy. She reported that her husband's mood improved when he was drinking, and he became more friendly and affectionate as compared to being "very nervous" and "quick-tempered" when sober. Their 11-year-old-son was described by his parents as a "worrier" who "sucks his thumb and bites his fingernails." He denied that his father's drinking affected him, except that he was annoyed by "getting him his beer from the refrigerator." He reported that his father "gets nicer after he drinks."

Clearly, in this family the father's drinking served to create a more congenial atmosphere, improving his mood so that other family members found him more approachable. Even the process of retrieving the father's beer served to bring father and son in contact with each other! In the short run, alcohol served to alleviate tensions in the family system; in the long run, however, the effects were more tragic.

Five years later, the father was diagnosed as having an advanced state of cirrhosis and lost his job because of frequent absences. Paradoxically, alcohol no longer relieved his feelings of depression. His wife divorced him, claiming she could no longer tolerate the financial and emotional stress. Their son was functioning adequately in school and peer relationships but continued to exhibit high levels of anxiety.

Case History 2

When first seen, Mr. Jones was a 49-year-old steel mill foreman who began drinking at age 12. His psychological profile indicated that he was an individual who often felt alternately angry and guilty. He drank variable amounts, occasionally stopping at a local bar for a few drinks, but often abstaining for several months. This consumption pattern was interrupted by drinking binges during which he would abandon his home and job for several days. His wife reported that he totally dissolved his $900 paycheck in a recent 10-day binge.

Mrs. Jones is a 44-year-old homemaker who described her husband as "stern" and "overcontrolled" when sober. When he returned from binges, he would be penitent and "the best husband in the world." The Joneses have two children, an 18-year-old daughter and a 14-year-old son. Their daughter was described as a good student with several friends. However, her father showed up "totally blasted" at her graduation party, and she moved out of the home shortly afterward. Their son was experimenting with alcohol and exhibiting behavior problems at school.

Although not clearly articulated, it appeared that in the Jones family the father's drinking tended to relieve a rigid home environment and to generate some improvement in the marital relationship. The father's behavior at his daughter's graduation party, a social marker of transition, would suggest that this family (or the father in particular) may have difficulty adjusting to change. Four years later, in a follow-up interview, Mrs. Jones said her husband's binges had caused a "total breakup of the family." Her daughter seldom visited, and her son was on the verge of expulsion from school. She said she remained in the marriage solely for financial reasons.

Conclusion

The Smith and Jones families are examples of the similarities as well as the diversities that exist among alcoholic families. Economic hardship, medical problems, employment difficulties, marital discord, child adjustment problems, tense relationships, and disrupted living patterns are common characteristics of these families. On a more intricate day-to-day level, however, families develop their own unique adaptation to abusive drinking. Because it provides a temporary solution to distressful tensions in the family, this adaptation becomes ingrained in their style of living and relating. A fuller understanding of these complex interactional patterns presents a challenge to both family researchers and family therapists. An expanding focus on the alcoholic family is evident in the development of more comprehensive theories, rigorous research programs, and published clinical observations. It is hoped that these efforts will lead to more effective treatment and prevention efforts than those that presently exist.

FAMILY ASSESSMENT PROCEDURES

There is a lack of family assessment procedures designed specifically to identify and evaluate families of alcoholics. The following questionnaires have been developed to address that need and may prove useful to the reader:

The *Children of Alcoholics Screening Test* (CAST; Jones, 1981) is a 30-item screening questionnaire designed to identify latency age, adolescent and adult children of alcoholics. It has a "yes-no" format and can usually be completed easily by children nine years of age or older. The CAST addresses the child's perceptions of parental drinking and family discord, as well as behavioral reactions and emotional distress associated with parental use of alcohol. Pilat and Jones (1984-1985) note that the questionnaire may also be helpful as a springboard for discussion in therapy.

Did You Grow up with a Problem Drinker? is a 20-item questionnaire published by Al-Anon (1984) that is applicable to anyone with a close association with a problem drinker. It is directed at how one's life may have been affected, with "yes-no" questions that pertain to one's current dysfunctional behavior and emotional difficulties.

The *Family Recovery Workbook* (Daley, 1987) provides a versatile comprehensive workbook for evaluating the impact of chemical dependence upon the family as a whole as well as on individual family members. It provides the reader with checklists and sections for written personal statements in a format that can be used in treatment settings or as an independent activity. Additionally, it provides guidelines for seeking help and maintaining recovery.

Although not specifically developed for alcoholic families, there are many family questionnaires that can provide information about the general functioning of alcoholic families and enable a comparison with other types of families. In *Family Assessment: Rationale, Methods, and Future Directions,* Jacob and Tennenbaum (1988) review existing and developing family assessment procedures. This review provides information about the background, typical questions, and psychometric properties of questionnaires, interviews, and observational methods that pertain to marital (e.g., Spanier, 1976; Snyder, 1981; Weiss, Hops, & Patterson, 1973), parent-child (e.g., Barnes & Olson, 1982; Jacob & Seilhamer, 1985; Schaeffer, 1965), and sibling relationships (e.g., Furman & Buhrmester, 1985), as well as whole families (e.g., Moos & Moos, 1981; Olson & Portner, 1983; Skinner, Steinhauer, & Santa-Barbara, 1981).

REFERENCES

Al-Anon. (1984). *Did you grow up with a problem drinker?* New York: Al-Anon Family Group Headquarters.

Bailey, M., Haberman, P., & Alksne, H. (1962). Outcomes of alcoholic marriages: Endurance, termination or recovery. *Quarterly Journal of Studies in Alcohol, 23*(4), 610-623.

Barnes, H. L., & Olson, D. H. (1982). Parent-adolescent communication. In D. H. Olson, H. I. McCubbin, H. Barnes, A. Larsen, M. Muxen, & M. Wilson (Eds.), *Family inventories: Inventories used in a national survey of families across the family life cycle.* St. Paul, MN: Family Social Science.

Bosma, W. G. H. (1972). Children of alcoholics—a hidden tragedy. *Maryland State Medical Journal, 21*(1), 34-36.

Clair, D., & Genest, M. (1987). Variables associated with the adjustment of offspring of alcoholic fathers. *Journal of Studies on Alcohol, 48,* 345-355.

Corder, B. F., Hendricks, A., & Corder, R. F. (1964). An MMPI study of a group of wives of alcoholics. *Quarterly Journal of Studies on Alcohol, 25,* 551-554.

Cork, R. M. (1969). *The forgotten children: A study of children with alcoholic parents.* Toronto: Alcoholism and Drug Addiction Research Foundation of Ontario.

Daley, D. (1987). *Family recovery workbook.* Bradenton, FL: Human Services Institute.

el-Guebaly, N., & Offord, D. R. (1980). The competent offspring of psychiatrically ill parents. *Canadian Journal of Psychiatry, 25,* 457-7463.

Ernhart, C. B., Wolf, A. W., & Linn, P. L. (1985). Alcohol-related birth defects: Syndromal anomalies, intrauterine growth retardation and neonatal behavioral assessment. *Alcoholism: Clinical and Experimental Research, 9,* 447-453.

Furman, W., & Buhrmester, D. (1985). Children's perceptions of the quality of sibling relationships. *Child Development, 56,* 448-461.

Goodwin, D. W. (1976). *Is alcoholism hereditary?* New York: Oxford University Press.

Jackson, K. (1954). The adjustment of the family to the crisis of alcoholism. *Quarterly Journal of Studies on Alcohol, 15,* 562-586.

Jacob, T., & Leonard, K. (1986). Psychosocial functioning in children of alcoholic fathers, depressed fathers and control fathers. *Journal of Studies on Alcohol, 47*(5), 373-380.

Jacob, T., & Seilhamer, R. A. (1985). Adaptation of the Areas of Change Questionnaire for parent-child relationship assessment. *American Journal of Family Therapy, 13,* 28-38.

Jacob, T., & Seilhamer, R. A. (1989). Alcoholism and family interaction. In M. Galanter (Ed.), *Recent developments in alcoholism* (Vol. 7, pp. 129-145). New York: Plenum.

Jacob, T., Seilhamer, R. A., & Rushe, R. (1989). Alcoholism and family interaction: An experimental paradigm. *American Journal of Drug and Alcohol Abuse, 15*(1), 73-91.

Jacob, T., & Tennebaum, D. (1988). *Family assessment: Rationale, methods, and future directions.* New York: Plenum.

Jones, J. W. (1981). *The Children of Alcoholics Screening Test (C.A.S.T.).* Chicago: Family Recovery Press.

Kalashian, M. (1959). Working with wives of alcoholics in an out-patient clinic setting. *Marriage and Family Living, 21,* 130-133.

Kogan, K. L., Fordyce, W.E., & Jackson, J. K. (1963). Personality disturbance in wives of alcoholics. *Quarterly Journal of Studies on Alcohol, 24,* 227-238.

Kogan, K. L., & Jackson, J. K. (1965). Stress, personality and emotional disturbance in wives of alcoholics. *Quarterly Journal of Studies on Alcohol, 26,* 486-495.

Macdonald, D. E. (1958). Group psychotherapy with wives of alcoholics. *Quarterly Journal of Studies on Alcohol, 19,* 125-132.

Moos, R. H., Finney, J. W., & Gamble, W. (1982). The process of recovery from alcoholism, II: Comparing spouses of alcoholic patients and matched community controls. *Journal of Studies on Alcohol, 43*(9), 888-909.

Moos, R. H., & Moos, B. S. (1981). *Family environment scale manual.* Palo Alto, CA: Consulting Psychologists Press.

Moos, R. H., & Moos, B. S. (1984). The process of recovery from alcoholism, III: Comparing functioning in families of alcoholics in matched control families. *Journal of Studies on Alcohol, 45*(2), 111-118.

Nace, E. P. (1982). Therapeutic approaches to the alcoholic marriage. *Psychiatric Clinics of North America, 5*(3), 543-564.

Olson, D. H., & Portner, J. (1983). Family adaptability and cohesion evaluation scales. In E. E. Filsinger (Ed.), *Marriage and family assessment* (pp. 299-315). Beverly Hills, CA: Sage.

Orford, J., & Guthrie, S. (1976). Coping behavior used by wives of alcoholics: A preliminary investigation. In G. Edward, M. A. H. Russell, D. Hawks, & M. McCafferty (Eds.), *Alcohol dependence and smoking behavior* (pp. 136-143). Westmead, Hants.: Saxon House.

Orford, J., Guthrie, S., Nicholls, P., Oppenheimer, E., Egert, S., & Hensman, C. (1975). Self-reported coping behavior of wives of alcoholics and its association with drinking outcome. *Journal of Studies on Alcohol, 36,* 1254-1267.

Orford, J., Oppenheimer, E., Egert, S., Hensman, C., & Guthrie, S. (1976). The cohesiveness of alcoholism-complicated marriages and its influences on treatment outcome. *British Journal of Psychiatry, 128,* 318-339.

Paolino, T. J., & McCrady, B. S. (1977). *The alcoholic marriage: Alternative perspectives.* New York: Grune & Stratton.

Paolino, T. J., McCrady, B. S., Diamond, S. & Longabaugh, R. (1976). Psychological disturbances in spouses of alcoholics. *Journal of Studies on Alcohol, 37*(11), 1600-1608.

Paolino, T. J., McCrady, B. S., & Kogan, K. B. (1978). Alcoholic marriages: A longitudinal empirical assessment of alternative theories. *British Journal of Addiction, 73,* 129-138.

Pilat, J. M., & Jones, J. W. (1984-1985). Identification of children of alcoholics: Two empirical studies. *Alcohol, Health and Research World, 9*(2), 27-33.

Prewitt, M. J., Spence, R., & Chaknis, M. (1981). Attribution of causality by children with alcoholic parents. *The International Journal of Addictions, 16*(2), 367-370.

Rae, J. B., & Forbes, A. R. (1966). Clinical and psychometric characteristics of the wives of alcoholics. *British Journal of Psychiatry, 112,* 197-200.

Rosett, H. L., & Weiner, L. (1982). Effects of alcohol on the fetus. In E. M. Pattison & E. Kaufman (Eds.), *Encyclopedic handbook of alcoholism* (pp. 301-310). New York: Gardner.

Schaefer, E. S. (1965). Children's reports of parental behavior: An inventory. *Child Development, 36,* 413-424.

Shaffer, J. B., & Tyler, J. D. (1979). Degree of sobriety in male alcoholics and coping styles used by their wives. *British Journal of Psychiatry, 135,* 431-437.

Seilhamer, R. A., & Jacob, T. (1990). Family factors and adjustment of children of alcoholics. In M. Windle & J. S. Searles (Eds.), *Children of alcoholics: Critical perspectives* (pp. 168-186). New York: Guilford.

Skinner, H. A., Steinhauer, P. D., & Santa-Barbara, J. (1981). *Family assessment measure.* Toronto: Addiction Research Foundation.

Sloboda, S. B. (1974). The children of alcoholics: A neglected problem. *Hospital and Community Psychiatry, 25*(9), 605-606.

Snyder, D. K. (1981). *Marital Satisfaction Inventory (MSI) manual.* Los Angeles, CA: Western Psychological Services.

Spanier, G. (1976). Measuring dyadic adjustment: New scales for assessing the quality of marriage and similar dyads. *Journal of Marriage and the Family, 38*(1), 15-30.

Steinglass, P. (1981). The alcoholic family at home: Patterns of interaction in dry, wet, and transitional stages of alcoholism. *Archives of General Psychiatry, 38,* 578-584.

Steinglass, P., Bennett, L. A., Wolin, S. J., & Reiss, D. (1987). *The alcoholic family.* New York: Basic Books.

Steinglass, P., Davis, D., & Berenson, D. (1977). Observations of conjointly hospitalized "alcoholic couples" during sobriety and intoxication: Implications for theory and therapy. *Family Process, 16,* 1-16.

Steinglass, P., Weiner, S., & Mendelson, J. H. (1971). A systems approach to alcoholism: A model and its clinical application. *Archives of General Psychiatry, 24,* 401-408.

Steinhauser, H., Nester, V., & Spohr, H. (1982). Development and psychopathology of children with the fetal alcohol syndrome. *Journal of Developmental and Behavioral Pediatrics, 3,* 49-54.

Tarter, R. E. (1976). Personality of wives of alcoholics. *Journal of Clinical Psychology, 32*(3), 741-743.

Warner, R., & Rosett, H. L. (1975). The effects of drinking on offspring: An historical survey of the American and British literature. *Journal of Studies on Alcohol, 36,* 1395-1420.

Weiss, R. L., Hops, H., & Patterson, G. R. (1973). A framework for conceptualizing marital conflict: A technology for altering it, some data for evaluating it. In R. W. Clark & L. A. Hammerlynck (Eds.), *Handbook for behavioral assessment* (pp. 309-342). New York: John Wiley.

Werner, E. E. (1986). Resilient offspring of alcoholics: a longitudinal study from birth to age 18. *Journal of Studies on Alcohol, 47,* 34-40.

Whitfield, C. L. (1981). Children of alcoholics: Treatment issues. *Services for children of alcoholics.* Research Monograph No. 4, DHHS Pub. No. (ADM) 81-1007. Rockville, MD: National Institute on Alcohol Abuse and Alcoholism.

Wiseman, J. P. (1975). An alternative role for the wife of an alcoholic in Finland. *Journal of Marriage and the Family, 87,* 172-179.

Wiseman, J. (1980). The "home-treatment": The first steps in trying to cope with an alcoholic husband. *Family Relations, 29,* 541-549.

Wolin, S. J., Bennett, L. A., & Noonan, D. L. (1979). Family rituals and the recurrence of alcoholism over generations. *American Journal of Psychiatry, 136,* 589-593.

Wolin, S. J., Bennett, L. A., Noonan, D. L., & Teitelbaum, M. A. (1980). Disrupted family rituals: A factor in the intergenerational transmission of alcoholism. *Journal of Studies on Alcohol, 41*(3), 199-214.

Woodside, M. (1988). Research on children of alcoholics: Past and future. *British Journal of Addiction, 83,* 785-792.

Chapter 8

FAMILY RECOVERY ISSUES AND TREATMENT RESOURCES

CAROL KOFFINKE

In 1980, a Gallup poll indicated that one out of every four Americans felt that alcohol-related problems had adversely affected his or her family. More recent data suggest that as many as one out of every three Americans live in a family where there is alcohol abuse (National Association of Children of Alcoholics, 1983). Consequently, most helping professions will have the opportunity to assist a family suffering from the effects of chemical dependence. This chapter will help these professionals understand the family's recovery process. Professionals who generally do not deal with problems of chemical dependence can play an important role if they are able to assess the situation accurately, provide the appropriate kind of support, and make proper referrals. Professionals who normally deal with chemical dependence may be better able to treat the addict and/or family if they are aware of the dynamics of family recovery. This chapter will examine various symptoms of alcohol-related disease in the family and their impact on recovery, assessment, the healing process, the prevention of family relapse, and resources for treatment.

In this chapter, the term *family* refers to those individuals who have the closest or most significant relationships with the chemically dependent person. Family members include spouse and children, parents, roommates or close friends, siblings, or some combination of these. These are the individuals who will feel the greatest effect of the chemical dependence and who may need to be treated if they are to move into recovery themselves, have a positive influence on the patient's recovery, and participate in the healing of the family system.

The family of a chemically dependent person must often participate in treatment if the addict is to have the best chance to recover, and if the healing process is to take place. The family's effect on recovery can be powerful, either positively or negatively. To treat a chemically dependent person, one must realize that the addict does not exist in a vacuum. The addict's life situation has a definite impact on his or her recovery. This includes work, friends, recreational choices, and family. These involve people with whom the addict will interact. How do they feel about recovery? What issues are they struggling with that may cause conscious or unconscious sabotage of the recovery process? How are they supposed to heal from the effects on their own physical, emotional, and spiritual selves? If the goal is to be the healing of families, each person has an important part to play. The result can be healthy family relationships and an environment that is conducive to ongoing recovery for all involved.

OVERCOMING FAMILY DENIAL

Denial is one of the first stumbling blocks encountered in helping the addict and his or her family. Until denial is dealt with, no significant progress can be made. Family members tend to suffer from a distortion of reality from two perspectives. Not only do they usually deny the chemical use of the addict/alcoholic, but they also tend to deny that it has affected them to the point where they, too, may need help.

Family denial takes many forms. The addict's unacceptable behaviors can be rationalized by making excuses for the substance abuse, or the family member may rationalize his or her own unacceptable behavior. This is commonly heard in statements such as "He made me mad," or "He doesn't care, so why should I?" Minimization is another manifestation of denial. Examples include: "He still gets to work every day," "He only drinks beer," "It's not that bad," and "It doesn't bother me."

Because the lack of an odor, drug abuse is often harder to detect than alcohol abuse. Family members may observe a behavior change that concerns them. If the addict denies that there is a chemical involved, however, the family is helpless to make a definite determination, unless they find the chemical or related paraphernalia. Unfortunately, the family's denial can feed that of the addict, and both can work together to fuel the ongoing addiction. The following case illustrates this:

> Don is an 18-year-old who was admitted to inpatient treatment for cocaine addiction. When the family was assessed, the mother appeared in shock that her son needed treatment for drug addiction, even though Don still lived at home. She went to great lengths to tell what a good boy he always was, and how he always came home during the week. She accepted without question that he did stay out very late on weekends and then slept all day. She refused to accept that her son was a cocaine addict and that the family needed to work together to give him the best possible chance to recover. She protected with a vengeance her fantasy that everything was all right and believed that everything would magically be better after treatment. Don remained drug free for only one day after discharge.

There is always someone who is worse, and families tend initially to exclude their loved one from their definition of alcoholic or addict. Education to help the family understand the disease and the many faces of addiction is very important in helping them accept the disease. Even after acceptance, many family members still believe that they are the "healthy" ones who do not need help. This attitude can be very detrimental to making the kinds of changes recovery requires. For the individual, the effects are sometimes subtle and covert.

A simple therapeutic task is to ask the family to identify how they have been affected by the problem of chemical dependence. Each family member lists the physical (e.g., loss of sleep, headaches, change in appetite, and smoking more cigarettes), emotional (e.g., fear, hurt, frustration, anger, and guilt), and behavioral effects (e.g., lying, threatening, and reducing social activities). This helps family members face the reality of *their* pain and can enhance motivation to become involved in recovery. Professionals working with the family can also ask: (1) What excuses have you used to justify the addict's behavior? (2) How have you tried to minimize the seriousness of the problem? (3) Why are you here now? and (4) How have you tried to avoid what is going on in your family? (Potter-Efron & Potter-Efron, 1989). The involvement of children in the treatment process can help to break denial. Parents occasionally refuse to acknowledge that their child has been affected, perhaps because this admission would create pain and guilt. However, the honesty and special bonding ability of children may help the addict and the nonaddicted spouse accept reality.

The following case illustrates the power that children have in breaking denial:

> Tom is a 38-year-old who was admitted for inpatient treatment of alcoholism. His wife of 18 years had never known him when he had not drunk nearly a case of beer a day. She had accepted the fact that he had numerous affairs and that he would not come home for days at a time. Tom began sexually abusing their 14-year-old daughter during the last 18 months. The wife found out about this from the mother of her daughter's best friend. She and the daughter immediately confronted Tom, and he swore that he had no recollection of this because of blackouts. He stated, however, that he believed that his daughter would not lie about this, and he volunteered to come into treatment, fully aware of the legal implications of the sexual abuse. The daughter's plea for help is what broke through the wall of denial for both Tom and his wife.

ENABLING

The following case highlights the "enabling" concept:

> Charlie does not show up for dinner. No one mentions it. His wife makes up a plate and puts it in the microwave for whenever he comes home. The phone rings. Charlie's boss needs to talk to him immediately about an emergency at work. His wife lies and says that he is on the road because of a family emergency and that he cannot be reached. After dinner the family, except for Charlie, goes to the school concert in which his son plays the saxophone. Afterward, the son's friends ask him where his father is. He lies and says that he has the flu. At bedtime Charlie still isn't home. The children go to bed, but Charlie's wife stays up. At midnight she starts calling the local bars. No luck. At 4:00 a.m. she finally dozes off. At 7:00 a.m. Charlie staggers home. He asks his wife to call work and tell them that he has the flu. She complies. Then she tells each child to kiss their father good-bye before leaving for school. They are instructed to be kind—"Daddy" has had a rough night.

This alcoholic is being enabled. Normally, enabling involves a positive action of helping someone. Once substance abuse is introduced into a family, however, the term's meaning changes to a very negative one. By helping the addict avoid the negative consequences of his or her addiction, the enabling family member actually helps the addict stay addicted. These negative consequences are one of the main motivations for an addict to risk giving up a chemical. Most family members are unaware that their enabling behavior helps their loved one remain addicted.

The professional working with the family of a substance abuser can help evaluate enabling behaviors. Once family members realize that protecting the addict and assuming his or her responsibilities is detrimental to the addict's potential recovery, they are more willing to assess their enabling behavior. Common examples of enabling include:

- Making or canceling appointments
- Diluting or hiding the chemical
- Bailing the addict out of jail
- Taking over financial responsibilities
- Riding around in an effort to locate the addict
- Threatening to leave and not following through
- Nagging or scolding
- Agreeing with the addict that the real problem is something else
- "Walking on eggshells"

Any behavior that protects the substance abuser from experiencing the natural consequences of the addiction is considered enabling. The abuser can be motivated to change only by directly experiencing the pain and problems resulting from the chemical use.

This attempt to bring awareness to the family can be taken a step further. Family members should be allowed to explore how it *feels* to enable as well as the consequences to themselves and the addict. When they see that all of their efforts did not help to achieve sobriety, but actually resulted in negative feelings and consequences for themselves, they become more willing to risk new nonenabling behaviors.

Enabling must stop if family members are to experience recovery. Because many family members equate enabling with their love for the addict, it is very difficult to terminate their behavior in order to allow the addict to experience the natural consequences of his or her own behavior, to help the addict make a direct connection between the pain and the addiction, and to gain the initial motivation for recovery.

The following case illustrates this point:

Jane is a 71-year-old widow who participated in the family program of an inpatient drug and alcohol facility. Her 50-year-old son was in treatment for alcoholism. Ever since the patient had moved out of her home 22 years ago, she cleaned his apartment every week, did his grocery shopping for him, cooked for him several times a week, and provided transportation because he had lost his driver's license several years before. Her son had never married. Her enabling behavior kept him in the position of a child that needed to be cared for.

CODEPENDENCE ISSUES

Once family members accept the reality of the addiction and its effect on them, they tend to be more open-minded in terms of examining the issues concerning recovery. The term *codependent* has many definitions and is used generically. Generally, the term refers to a person who is experiencing physical and emotional stress as a result of a significant relationship with a chemically addicted person (Subby & Friel, 1984). Symptoms that typically develop as a result of this relationship are: excessive or inappropriate dependence on another person, preoccupation with people or things outside oneself, lack of self-identity, repressed feelings, and caretaking and rescuing behaviors. There are often control issues and a tendency to compulsion in some area such as work, eating, cleaning, or perfectionism.

A codependent is usually very focused on the alcoholic or addict. There are frequent problems, crises, and opportunities for worry and preoccupation with the addict. This is especially the case when the codependent grew up in a dysfunctional family, in which crises and hypervigilance (maintaining an acute awareness of the environment) were common. This may be part of the unconscious motivation for some adults to choose this kind of relationship. Continuing this relationship is familiar and more comfortable than a relationship where conflict is minimal and one is expected to relate on an emotional level.

Codependents may become so preoccupied with the addict that they lose their own sense of identity. Their emotional well-being becomes very dependent on the addict's moods. They become extremely hypervigilant with regard to whatever is happening in the immediate environment. If they are to survive, codependents must repeatedly readjust and respond to the situation as opposed to their own needs. As codependents continue to focus their energy and awareness outside of themselves, they lose more and more contact with their own identities. Even when the addict is not physically present, the codependent still maintains an emotional connection with this person to whom his or her identity is attached by excessive worrying, feeling victimized, or becoming enraged.

Caretaking and rescuing often become a way of life. The codependent feels compelled to fix the problems that result from the chemical dependence and to protect the addict from its consequences. The codependent typically protects the addict by refusing to discuss the reality of various problematic situations caused by the addict, or by rationalizing them away. Isolation from friends and extended family is also common among codependents. After so much energy is spent attempting to fix the problem and to repress the flood of negative feelings, there is little left for social interaction. Emotionally, the codependent often responds with some degree of repression. Because of the wide range of negative emotions that are experienced within the relationship (fear, anger, hurt, guilt, resentment, frustration), the codependent feels emotionally overwhelmed and tends to block the experience of the feelings. Unfortunately, this also blocks the opportunity to release these feelings and results in a buildup that may contribute to medical problems, such as migraines or ulcers, and emotional problems, such as depression or anxiety.

ASSESSING THE IMPACT OF ADDICTION ON SELF AND OTHERS

A close look at the effect of the addiction is an important first step for the family member. This assessment facilitates the breakdown of denial and encourages involvement in the recovery process. It is more comfortable for many family members to say, "It's his disease," or "It's his recovery." Yet, as already noted, the family plays an important part in this process. Realization of the impact of addiction, however, helps the family move past this self-defeating attitude. There are four major areas of assessment: physical, psychoemotional, spiritual, and social.

A variety of medical problems may result from the stress associated with living with an addict. Physical side effects can include migraines, ulcers, and colitis (Wegscheider, 1976); arthritis, asthma, insomnia, and heart arrhythmias (Whitfield, 1989); and rashes, hormonal imbalance, and heart attacks (Schneider, 1986). In his film, *The Medical Aspects of Co-Dependency,* Dr. Max Schneider draws a striking similarity between the organs of the body affected by substance abuse and codependence. He illustrates that there are few organs in the body *not* affected by the stress resulting from the chronic repression of feelings symptomatic of codependence.

Psychoemotional assessment encompasses anxiety levels, emotional outbursts, inability to concentrate and to accomplish tasks, obsessive focus or chronic worry about the addict, and mood disturbances such as depression. When the family member looks at these symptoms one at a time, he or she begins to see that the level at which he or she is currently functioning lacks peace of mind and positive feelings such as joy, love, and hope. At a minimum, he or she should see that the emotional balance between experiencing positive and negative feelings has been lost, and that the balance is heavily weighted on the negative side.

Spiritually, the person may lose a sense of meaning or purpose in life and feel alone or hopeless. This leads to a lack of motivation to address the situation. Changes in spiritual practices such as church attendance, prayer, or meditation are characteristic of the spiritual side effects of codependence.

Social isolation should also be addressed, for many codependents withdraw from friends and outside activities (Beattie, 1987). The effort to maintain both image and secrets can be overwhelming, and it is easy for codependents to remain home. Additionally, the emotional turmoil makes it difficult to relate to others in a relaxed manner. If a wife wonders whether her husband is going to make it home from the bar without killing himself or someone else, she will have difficulty relating to a friend's dilemma about what to wear to the party next week. Family members may also discontinue previous involvement in a 12-step program, or perhaps discontinue counseling as a symptom of isolation.

Family issues that can also be assessed are quality of overall family relationships, role reversals, discipline problems, and dysfunctional rules such as those that prevent the family from communicating about what is really happening.

EDUCATION ON ADDICTION AND RECOVERY

Understanding of the following content areas is crucial to the recovery process:

- Chemical dependence as a disease
- Causes and effects on the addict
- Effects on the family system and its individual members
- Codependence
- Recovery for addict and family to include resources
- Relapse

Education on these topics tends to reduce resistance to new concepts. This begins the process of changing ideas, attitudes, feelings (anger and guilt), and behaviors. Education can have a significant impact on the motivation to change and the willingness to continue in a direction that may be growth enhancing but is, at the same time, unfamiliar, uncomfortable, and frightening. For this reason, education is an integral part of family recovery (Cermak, 1980).

The family needs to understand chemical dependence as a disease. An individual will often respond affirmatively when asked if he or she believes the addict has a disease. Yet, as he or she goes on to blame the person for lack of willpower, or to blame the addict's job, friends, husband, and so forth, it becomes apparent that this individual lacks a clear understanding of the nature of this disease. Once the family members become more informed, they can reinterpret what has transpired in a way that facilitates forgiveness and a fresh perspective on recovery. Education about the effects of chemical dependence on the family is usually necessary before family members accept their own role in recovery. Many readings, films, and audio tapes are available to facilitate family members' understanding of addiction and recovery.

Family members need to be educated about the dynamics of the chemically dependent family and the "survival roles" that members tend to assume. The family may observe a direct correlation between offspring and these classic roles, facilitating acceptance that the children have been affected. In addition, if the nonaddicted spouse happens to be an adult child of an alcoholic or addict (ACOA), identification with a particular role or blend of roles seems to increase the motivation to change.

Finally, education on 12-step programs, and the recovery process in general, should be provided. The family member must learn to be responsible for his or her own recovery and not for the addict's. It is important for the family to understand that recovery will not occur if someone is responsible for another person's recovery.

204 TREATING THE CHEMICALLY DEPENDENT AND THEIR FAMILIES

OVERCOMING GUILT AND SHAME

Guilt and shame are experienced to one degree or another by all codependents. Guilt is the feeling associated with actions we have taken or failed to take; shame is the feeling associated with who we are (bad, defective, worthless).

The manifestation of guilt and shame depends on the relationship with the chemically dependent person. Spouse, child, and parent tend to experience these feelings differently. The spouse feels guilt for nagging, controlling behaviors, angry outbursts, and lying. Shame is experienced in the belief that one is not a good spouse, parent or housekeeper, and is not sufficiently smart or attractive to make the addict happy.

The young child often feels it is his or her fault if a parent becomes upset (guilt), and he struggles with the fact that he is not lovable (shame): "If Mom really loved me, she wouldn't drink or take drugs." The adult child tends to feel guilty when he or she experiences happiness because his or her parents are still addicted or miserable in their codependence. The shame of not being worthwhile or lovable can affect later adult relationships. The adult child of the alcoholic may have a compulsive need for validation or may avoid intimacy in an effort to remain safe from finding out the "truth" that he or she secretly fears—that he or she is not "okay."

Parents usually question the quality of their parenting and believe that they should have saved their child from addiction. They feel guilty when they experience negative feelings toward the child. Parents who were raised in dysfunctional homes may become so enmeshed with their children that the child's "failure" (chemical dependence) becomes an indictment of their own worthlessness. They believe they must be flawed to have a child who is an alcoholic/addict.

The family members benefit by exploring these feelings in a group setting where their experiences are validated by others who struggle with similar feelings of guilt and shame. Once they realize that feelings are not "good" or "bad," but human responses to what is happening in one's life, they can begin to accept rather than repress these feelings. This facilitates the expression of the feelings, a process essential to recovery.

Overcoming feelings of guilt and shame is often a long-term process of advances and retreats. The 12-step programs can provide validation for these feelings and promote further emotional growth. In addition, counseling, ACOA groups, and residential family services associated with chemical-dependence programs are resources to help a family member reduce or relieve guilt and shame.

SHARING PERSONAL PAIN

If one is to work through the personal pain, it is essential that it be shared with at least one other person. As the family members hear about the problems of others, they realize that they are not alone in their pain. This helps dispel the myth that there must be something wrong with us if we experience problems in our life. Some family members who have been abused verbally, physically, or sexually experience a deep sense of shame and feel that they must have deserved the abuse. Listening to others talk about their pain permits the listener to share his or her pain as well.

Sharing the pain means sharing feelings, disappointments, and experiences. As the negative feelings are processed, healing begins. The person reconnects to his or her positive feelings. Because codependents tend to repress emotions, positive feelings like love, joy, and compassion are also locked away. The release of negative feelings allows the positive feelings (always there, but unattainable) to be experienced.

Anger is also found in a chemically dependent family. Promises are broken, family life revolves around the unpredictable addict, and the child may be left to his or her own devices. Not all family members are aware of their anger, and some may have repressed it completely. Expression of this anger is an integral part of the emotional healing, and the individual may need to learn that all people have this feeling. Anger is not a sin, not even anger toward a parent, and is not equated with lack of love. The adult child may be surprised to find, while working on his recovery, that he or she is often more angry with the nonaddicted parent than with the addict. Sometimes this anger may be self-directed and be manifested in self-defeating behaviors such as chemical use, antisocial behavior, or the sabotage of opportunities for happiness and success.

Grief is also a part of the pain that needs to be released. It is the sadness that is experienced as a result of any significant loss—addiction is fraught with losses for both the addict and the codependent. As with the death of a loved one, the person must grieve if he or she is to heal. The support of a group, a sponsor, a counselor, or a close friend can facilitate the expression of this intense emotion necessary for the healing process to begin.

The kinds of losses vary somewhat for different members of the family. Spouses lose their relationship with the addict, self-respect, and a portion of their lives. Children lose one or both parents, their childhood, and/or their selves. Parents lose hopes and dreams for children, and/or the children themselves. The joy of parenthood can become the terror of parenthood.

LEARNING DETACHMENT

The process of removing oneself from the pain of involvement with a person or problem is called *detachment* (Beattie, 1987). Most families struggle with detachment. Learning about the disease of chemical dependence helps family members realize that the addict's behaviors are not aimed at hurting them. As they learn not to take the behaviors personally, they can "detach from the disease" but still connect to the person. The family then needs to examine its own enabling behaviors. To be fully detached, one must cease all attempts to be responsible for, rescue, or protect the addict.

The goal for the codependent is to learn detachment with love as opposed to abandonment with hate. Some family members cut themselves off from the addict out of anger and revenge. These situations (incorrectly referred to as detachment) are characterized by guilt and resentment.

Detachment with love does not mean that one must experience particularly warm feelings toward the addict. It means that one lets go of control and rescue because the addict will be motivated to give up the chemical only if he or she is allowed to experience the natural consequences of the dependence. This love is a much higher form than protection, where one may be keeping the addict from getting fired, or from spending the night in jail. Such behaviors unintentionally support the addict's continued use of chemicals by shielding him or her from the adverse consequences of the addiction.

Teaching family members to focus more on themselves than on the addict will facilitate this process. If family members try to stop rescuing, but continue to keep all of their energy directed to the addict, they will find themselves confused, guilt ridden, and paralyzed with fear. One of the "payoffs" of codependence is distraction from the self and one's own pain. A self-help group and/or counseling can provide consistent feedback to allow the codependent to see where his or her focus is. This will allow him or her to shift the focus away from the addict and onto himself or herself.

The first step of the 12-step program of recovery deals specifically with detachment: "We admitted we were powerless over the alcoholic/ addict, that our lives had become unmanageable." Once this is accepted, the person can work on serenity, another integral part of self-help programs. The Serenity Prayer is a reminder to the codependent that one must learn to distinguish what is and what is not possible to control or change: "God, grant me the serenity to accept the things I cannot change, courage to change the things I can, and the wisdom to know the difference."

Detachment from the addict can be done in a positive and healthy way. Many family members are afraid that detachment means that they may not be able to have a relationship with this person. Addicts are afraid that the family is being advised to leave them. These are misinterpretations. The healthy message of detachment is: "I have chosen to go down this path—recovery—and I want you to share the journey with me. However, if you choose the other road, you need to know that I will not go with you."

BUILDING SOCIAL RELATIONSHIPS
AND REDUCING ISOLATION

Social isolation is a common problem with codependents. Spouses may not entertain and may socialize less with friends. Children may stop bringing friends home. Parents are too worried about the addict to leave the house comfortably, so they become isolated from others. Contact with extended family members may decrease as well. An exaggerated sense of loyalty develops as the family system becomes closed. This isolation contributes to a growing sense of hopelessness and aloneness, compounding a situation where the family already feels it is "drowning."

Self-help groups are a good place to begin the social reconnection. Most self-help groups sponsor a wide variety of social activities, such as dances, picnics, banquets, and cruises. As family members attend meetings, they realize that they are not alone, and the interaction provides an opportunity to restore hope as they meet people who are recovering.

Sponsorship is an element of self-help groups that encourages a more personal involvement for the family member. A sponsor is an individual in a self-help group who personally monitors a newcomer's recovery. The sponsor enables the family members to connect with someone who can be called upon any time support is needed, and who helps the individual express his or her feelings of anger, fear, hurt, or resentment. This allows ventilation, necessary in getting past negative feelings. The relationship with a sponsor is important in attaining maximum benefit from a self-help program. Members are encouraged to select one within a reasonable length of time.

In addition, the family should be encouraged to reestablish relationships with friends and to initiate new social activities. There may be some resistance to this because of the tendency to isolate oneself when dealing with negative emotions.

When one family member is alone in his or her journey of recovery, he or she may find it necessary to create a supportive system where he or she can continue in a positive direction. Self-help groups can provide the kind of support that most people hope to get from their own families. As the recovering individual has a safe place to explore and express himself or herself, he or she is better able to find new, acceptable ways to remain connected to his or her family.

Social reconnection is important. When the family member moves past the initial resistance, he or she will be participating in a part of life that can be nurturing and uplifting.

RESTORING FAMILY COHESIVENESS

Families need to be guided to see what works well in the family system. They need to explore issues such as the expression and validation of feelings and ideas, rigidity, boundaries, consideration for others, and parental coalition. Rules such as "Don't talk, don't trust, and don't feel" need to be broken (Black, 1982). Families need to be reminded that the recovery process takes time and that patience is required.

Many believe that a healthy family does not experience problems. However, as M. Scott Peck (1978) writes in *The Road Less Traveled,* "life is difficult." If the individual understands that problems are a natural part of personal and family growth, he or she will be less likely to feel like a failure when the first hurdle is met in recovery. The parents will be less likely to be resentful toward the children for not being perfect, and the children will better be able to keep their own problems in perspective.

It is important to establish better-quality relationships among the various family members. This is best done on a one-to-one basis, where parents have quality time together without the children, each parent has time with each child, and the children share projects. This may be difficult in a large family. When only two individuals are together, however, there are fewer distractions and less chaos to interfere with the process of relating. The child can feel special for having the parent all to himself.

If it is a dual-parent family, the parents should act as a team as much as possible. Even if they do not always agree, it is essential to present a united front. This can be accomplished by "stall tactics," such as "I need time to think about this," or "Your father and I want to discuss this before making a decision." This allows time for discussion and resolution by the parents.

Rules need to be stated plainly and to be enforced consistently. Children feel more secure when boundaries are clearly defined, and they are much less apt to test them. Some testing of the limits is natural at certain stages, but these behaviors are less frightening and more manageable when they are a result of the child's natural development, as opposed to a symptom of a disintegrating system.

Parents need help in assessing the quality of the family's relationships. Does one parent tend to mediate between the other parent and children? Are there personality conflicts between certain family members? Who needs help communicating better, and how can this be accomplished? How are listening skills? Are there role reversals that need to be addressed?

Sometimes, depending on the ages of the children and the willingness of each member, a family meeting can be used to discuss problems in the recovery process. Rules should be established for this kind of meeting and guidelines explained to each person. No one person can be more important or powerful than anyone else during the meeting.

Finally, the inclusion of all family members in the recovery process is beneficial. If one or both parents are involved in a self-help group, the children can be involved as well. If this is not possible, parents can share with their children what they are learning about themselves. Family counseling is indicated when the family lacks the skills necessary to make the required changes on its own. Also, significant dysfunctions such as physical or sexual abuse require professional help if the devastating effects are to be modified and the healing to occur.

GAINING HOPE

The most direct approach to helping a family gain hope is to encourage the involvement of its members in a self-help group. An individual who is in crisis is powerfully affected by exposure to others who have survived the same crisis. Faces are different and stories vary, but the crisis is the same—loss of someone because of chemical dependence and loss of themselves in the process. The family members see that things can really change, and this allows them to accept this as a possibility for themselves.

It is more difficult to be hopeful when the substance abuser has relapsed repeatedly. Self-help groups provide multiple opportunities to learn about and meet those who experienced multiple attempts before they could ground themselves in recovery. Through a self-help group the family member can experience a sense of power in terms of his or her own recovery. He or she begins to understand that powerlessness results only when all of his or her energy is focused on someone else. As the focus is shifted to self, he or she can begin to experience the power that lies in making choices—he or she does not have to choose to be the victim.

Programs based on the 12 steps of recovery address spirituality in the second step. The individual has an opportunity to explore his or her own spirituality—a part of the healing process that is vital to most people. Spirituality is not precisely defined, and the term "higher power" is used to allow individual interpretation.

Finally, the family needs to be reminded to have reasonable expectations. There will be ups and downs, good and bad days, happy and sad moods. These are normal and predictable and should not be interpreted as backsliding.

ADJUSTING TO THE SOBRIETY OF THE ADDICT

Family members often do not believe that there will be a rough adjustment period when the addict moves into recovery. The recovery is what they have been waiting, praying, and longing for. Many believe that when the addict makes this commitment, all of their problems are solved.

Issues of trust and fear emerge almost immediately. Dishonesty, manipulation, and broken promises are common effects of chemical dependence. It is impossible for most people suddenly to forget the past and fully trust the addict. Trust takes time to build. Both addict and family need to realize that this is a normal response to the situation. The addict should not be overly frustrated in his or her attempts to reassure the family, and the family members should not feel inadequate because they "can't let go of the past."

Most family members fear that the addict will relapse. This fear is ever present as the addict faces people, situations, and activities that are associated with chemical use. If family members have not received the education and treatment necessary to accept their own powerlessness, they tend to want to become "AA/NA policemen." This has a negative effect on recovery; it again places the addict in the inferior/childlike role. The family should instead focus on its own program of recovery, giving the addict the space needed to work on his or her own. The addict must be responsible for his or her own sobriety.

Family members often wonder how they can show support without taking control. It is important that the addict and family discuss this topic. Simple statements that voice support but not control put the responsibility on the addict and permit the family members to work on their own recovery.

Old patterns such as "walking on eggshells" need to be broken. Family members need to learn that they cannot be "bad" enough to cause the addict to relapse, nor can they be "good" enough to keep him or her sober.

Some families may feel confused and insecure with the unpredictability of the recovering family system. They may not like the addict initially, as everything that they came to expect changes. If one gets tripped every time one walks through the front door, one quickly learns to prepare before opening the door. However, if that is suddenly no longer the case, one tends to let one's guard down and, therefore, it is possible to get hurt if the tripping starts again. Family members may have felt safer in the old system because they knew what to expect. This insecurity in newly recovering families may be perceived as ambivalence toward recovery.

Again, patience is required. Family cohesiveness is not created overnight, nor is it a smoothly progressing process.

ADJUSTING TO A SOBER FAMILY

When an individual who has been abusing substances is sober and wants to be part of the family again, it can upset family equilibrium. The spouse may have been responsible for all the child care and resent the fact that the addict suddenly wants to have a say in it. One child may have taken over the mother's or father's role and feel lost when the parent resumes the position. The children may be used to independence and resent the parents suddenly telling them what to do. The main conversation for a number of years may have been one child's drug abuse. What is everyone now supposed to talk about, and how do they find new ways to relate?

These are examples of the kinds of adjustments that are part of a newly recovering family system. If the family members are to be assisted in their readjustment, the roles each have played in the addiction need to be examined, including the survival roles that the children have assumed. Assessment of these roles indicates the recovery needs of the system and the individuals.

One fairly predictable adjustment involves the recovering person's program. The addict was not there for other family members for so many years because of the chemical dependence. Now, in sobriety, the person still is not there because of his or her meetings. The usual "90 meetings in 90 days" approach may sound fine at first, but may wear thin for some family members before it is over. This initial recovery period will progress much more smoothly if family members are involved in a program as well. They may need to be reminded that the ultimate goal is *balance* or equilibrium, and that a maintenance program will be established in time.

Patterns of communication will most likely have to be changed. During the active phase of chemical dependence, the mode of problem solving tends to be family members, minus addict, huddling together to make decisions. In recovery, family members need to ask questions of the addict directly, instead of leaving him or her out of this process. This interaction must occur, even if it involves an uncomfortable subject.

Family counseling, couples counseling, parenting classes, or individual counseling for a particular family member may need to be pursued in order for family recovery to start or for the process to be enhanced. Appropriate recommendations and referrals can be given.

FAMILY RELAPSE PREVENTION

Family members who have never experienced an addict's relapse during recovery often resist examining this possibility. The idea is very frightening in light of their experiences during the addiction. Yet, the possibility of relapse is present for every recovering person. To be fully prepared, family members need to learn about the process involved (i.e., warning signs) and the factors that contribute to the addict's return to chemical use.

Eliminating enabling behaviors can be a deterrent to relapse. If family members refuse to participate, the addict gets a clear message that a relapse will be his or her responsibility, and one where others refuse to share his or her experience. The following case illustrates this:

> Sue was married to a recovering alcoholic. Both she and her husband had actively been working their programs. He had several challenges to face in his early sobriety after being fired and experiencing many rejections as he interviewed for new jobs. One evening, when Sue came home from work, her husband was passed out drunk in the living room. He had even left the empty bottle of whiskey on the kitchen table for her to see. Sue kept cool, went to bed, and before she left in the morning for work, she left a note attached to the bottle: "I want you to know that I will not go this route with you. You need to make a choice. I'm not going back." Her husband believed her because of the changes he had already seen in her behavior. He went to a meeting that day and that was the extent of his relapse. A hysterical reaction from Sue would have shown that she was still attached to his disease and would have given her husband an excuse to medicate his shame with more alcohol.

Addicts are not the only ones who can relapse. There is also a progression of relapse for the family member in recovery. Some symptoms of this are: failing to give attention to one's own program; a reemergence of controlling behaviors; social isolation; emotional changes (depression, mood swings, excessive worry); sleep and eating disturbances; an increase in compulsive behaviors; becoming defensive; and putting one's own needs last (Gorski, 1985). Family members need to be reminded that mistakes are to be expected, and one is not a "failure" if one makes a mistake or slips back into old behaviors.

TREATMENT AND RECOVERY RESOURCES

There is a wide variety of programs to assist families in recovery, including inpatient and outpatient treatment, and various counseling, educational, and self-help programs. Professionals may want to ask the following questions when determining what kind of treatment is indicated:

- How long has the addiction been present?
- How safe is the family environment?
- How dysfunctional has the codependent become?
- How is the codependent dealing with his or her emotions?
- How strong are negative family influences that resist recovery?

Based on the above, education and self-help groups may be adequate for those family members who seem to have been the least affected. Outpatient counseling (individual, group, or family) may be indicated for those who do not seem to have the ability to apply what they learn. For those whose lives are falling apart emotionally, personally, professionally, or physically, some form of residential treatment may be required.

A wide variety of residential programs is available for the codependent, ranging from weekend treatment to a 30-day program. Cost, geography, and the level of care most appropriate for treatment are issues to consider in referral. A 30-day program would be appropriate for someone who is experiencing significant dysfunction; a two-to-five-day program can potentially accelerate the recovery process for almost any codependent. Residential treatment should be specifically geared to meet the needs of recovery, whether they relate to adult children of alcoholics (ACOA), codependence, or parent-child issues. Familiarity with local resources and information on available programs can be obtained by contacting the local Drug and Alcohol Agency (or related county agency).

Most communities have counseling agencies that meet a variety of needs. When used as referrals for addicts and their families, counseling agencies should be experienced in the dynamics of the disease of chemical dependence and the recovery process. To ensure that the referral is appropriate, local drug and alcohol rehabilitation hospitals can be asked for suggestions. Counselors can be asked about their background in working with chemically dependent families. Individual, group, or family counseling options should be considered in meeting the various needs of the family.

There have been frequent references to self-help programs in this chapter. Following is a list of some of the well-established self-help groups for family members:

- "Al-Anon"—Family counterpart of AA (adults)
- "Al-A-Teen"—Children of Alcoholics (approximately ages 12-18)
- "Al-A-Tot"—Children of Alcoholics (approximately ages 5-10)
- "Nar-Anon"—Family counterpart of NA (adults)
- "Coc-Anon"—Family counterpart of CA (adults)
- "ACOA"—Adult Children of Alcoholics (adults)

For young children, there are structured recovery programs that assist the child in understanding the illness at his or her level and in dealing with the feelings that even small children experience. In addition, there are self-help groups for elementary-school-age children.

For teenagers and younger children, the county Drug and Alcohol Agency is an important resource for information about available programs. Al-A-Teen is a highly recommended self-help group that allows teens to speak freely about their experiences.

For ACOAs, there are several options: residential treatment, self-help ACOA groups, professionally led ACOA groups, and individual ACOA therapy. There are also frequent lectures, workshops, and conferences available in most areas. The ACOA may want to join the national association to be informed of significant events.

There are many ways professionals can help the chemically dependent family, both directly and indirectly. Most of the issues discussed in this chapter can be dealt with on the professional and/or self-help level. Most importantly, professionals must know the symptoms and dynamics of chemical dependence and codependence. This facilitates sound judgments in referring individuals to the proper level of care and providing the kind of support that encourages recovery.

REFERENCES

Beattie, M. (1987). *Co-dependent no more.* Center City, MN: Hazelden.

Black, C. (1982). *It will never happen to me.* Denver, CO: MAT Books.

Cermak, T. L. (1980). *Diagnosing and treating co-dependency.* Minneapolis: Johnson Institute.

Gallup Organization. (1980). *American families—1980.* Princeton, NJ: Author.

Gorski, T. (1985). *Relapse warning signs of co-dependency.* Hazel Crest, IL: CENAPS.

National Association of Children of Alcoholics (NACOA). (1983). *Charter statement of NACOA.* San Francisco, CA: Walker.

Ohlms, D. (1988). *Disease concept of alcoholism.* Belleville, IL: Whiteaker.

Peck, M. S. (1978). *The road less traveled.* New York: Simon & Schuster.

Potter-Efron, R. & Potter-Efron, P. (1989). Assessment of co-dependency with individuals from alcoholic and chemically dependent families. *Alcoholism Treatment Quarterly, 6*(1) 37-57.

Schneider, M. (1986). *Medical aspects of co-dependency.* Santa Barbara, CA: FMS.

Subby, R., & Friel, J. (1984). Co-dependency—A paradoxical dependency. In *Co-Dependency: An emerging issue.* (p. 31). Hollywood, FL: Health Communications.

Wegscheider, S. (1976). *Family trap* [Film]. Rapid City, SD: Onsite Training and Consulting.

Wegscheider, S. (1981). *Another chance.* Palo Alto, CA: Science and Behavior.

Whitfield, C. L. (1989). Co-dependence: Our most common addiction—some physical, mental, emotional and spiritual perspectives. *Alcoholism Treatment Quarterly, 6*(1), 19-35.

ABOUT THE AUTHORS

FRANCES A. CAMPBELL, R.N., M.S.N., is a Psychiatric Nurse who is certified as a Clinical Specialist in Adult Psychiatric Nursing and Addictions Nursing by the American Nurses Association. She has extensive experience in psychiatric treatment services in both inpatient and outpatient settings. For the past five years, she has been working in the chemical dependency treatment field and has held positions in a variety of settings specializing in the treatment of dually diagnosed clients. Currently she is employed by the University of Pittsburgh School of Medicine, Department of Psychiatry, as the coordinator of the Comprehensive Drug and Alcohol Treatment Programs.

She holds an adjunct faculty position at the University of Pittsburgh School of Nursing and is on the board of the National Nurses Society on Addiction. She is co-author (with Dennis C. Daley) of the book "Dual Disorders: Counseling Clients With Chemical Dependency and Mental Illness," plus other publications related to the dually diagnosed. She has lectured and presented workshops on the topic of dual diagnosis on a national level.

KATHRYN COLEMAN, L.S.W., C.A.C., is currently the Director of the Adult Chemical Dependency Inpatient Treatment Program at St. Francis Medical Center, Pittsburgh, PA. She had previously worked as a primary therapist on St. Francis' Adolescent Chemical Dependency Unit for 7 years and has spent 15 additional years in family and individual treatment in the Pittsburgh area. She is a Certified Addictions

Counselor and Trainer for the Office of Drug and Alcohol Programs in
Pennsylvania. In addition, she has trained for the Student Assistance
Program at St. Francis and has served as consultant for their Health
Assistance Program for Personnel in Industry. She is a member of the
Employee Assistance Program Association (EAPA) and the National
Association of Social Workers (NASW). She is on the faculty of
Pennsylvania State University-McKeesport campus for their Chemi-
cal Dependency Counselor Training Program and at the Community
College of Allegheny County in their Adult Education Division. She is
also a member of the Registry of Interpreters for the Deaf. Coleman
received her undergraduate degree in psychology from Indiana University of Pennsylvania. She completed her master's degree in social work
at the University of Pittsburgh.

DENNIS C. DALEY, M.S.W., is Assistant Professor of Psychiatry and
Director of the Office of Family Studies and Social Work, Department
of Psychiatry at Western Psychiatric Institute and Clinic, University of
Pittsburgh School of Medicine. For over a decade, Mr. Daley has been
involved in providing clinical services to patients and families, as well
as program development and management. He developed a psychoeducational model of relapse prevention and helped to design a dual-
disorders program for patients with chemical dependence and mental
illness. He has held adjunct faculty positions at several universities and
is also Assistant Professor of Sociology and Anthropology at Indiana
University of Pennsylvania. Mr. Daley has written many articles,
books, and recovery guides on the topics of addiction and recovery,
family recovery, relapse prevention, and dual disorders. In collabora-
tion with Gerald T. Rogers Productions he has written several educational videotapes. His practical recovery materials are used in many
treatment programs throughout the world. He has lectured widely in the
United States and Canada.

LOU GENE KINGERY-McCABE, M.D., is a psychiatrist in private
practice in the North Shore area of Massachusetts (Marblehead) and on
the staff of Salem Hospital. Prior to entering private practice she was
an Assistant Professor of Psychiatry at the University of Pittsburgh,
where she was instrumental in the development of an inpatient dual-
diagnosis programs at Western Psychiatric Institute and Clinic.

CAROL KOFFINKE received her M.Ed. in Counseling and Human Services from Boston University in 1975. She has worked extensively with the chemically dependent family and has designed and conducted intensive family treatment programs to facilitate the healing process of the individual as well as the family, treating over 1,000 family members in these programs. In addition, she is a consultant for the Institute of Alcohol and Drug Studies in Maryland, developing and teaching courses for professionals in the field of chemical dependence treatment. She has lectured and conducted workshops in several states and is in the process of completing her first book, which addresses the parenting issues of ACOAs. She is presently Director of Treatment at New Beginnings at Hidden Brook, a 54-bed freestanding substance abuse treatment facility in Maryland.

TOD R. MARION, M.P.H., C.A.C., is Director of Geriatric Services at St. Francis Medical Center, Pittsburgh, PA. He is responsible for the development of services to geriatric patients within psychiatry, medicine, and physical rehabilitation at the Medical Center. He has designed and implemented an inpatient drug and alcohol rehabilitation unit for the elderly, a comprehensive prevention education program, and a medication management center. Mr. Marion has worked in chemical dependence for nine years. He is a Certified Addictions Counselor and Trainer on Substance Abuse in the Elderly for the Office of Drug and Alcohol Programs in Pennsylvania. Prior to his experience in chemical dependence and geriatrics, Marion spent several years in international health care. He received a B.A. in anthropology and an M.P.H. in Health Services Administration from the University of Pittsburgh. He is currently a candidate for a master's degree in psychology from Geneva College, Beaver Falls, PA.

JOHN D. MASSELLA, B.A., M.Ed., is Therapy Manager for Gateway Rehabilitation Center (GRC). This position involves developing and implementing various GRC training and educational programs, such as Gateway's "referral source liaison program" and Employee Assistance Program (EAP) development and referrals, as well as marketing and planning GRC addiction treatment conferences. His strong marketing background is intertwined with a clinical background. He is also a Certified Addictions Counselor under the Pennsylvania Alcoholism and

Drug Abuse Office. During his tenure as the Therapeutic Coordinator of GRC's Clinical Assessment Unit, he helped develop various services to provide detoxification as well as appropriate treatment modalities for GRC patients. Currently, Massella is coordinating Gateway's new counselor internship program where he is in charge of the training manual and program for clinical interns. He also assists in training clinical interns in all procedures related to Gateway's therapy programs and aftercare treatment. Massella has lectured on adolescent drug and alcohol abuse. His subspecialties include ACOAs and treatment of mood disorder clients.

MIRIAM S. RASKIN, Ed.D., A.C.S.W., is Associate Professor and Acting Chair of the Social Work Department at George Mason University, Fairfax, Virginia. She received her M.S.W. from the University of Maryland School of Social Work and Community Planning and her Ed.D. from Virginia Polytechnic Institute and State University. Her research and teaching interests include social work education, field instruction, child welfare, and women/family issues. Her work in public and private agencies includes clients who were chemically dependent. She is active in the community and serves on social service agency boards and county commissions. She has presented numerous papers and workshops at national and international conferences, serves as a reviewer for several journals, and provides consultation to social service and professional organizations.

RUTH ANN SEILHAMER, Ph.D., is a clinical psychologist who is Senior Program Coordinator of the Family Research Project at Western Psychiatric Institute and Clinic, University of Pittsburgh School of Medicine. This broad-based research program focuses on the interaction patterns of families of alcoholics as well as predictors of risk for children of alcoholics. Her clinical background includes individual and family interventions with substance abusers. She has authored several book chapters and publications about families of alcoholics.